The Changing Dimensions Of Business Education

Published by:
National Business Education Association
1914 Association Drive
Reston, Virginia 20191

THE CHANGING DIMENSIONS OF BUSINESS EDUCATION

Copyright 1997

NATIONAL BUSINESS EDUCATION ASSOCIATION
1914 ASSOCIATION DRIVE
RESTON, VIRGINIA

ISBN 0-933964-50-1

Preface

Business educators expect change as a way of life. As changes occur, work and individual lives are profoundly affected. Managing pervasive changes with a degree of success requires flexibility and preparedness. The material in the 1997 NBEA Yearbook may serve as a basis for change in both course content and methodology as business educators prepare for the future.

The Yearbook is divided into six parts:

The Yearbook is divided into six parts:

Part I provides an historical perspective for the changing dimensions in business education. The history of the business education discipline serves as a background for understanding the present and for coping with the future.

Part II describes forces that impact changes in business education. Within the United States, demographic, social, and environmental developments affect all of education. In addition, globalization has brought many changes that must be considered. These forces have resulted in the enactment of numerous reforms and regulations.

Part III identifies specific technologies that enable changes in business education. Given the fact that technology changes constantly, the material in Part III serves as a foundation upon which educators may build. However, changing technologies require ongoing adaptation of both content and methodology.

Part IV presents traditional and innovative approaches to preparing, retaining, retraining, and rewarding business educators. Teachers are challenged to search for additional ways to enhance their professional lives.

Part V focuses on how business education can accommodate change. Highlights include the global economy, entrepreneurship education, future work, and the job-seeking process.

Part VI concludes with a career vision, a practical plan for lifelong learning.

The Changing Dimensions of Business Education is a refereed yearbook. Chapters were reviewed by at least three persons. Members of the editorial review board were:

Vivian Arnold, East Carolina University,
   Greenville, North Carolina
Linda Bloom, Pensacola Junior College,
   Pensacola, Florida
Dale Brewer, Warrington Campus, Pensacola Junior College,
   Pensacola, Florida

Carolyn Hagler, University of Southern Mississippi,
    Hattiesburg, Mississippi
Donna Holmquist, University of Nebraska,
    Lincoln, Nebraska
Betty Johnson, Stephen F. Austin State University,
    Nacogdoches, Texas
Colleen Vawdrey, Utah Valley State College,
    Orem, Utah
Bonnie White, Auburn University,
    Auburn, Alabama

Clarice P. Brantley, Co-editor
Bobbye J. Davis, Co-editor

Contents

PART I
HISTORICAL PERSPECTIVES

PART II
FORCES THAT IMPACT CHANGES IN BUSINESS EDUCATION

PART III
TECHNOLOGIES THAT ENABLE CHANGES IN BUSINESS EDUCATION

PART IV
INITIATIVES THAT EMPOWER BUSINESS EDUCATORS

PART V
BUSINESS EDUCATION FOCUSES ON CHANGE

PART VI
CAREER VISION

PART I
HISTORICAL PERSPECTIVES

CHAPTER 1

Historical Perspectives: Basis for Change In Business Education

Lloyd W. Bartholome
Utah State University, Logan, Utah

Business education as defined in this paper is education for and about business. Before the term "business" was used in the Western World, the term "commerce" existed because the roots of business are in commerce, which dates back to ancient civilizations. The concepts and practices of education for and about business have evolved through time. The purpose of this chapter is to summarize these different historical perspectives that have greatly influenced business education in the United States and thus provide a framework for business education today. Because business education in the United States mostly evolved from European practices that have developed over the centuries, this chapter concentrates on the history of business education in the Western Hemisphere.

Ancient Civilizations

Ancient civilizations before 1000 B.C. participated in the general trade of goods. Cities such as Babylon and Alexandria were of considerable size. Traders had to keep track of ideas by pictures since there was no written language. Picture-writing, however, was very unwieldy; and the Phoenicians were the first to develop a more-or-less simplified alphabet. In approximately 500 B.C., the Greeks improved upon this simplified alphabet by adding vowels, and the Greek language was predominant because of the advanced civilization in Greece. Even at this time no schools existed. Only the privileged could afford private tutors to learn to read and write.

In about 400 B.C. many Greeks settled in various parts of the Roman Empire. Computing came into existence, and the abacus was probably the first business machine in general use. As early as the first century A.D., the Roman Empire allocated public funds for education. However, these schools were primarily for grammar and rhetoric. The schools did not have much impact on the masses and fell into disrepute. Roman Empire schools were closed in 529 A.D. because Emperor Justinian believed that the schools were unfriendly to Christianity since schools gave reasoning priority over faith.

The Dark Ages

The Romans created the Roman numeral system, which was a great improvement to other systems. Since this system had no zero, calculations were difficult. The Hindus of India were the first to adopt the Hindu/Arabic systems of numerals and to use the zero. Numerals were found in inscription as early as the third century B.C. Intellectualism in the Western world was almost null, and strict controls on thought and action were universally imposed by the Roman Empire.

During this time the teachings and philosophy of Mohammed became widely accepted, and Mohammed's influence was extended from Spain to India. Civilization continued to develop in some areas to include the emergence of unique architectural styles, glasswork, pottery, and leather work. Mathematicians, scientists, and astronomers made major contributions to human knowledge. However, illiteracy prevailed in Western Europe. Most of the influential rulers could neither read nor write.

Then, in the 12th and 13th centuries A.D., the Crusades extended the influence of the Roman Catholic Church over the Holy Land, which was controlled by the Muslims, and the first universities were founded. At that time an atmosphere of acceptance for scientific, practical, and business education began to emerge.

Intellectual Awakening

Although the first inked impression on paper was made in China about the fifth century A.D., it wasn't until around 1440 when Gutenberg introduced the printing press to the Western world that printing became somewhat common in Europe. With printing becoming common, universities began to grow in Western and Central Europe from the 12th to the 15th centuries. The curriculum usually consisted of civil and canon law, medicine, philosophy, and logic. Much of the learning had a strong classical basis with the theories of Plato, Aristotle, Ptolemy, and Socrates predominating.

Francesco Petrarcha (Moreland, 1977) was a primary critic of the medieval system of education. Petrarcha inspired people to speak out against the restrictions of thought and expression that inhibited progress in all areas. He was joined by other intellectual leaders in Italy. Petrarcha was considered to be at the forefront of the Renaissance and the rebirth of learning and creativity in Italy, especially in the fields of literature, art, sculpture, architecture, and commerce.

Erasmus (1466-1536) was probably the greatest humanist of the 16th century, and he was as potent as Petrarcha. Erasmus was an outstanding scholar, and his books on Latin grammar and correspondence were used for many years in the secondary schools in Europe.

Business Training for the Working Class

Meanwhile, the upper and middle classes of England relegated the aspects of training for business to the working classes, and thus education for business was stigmatized. The privileged classes clung to the classics.

The philosophy on the European continent was quite different. For instance, Martin Luther advocated teaching all children, rich and poor, a trade or useful art. This was probably the first mention of providing basic working skills for all people. In contrast, John Locke proposed working schools for the poor. Thus, instruction in business education was given much more national recognition in Germany and the European continent than in England.

The study of handwriting was also in low repute in Renaissance England. Although monks in monasteries copied the beautiful manuscripts, the introduction of printing made copying more or less obsolete. As far back as the Renaissance period, businessmen complained of the illegible writing of most clerks that spread confusion and error. However, the educational institutions gave little attention to handwriting. Governors of some of the grammar schools felt that the image of their schools would suffer in the eyes of the public if handwriting were taught. Consequently, many private schools were established to teach handwriting.

During this time the aristocracy preferred to hire private tutors for their children, but comprehensive education was offered in public schools in England. The problem was that only the sons of well-to-do upper classes could afford to attend. Apart from a curriculum that concentrated almost exclusively on humanities, only physical education and sports were emphasized. Almost no instruction was provided in mathematics, science, languages, and history.

Moreland (1977, p. 24) stated that Sir Frances Bacon in his *Advancement of Learning* deplored the fact that "The wisdom touching negotiation or business hath not been collected into writing to the great derogation of learning and the professors of learning." Thus most business education in the medieval age was relegated to apprenticeship or private instruction.

Nineteenth Century Business Education in Europe

During the 19th century, industrial leaders complained about the shortages of clerks and bookkeepers. At the same time people were being educated in the classics and foreign languages rather than the practical arts. Steps were not taken until 1825 to start a third university to suit the needs of the times. The University of London was begun in 1827, and classes were opened in the arts, law, and medicine; but negative reactions from Oxford and Cambridge helped to delay the granting of the charter for the University of London. This university immediately began to give instruction in business education.

Germany opened a state school to provide instruction in business education in 1747. The school was very popular and became known as the Royal Realschule. The curriculum related to the needs of the community in general and business in particular. Business education was given prime consideration in Germany and, at the end of the 19th century, Saxony had the largest number of commercial schools per unit of population. The first specialized commercial high school founded in 1898 included the subjects of German, English, French, correspondence, mathematics, commercial arithmetic, commercial geography, commercial history, commercial law, bookkeeping, economics, physics, chemistry, writing, and stenography.

Other Western European countries followed the patterns of England and Germany. In 1820 Brodart and Legert opened a commercial school in France.

This school met a very urgent need in the mercantile area, but commercial schools were not welcomed by the conservative system. After 10 years the owners were forced to close the school. By the beginning of the 20th century, France had a well-established system of commercial schools. The system included about 200 lower or practical schools of commerce and 13 high schools of commerce in Paris, Bordeaux, and Marseilles.

The unification of self-governing states in Germany and Italy left educational control under the authority of the individual states. Thus education was allowed to change. Business was the lifeblood of each of the states. In 1868 the first high school of commerce was opened in Venice. Other commercial high schools were opened, and they attracted good quality teachers and students. Other countries on the European continent followed the examples of Germany, France, and Italy.

Early American Business Education

The 1492 voyage of Christopher Columbus initiated the Age of Discovery of the Americas. This age changed the course of the history of the world. Amerigo Vespucci also made several trips to the New World. He published much of this information in a letter proclaiming his discoveries. Based on his findings, mapmakers promptly drew up maps and commemorated Amerigo Vespucci's name in North, Central, and South America.

After the voyages of Columbus and Vespucci, settlers began to arrive in the New World. In 1601 King James I of England issued a charter to the London Company to settle in the New World. Colonists sailed up the James River in Virginia and established a settlement in what is now called Jamestown. In 1620 the Pilgrims established a settlement in Massachusetts at Plymouth. Others seeking religious and political freedom continued to settle the New World. The Puritans went to New England and the Roman Catholics to Maryland. By 1688 the population of the New World had risen to 300,000. Freedom was important for these early American settlers, and their educational system and their free enterprise approach to business were based upon this important aspect of freedom.

Although more than 75 percent of the population in the New England colonies could scarcely read and write, provision for schools was sporadic. Probably the strongest impetus for schools came from the colony of Massachusetts. In 1647 the Massachusetts General Court made the first educational move. All settlements of 50 families or more were required to maintain an elementary school; towns of 100 families or more had to provide a secondary school to prepare boys for college. Fines were levied on townships that did not comply. Some townships found the paying of fines cheaper than establishing the school. Nevertheless, a pattern was begun to support elementary and secondary schools.

Progress in the curriculum was very slow. Naturally, the class distinction favored the provision for universities before secondary schools. Harvard, the first American college, was opened in 1636 and plagued by low enrollments. For 60 years Harvard was the only degree-granting college in the colonies. During this entire period the average number of graduates per year was only eight.

At the same time, Latin grammar schools existed by law but never won popular support because the classical curriculum was not considered relevant, and many Latin grammar schools did not produce a single graduate. In fact, students frequently applied for release time to study subjects with some value. Schools then excused them on a scheduled basis to take courses in handwriting, arithmetic, bookkeeping, and English. These courses were offered by private schools and tutors in return for payment of a tuition fee. Hence, the first commercialization of education in America began.

Prominent leaders in this colonial era urged the adoption of useful subjects. William Penn advocated teaching children useful knowledge consistent with truth and godliness. Benjamin Franklin set forth many proposals to educate the youth of Pennsylvania, including an educational program for the commercial and productive classes. Franklin was also deeply interested in history because he had not received an education in the field. His leadership led to the founding of the Philadelphia Academy which, in its original program, supported his philosophy of educational realism. The Franklin Academy was the forerunner of local school systems managed by boards of trustees operating under the terms of colonial or state charter. Instead of slavishly following the classical curriculum, the academies encouraged diversification; many offered commercial courses such as handwriting, commercial arithmetic, and bookkeeping. Some were boarding schools and some even admitted girls to the courses. However, the children of the poor were largely ignored and teachers' salaries were low. But in the new spirit of nationalism in the Revolutionary War, leaders began to realize that the future of their nation depended largely on the capabilities and the education of its citizens. Thus began the new structure for education in America.

Early U.S. Education

The conflict between liberal and practical education continued. Besides William Penn and Benjamin Franklin, other distinguished educators emerged during early American times. Thomas Jefferson was a very influential person who supported the primary schools. Horace Mann was one of the most influential educators of this time. He built an excellent system of schools in Massachusetts, and several other states followed his example. Mann assisted in levying the first effective school tax in 1827, and he helped institute free schools in 1834. Horace Mann also established the first teacher training institutions or "normal" schools. His attitude was, "Why should algebra, which not one man in a thousand ever uses in the business of life, be studied by twice as many as bookkeeping which everyone, even the day laborer, needs?" (Moreland, p. 44). The same question is being asked in 1997.

On the other hand, Charles W. Elliott, an academician, considered bookkeeping to be useless and algebra of great value because it stimulated the human intellect. Elliott, a distinguished graduate of the Boston Latin School, was president of Harvard University from 1869-1909. However, the Harvard Business School has since gained worldwide recognition and today attracts outstanding scholars from all over the world.

The first business colleges. As the rivalries between the academic point of view and the utilitarian point of view continued, business colleges came into existence. James Gordon Bennett established the first business college in the United States in 1824. Instruction was offered in reading, penmanship, arithmetic, algebra, astronomy, history, geography, commercial law, and political economy. Bennett is more remembered as a founder of the *New York Herald,* first published on May 6, 1835, at a price of 1 cent per copy.

Benjamin Franklin Foster opened the first successful and continuing business school in the United States in 1827. A demand for better business education continued. James Garfield, who later became president of the United States, reflected the views of many of these leaders when he stated that "The business colleges which this country originated are a protest against that capital defect in our schools and colleges which consists in their refusal to give a training for business life" (Moreland, p. 46).

Business college chains. The first chain of private business colleges was established by H. B. Bryant and H. D. Stratton in 1853. Ten years later they had more than 50 schools under management. Many of these schools are still in operation although most of them are now privately owned and managed.

Several American business and public leaders received all or part of their training in private business schools. Herbert Hoover studied at Capital Business College in Salem, Ore. Henry Ford was a graduate of Detroit Business University. John D. Rockefeller and Harvey B. Firestone were graduates of Dyke College in Cleveland, and Thomas B. Watson of IBM graduated from Elmira (N.Y.) School of Commerce.

The first major effort to place business education at the university level was made in 1881 when the Wharton School of Commerce and Finance was established with a $100,000 grant from Joseph Wharton. This curriculum started with a three-year curriculum but was soon reduced to two years. By 1889, however, the enrollment of the school had grown and a four-year program was initiated. This program offered a comprehensive business curriculum including classes in accounting, economics, finance, law, political economy, industrial history, money and credit, politics, etc. Standards were very high, and no college or university at the time was in a position to match the comprehensive extent of this business program.

Business colleges also had detractors, including Edmond James. James believed that training in business schools, with few exceptions, could not be called higher training at all. However, James changed his views; he later became director of the first active collegiate school of business, the Wharton School of Commerce and Finance at the University of Pennsylvania. Thus, James became a true pioneer of commercial education at the university level.

Business colleges justified their existence by preparing workers for a growing economic system in the industrial age. Specific business school programs supplied trained office staff and capable management personnel.

The Industrial Revoluation

The Industrial Revolution in the 19th century was without precedent. All of the following inventions enhanced the "world of business." The telegraph was invented by Samuel B. Morse in 1844. Alexander Graham Bell invented the telephone in 1874. The first transatlantic cable was laid in 1886. Christopher Sholes invented the typewriter in 1868; and Thomas Edison invented the phonograph in 1877. In addition, the discovery of wireless telegraphy by Marconi in 1895 helped to revolutionize the communications system throughout the world.

To assist in this communication revolution, attempts were made to reduce the time and labor involved in recording both the spoken and written word. As a result, many written shorthand systems came into existence. Probably the two best-known systems were the Pitman Shorthand system, perfected by Isaac Pitman in 1837, and Gregg shorthand, invented by John Robert Gregg in 1888. Changes in communications systems are often abrupt. Manual shorthand systems developed because of early communication technologies. However, these systems almost no longer exist and are rarely taught today in our public schools because of new communication technologies.

Even though the typewriter was invented in 1868, the all-finger system of typewriting was developed by Frank McGurrin 10 years later. In international typewriting contests, McGurrin defeated all challengers, and the touch system was quickly adopted. This touch system is still taught in schools and used in business on typewriter-like keyboards that have been adapted for computer use.

Other business machines contributing to the rapid growth of business and communication in the 19th century included the adding machine invented by Charles Xavier Thomas in 1820; the cash register invented by James Ritty in 1879; the gelatin process duplicating machine invented by Alexander Shapiro in 1880; and the forerunner of the computer, the statistical machine, invented by Dr. Herman Hollerith in 1887. Believe it or not, the dictating machine was also invented in 1887 by Alexander Graham Bell. The coin changer was invented by William H. Stoates in 1890. Because of the industrial revolution, almost 20 percent of the population of the United States was associated with business in one way or another by 1930.

Twentieth Century Business Education

Following the end of World War I in 1918, many public educational systems adopted the 6-3-3 organization, and junior high schools were established as an attempt to decrease the drop-out rate and to assist in the crowded conditions at many high schools. The junior high schools adopted the traditional curriculum, but later they tended to shift certain commercial courses from grades 10-11 to grades 8-9. Much of this commercial shifting did not last. However, at least two courses endured. These courses were typewriting, primarily for personal use, and introduction to business, which is often called general business.

Fred Nichols in 1919 advocated the first course in junior clerical training, later called general business. This course was to be expansive rather than intensive and included topics such as communications, record-keeping, and occupational material. Junior clerical training became very popular in the junior high schools until legislation raised the age level for enrollment of youth in vocational education from junior high school-to high school-age youth.

Teacher training. During the late 1800s and early 1900s, commercial teachers often were recruited from business colleges. One- and two-year normal schools came into existence, and eventually training programs were provided for commercial teachers. Many educational leaders felt that to ensure professional competency in business teacher education, two requirements were essential: on-the-job experience and attendance at a university or teacher's college. This prevailing requirement continues to the present.

Business education associations. The forerunner to the National Business Education Association was also formed in the late 1800s. According to Nanassy, et. al., (1977) the Business Educators Association was formed in 1878. Annual monographs were published that included topics such as ethics, teacher education, the place of women in business, equipment, facilities, and other relevant topics. The Business Educators Association became affiliated with the National Education Association (NEA) in 1893 as the Department of Business Education.

Business school personnel were not happy with this affiliation, and they formed their own organization called The Eastern Business Teachers Association (EBTA) in 1894. The National Commercial Teacher's Federation, later known as the National Business Teacher's Association (NBTA), was formed at about the same time. The NBTA became the North-Central Business Education Association (NCBEA), one of the five regional branches of the National Business Education Association.

In the early years of the Department of Business Education, an affiliate of NEA, growth was rather slow; and in 1946 under the leadership of Hamden L. Forkner, the NEA Department of Business Education was organized into the United Business Education Association (UBEA). This became the largest business teacher association in the country and subsequently became the National Business Education Association (NBEA). The UBEA did not plan a national convention and had no meetings except its meetings with NEA held annually in June. UBEA was conceived as an umbrella organization to unite various regional groups. The Southern Business Education Association soon became a member, as did the Western Business Education Association, the Mountain Plains Business Education Association, and finally, the North-Central Business Education Association. A few years later, the Eastern Business Education Association joined NBEA. In 1962 UBEA changed its name to the National Business Education Association. It was not until 1972 that the EBEA became a region of NBEA.

Business education and marketing education are now both involved with the American Vocational Association (AVA). It was not until the passage of the Vocational Education Act of 1963 that business education was given federal subsidization as part of vocational education. Prior to that, business teachers were given no federal subsidies and displayed little interest in the American Vocational Association. Subsequently, subgroups of the American Vocational Association have been established for business educators.

The business curriculum. Commercial education, the forerunner of business education, was established in the late 1800s. By 1900 good courses in commercial education were offered in most public high schools. At first, commercial work was provided for those students who could not qualify for the regular classical courses. Later on, educators realized that students should be prepared for the business world and that better organization was needed to prepare teachers and students for the business world and the public schools. Standard curriculum in the early 1900s was English, mathematics, American history, bookkeeping, typewriting, and stenography, with additional options in commercial geography, penmanship, and commercial law. Office practice or clerical procedures courses were not offered. Bookkeeping was theoretical with no practice.

World War I gave a tremendous impetus to a better type of commercial work. At that time, commercial education also made great inroads into the junior high schools that were established in many school districts. Also during the same period, economic theory was introduced, and this made high school economics very important. During the first 25 years of the 20th century, commercial education students were also taught human relations skills such as courtesy, professional dress and appearance, and social skills. Students in English classes were taught practical matters such as how to write telegrams, letters, and additional forms of correspondence. Although foreign language was advocated, it was not generally taught for commercial students. Students were also given some training in actual business practices. In 1926 Elwood P. Cubberley, dean of the School of Education at Stanford University, said, "In the future competition will be keener than ever before. The European continent, with the possible exception of Russia, has today a different idea as to what war means. They realize that war does not pay . . . . Far keener competition than ever before is ahead. Commercial preparation is the watchword" (Business Education - A Retrospection, p. 9).

Growth of business education. From World War I to World War II, business education and business teacher education thrived. Some of the primary institutions providing collegiate business education as well as commercial education for business and industry were New York University; Indiana University; University of Pittsburgh; and University of California, Los Angeles.

The two most popular business subjects at the secondary level were typewriting and bookkeeping. Historically, typewriting has been the public school business subject with the greatest student enrollment. Keyboarding/word processing classes still contain the largest student enrollment of any business education subject in the public high schools.

After its invention in the late 18th century, shorthand made inroads into the public high school program. In 1940 the decision was made that transcription skills were also important, and classes for shorthand transcription were developed. Some of the leaders in this field were Louis Leslie, S. J. Wanous, A. R. Russon, Hamden Forkner, and John Robert Gregg, the originator of Gregg shorthand.

During the first part of the 20th century, basic or general business also grew considerably. In many high schools and junior high schools, general business was one of the required classes for all students. This class was considered important for both personal and occupational business use.

By 1950 business teacher education had a firm foundation in the colleges and universities, and business education was one of the most popular elective areas in the public high schools in the United States. In most instances, business teacher education and business education were housed with other business subjects at the college and university level. In fact, one of the most prevalent majors from the beginnings of land grant institutions of higher education in the United States (1860s until 1950) was the area of office education. Office education included the subjects of typewriting, shorthand, and bookkeeping.

The Gordon/Howell Report

By the 1950s schools of business were becoming firmly entrenched at the college and university levels. A single report from the American Assembly of Collegiate Schools of Business (AACSB) commissioned by the Carnegie Foundation and published in 1957 had far-reaching impact not only on business education at the university levels but also business education at the high school levels because of the report's negative influence on office education and business teacher education (America's Business Schools: Priorities for Change, 1985). This report, called the Gordon/Howell Report, enabled business schools to implement a number of key recommendations. Most of these recommendations included a move from practical training in business schools to a systematic study of the business environment. These changes included a greater emphasis in finance, marketing, mathematics, economics, and the behavioral sciences. The purpose of the report was to have business schools receive greater acceptance and integration into the university community and to increase the quality of instruction and research in various business-related disciplines. While these changes made improvements in the so-called functional areas of business, including marketing, management, finance, and economics, the changes had a negative impact on business teacher education and business and office education at the university level. This negative impact eventually reached high school business education.

High School Business Education from 1950-1980

Although university business education and business teacher education were negatively impacted by the Gordon/Howell report, the impact on high school business education was not felt for almost 30 years. In the meantime, high school business education thrived.

Nanassy, Malsbary, and Tonne (1977), using actual enrollments in 1948-49 and estimated enrollments in 1980, indicated that in those approximately 30 years, general business enrollments increased 50 percent; business arithmetic enrollments increased 31 percent; accounting enrollments increased 57 percent; shorthand enrollments increased 27 percent; and typewriting enrollments increased more than 125 percent. Typewriting enrollments included almost one-fourth of all students taught in the public high schools of the United States.

By the 1960s virtually every state in the United States had a business education specialist at the state level. However, with the inclusion of business education as a vocational area in the Vocational Education Act of 1963, many states had not only a state specialist for business education as a general public school class, but also had another specialist for vocational business education. Eventually with cutbacks at the state levels, the general specialist for business education became extinct, and business education was governed primarily by the vocational divisions of state departments. Thus, the general aspects of business education suffered, and enrollments in various general business subjects such as introduction to business, business law, business mathematics, etc., declined considerably because of lack of funding and lack of emphasis.

Preparation for Work or College

During the rapid growth of business education in the 20th century, local school boards in various states in the United States emphasized the preparation for work. Much of this emphasis was due to the immigration of citizens from Europe in the late 1800s to homestead free land in the United States. These people were raising children, and they wanted their children to have work skills to earn a living.

The Eight-Year study. The Eight-Year study reported in 1932 (Best, 1959) indicated that the traditional college curriculum was not necessarily the best plan for preparation for college. This study provided evidence that preparation for work may also be good preparation for college.

As a vital part of the Eight-Year Study, several universities agreed to accept students from a group of 30 selected secondary schools without entrance examinations and without regard to the pattern of course requirements ordinarily required for admission. The only requirements for admission were to be recommendation of the principal, the complete record of the student's academic and extra class activities, and his or her scores on scholastic aptitude and achievement tests given during the secondary school years. These universities were concerned with establishing effective secondary school curriculums. Freed from the traditional college entrance requirements, schools could then build the type of curriculum believed to be best. The hypothesis was that youth could be prepared for college through various curriculum plans.

While the programs of the 30 schools were of widely differing patterns, some common elements did exist. The programs emphasized teacher-pupil planning, laboratory-type learning experiences, democratic procedures, and the problem-solving approach to learning. Participants were also uninhibited by usual restrictions of course unit requirements found in conventional secondary school programs. By 1940 the first class had completed the four-year college program. The results of the study were based upon students who entered college in 1936 and graduated in 1940. Results included the following:

- Experimental students earned a slightly higher grade point average in all subjects except the foreign languages. They received slightly more academic honors and a higher percentage of non-academic honors.

- They were more often judged to possess intellectual curiosity and drive and to be precise, systematic, and objective in their thinking.

- They participated more frequently and more often appreciated experiences in the arts and participated more in all organized student activities except those of a religious or service nature.

- They were more often judged to have developed clear ideas about the meaning of education, a better orientation toward the choice of a vocation, and more active concern for what was going on in the world.

This study contributed greatly to different curriculum patterns for secondary schools in the United States, a trend that continued until the *Nation At Risk* report in 1983.

A Nation at Risk. On August 26, 1981, T. H. Bell, U.S. Secretary of Education, commissioned the National Commission on Excellence in Education to report on the quality of education in America (The National Commission on Excellence in Education, 1983). He appointed his friend, David P. Gardner, president of the University of Utah, to chair this commission. The commission consisted primarily of educators with five of the 17 members being educators from higher education.

The commission recommended strengthening liberal education at the high school level and increasing the number of college preparation subjects. The age-old battle of liberal versus practical education was, again, being waged.

The commission also recommended that high school students take five new basics including four years of English, three years of mathematics, three years of science, three years of social studies, and one-half year of computer science. For the college-bound student, two years of foreign language in the high school were strongly recommended in addition to the other requirements. Part of the problem with the recommendation was that the four years of English were not identified as grammar, spelling, writing, etc.; and even now, the four years of English include primarily the study of literature rather than the study of the English language.

By 1986 virtually every state in the United States had changed its admission standards to implement the so-called new basics. Obviously, the practical subjects, including business education, suffered, and high school business instruction was negatively affected. Implementation of the *Nation at Risk* report further weakened the preparation of business teachers and business education at the collegiate level. The Gordon/Howell Report implemented in 1957 started the decline of business teacher education programs in the United States, and the *Nation At Risk* report almost led to its demise.

The Information Age

The emergence of the Information Age has developed during the entire 20th century. In 1885 Hollerith invented the Hollerith Code, and computers began to evolve. Other computer milestones were as follows:

- 1937: Aiken proposed the fully automatic calculating machine.
- 1944: Harvard Mark I was completed.
- 1946: Electronic Numerical Integrator and Calculator (ENIAC) built.
- 1951: Remington Rand sold the first Univac to the Bureau of Census.
- 1951: Commercial sales of first generation hardware began.
- 1964: IBM announced the 360 timesharing computers.
- 1964: A variety of manufacturers produced computers.
- 1970: Large scale integration was implemented.

Large scale integration (LSI) was possible by allowing a number of elements to be created on a single computer chip. LSI used a technique called photo lithography that allows circuits to be photographed and reduced. Photo lithography and reduction of circuits to crystals of silicon chips were essential to the development of personal computers.

At first, personal computers were used primarily by those who wished to craft their own computers. However, by the late 1970s Apple Computer was formed, and its products were being placed in many of the public schools in the nation. At the same time the CPM operating system was developed by Digital Research, and competition for Apple was provided by Adam Osborne and other CPM microcomputer manufacturers. During this period of time microcomputers used proprietory operating systems.

The use of personal computers did not expand rapidly until IBM introduced its first PC and shared its code in the early 1980s. Since then, the IBM or IBM-compatible personal computer has taken over the market in business with word processing, spreadsheets, database, and other forms of computerization absolutely necessary to operating businesses in this information age.

As business began to utilize personal computers, business educators began to see opportunities for instruction on personal computers. Business education was beginning a new growth mode.

In the meantime, the speed and power of microcomputers have progressed rapidly from 64 kilobytes of RAM memory to 64 megabytes of RAM memory. The advent of the hard disk drive also greatly enhanced microcomputers. World-wide electronic communication is now possible through the use of personal computers.

Several years ago the federal government, through the National Science Foundation, funded a project for research universities to communicate electronically via computers using a system called Bitnet. This system expanded to make electronic communication available throughout the world via a system called the Internet. By 1995 many business education teachers were including Internet, World Wide Web, and Hypertext Markup Language as part of the business curriculum.

The Changing Face of Business Education

By 1979 members of the business education profession began to make paradigm changes. These changes were designed to further move business education into the information age.

Snowbird report. Recognizing that business education needed to change, 50 business education professionals met at a conference in Snowbird, Utah, in September, 1979 (New Directions for Business Education, 1979). These educators singled out new directions for business education. The new directions included the areas of office management, modern office technology, information management (including records management and data processing), management information systems, and word processing. The Snowbird Report recommended that "Business education must carefully evaluate its curriculum in terms of its business teacher education offerings" (p. 5). These recommendations included updating business educators to teach emerging technologies in office and distributive education. The Snowbird group met again in February 1981, in Tempe, Ariz., and reaffirmed the commitment that a major aspect of business education must include information systems at the secondary and postsecondary levels.

NBEA task force on new concepts and strategies. A contingent of the Snowbird/Tempe group and officers from major national business education associations met in Dallas, Texas, two additional times. On May 1, 1983, the group made business education recommendations for the next five to 10 years. This group was known as the NBEA Task Force on New Concepts and Strategies for Business Education. Members of the Task Force were Gerald Maxwell, chairman; Lloyd W. Bartholome; Gay Sweet-Harris; Charles Hopkins; June Atkinson; and Elizabeth Iannizzi. Walter A. Brower and Gordon Culver served as consultants. The recommendations were reported in the November 1983 issue of the *Business Education Forum*. Fourteen years later many of these recommendations have come to fruition. Others still need to be considered. Primary recommendations were that:

- Business educators should be prime deliverers of general education computer literacy courses. Every business education course should be interfaced with a computer.

- In business education programs computer literacy and keyboarding should become basic skills. Courses in introductory and advanced computer applications should be available.

- Because of worldwide linkages available, business students should receive instruction on national and international practices used in processing information.

A major recommendation for collegiate business education instructors was to accept the role of information systems management as a functional area of primary responsibility.

Information age challenges. Business educators are still attempting to meet the challenge of change for the Information Age. As stated by Bartholome (1991, p. 15), "If business education is to be at the forefront of education in the twenty-first century, business educators must continue to change with the changing times. Part of that change may be changing the thrust and name of the discipline. The content and name of the discipline need to be considered by business education strategic planners." Bartholome further stated, "Indeed the Information Age is here. This is an area in which knowledge has overtaken steel, oil, and wheat as a source and measure of wealth and strength . . . education and business education must keep up with this revolution in information technology." Business educators have met that responsibility so far in the Information Age by offering classes in word processing, spreadsheets, and database. They must now begin to offer classes using global electronic communication. Indeed, business educators must participate in global education. In addition, they need to rethink teaching and learning in the public schools as well as in higher education.

What Happens in the 21st Century

New information systems tools and additional knowledge regarding learning provide opportunities for new and better systems of learning in the 21st century.

Emphasis on learning. What will happen in the 21st century? A growing emphasis on learning rather than teaching and increasing support for innovation in learning will be benchmarks. Students in the secondary and post-secondary schools will be able to learn via computers at home and/or at school. Students in isolated areas will be able to receive instruction that is as good or better than instruction received by students in urban areas. Studies indicate no significant difference in learning between students in a conventional classroom and students involved in distance learning, regardless of the nature of the content, the educational level of the students, or the media involved (Moore and Kearsley, 1996). Also, multimedia will replace, in many instances, contact in laboratories to reduce the costs of laboratory instruction. Master teachers will be able to present instruction, via television and computers, to virtually all students in the United States. Students will have access to global information networks via the computer and unlimited library collections using some form of the Internet, CD ROM encyclopedias, and other information resources. Students will also be able to work on flexible schedules with lifelong support for learning through the use of the computer (Dolence and Norris, 1995).

New technologies for learning. According to John Sculley (1995), new technologies and support of a learner-centered model will excite educators in the next 10 to 20 years. At the same time, he is concerned about the huge segments of our society who may not have the motivation to learn or who may be denied access to some of the new learning technologies. Sculley also states that the information superhighway is not a highway at all but more of a web or marketplace.

Sculley further states that ". . . one has to be careful not to over-react too quickly because all of our content is shaped on where we have been, and we are just at the beginning of the road. This is just the beginning of the journey in what this new networked society is all about" (Sculley, p. 31).

Summary

Commercial (business) education in the Western Hemisphere was born of a need to communicate and transact business more than 2,000 years ago. As technology and communication have become more sophisticated, business education has had to change with the times to survive. From the beginnings of instruction in business education in the Western World, a rivalry has existed between a practical education in business and a liberal arts education.

However, historical forces have allowed business education to survive when business education has adapted to change. During the Industrial Age the typewriter and telephone were invented, and business education incorporated these tools into the curriculum. Business educators embraced shorthand instruction until its use was superseded by voice transcription, microcomputers, and other information aids.

The office has been transformed from a labor-intensive office to a highly technical machine-intensive office. Business instruction has changed from the use of the blackboard and the textbook to the use of computers and television. Federal legislation such as the Vocational Education Act of 1963 has impacted business education. Also, reports sponsored by special groups have impacted business education. These reports include the Gordon/Howell Report, the Eight Year Study, and *The Nation At Risk* report.

Thus, historically, as social, political, and business needs emerge, business educators change to survive. The curriculum must always change to meet the needs of business. Business educators must continue to rethink how people learn in a global information society because learners assume different roles in an information age. Active learning will be more popular, and learning will be a lifelong process. Learners must be able to assume greater responsibility for the learning at all levels of instruction. Business education must continue to adapt effectively, or other disciplines will surely take up the challenge.

References

Bartholome, L. W. (1991). Preparing business education for the 21st century. *Business Education Forum, 46*(2), 15-18.

Bartholome, L., Bieber, J., Boggs, L., Clark, M., Hertz, D., & Maxwell, G. (1980). *New directions for business education.* (Research Rep. No. 9). New York: McGraw-Hill.

Best, J. W. (1959). *Research in education.* Englewood Cliffs, NJ: Prentice-Hall.

Business education - A retrospection. (Monograph 133). (1978). Cincinatti, OH: South-Western Publishing.

Dolence, M. G., & Norris, D. M. (1995). *Transforming higher education, a vision for learning in the 21st century.* Ann Arbor, MI: Society for College and University Planning.

Moore, M. G., & Kearsley, G. (1996). *Distance education: A systematic view.* Belmont, CA: Wadsworth Publishing.

Moreland, P. A. (1977). *A history of business education.* Toronto, Canada: Pitman.

Nanassy, L. C., Malsbary, D. R., & Tonna, H. A. (1977). *Principles and trends in business education.* Indianapolis, IN: The Bobbs-Merrill Company.

Future directions and recommended actions for business education.(1983, November). *Business Education Forum, 38*(2), 3-6-8-1—11.

The National Commission on Excellence in Education. (1983). *A nation at risk.* Washington, DC: United States Department of Education. April, 1983.

President's Commission on Industrial Competitiveness. (1985). *America's business schools: priorities for change.* Washington, DC.

Sculley, J. (1995, September/October). Building blocks of a new society. *Educom Review,* 29-31.

PART II

FORCES THAT IMPACT CHANGES IN BUSINESS EDUCATION

CHAPTER 2

Demographic and Social Changes

Pauline A. Newton

Presentation High School, San Jose, California

Stop and think: what was life like in the United States in 1900? William McKinley was president. The population was about 76 million. Only men could vote. Electric power and telephones were relatively new and not yet universal. Automobiles were a rich person's curiosity. Most people traveled short distances by foot, horse or streetcar, and long distances by train. Television was non-existent. So were antibiotics.

Immigration from Europe, especially southern and eastern Europe, was growing. The West was being developed. Monopolies and trusts dominated business, and unions were forming muscle. The average worker labored for 50 or 60 hours a week to make about $12. Public school systems were expanding rapidly with public high schools more popular than private academies. There were no public community colleges.

Stop and think: what will life be like in the 21st century? Change is certainly inevitable. Many current trends already are well established: the U.S. population will continue to grow and the ethnic mix will shift. More people are living in the South and the West. The elderly will make up a bigger part of the population. More mothers are working and many children live in single-parent homes. The typical 9-to-5 workday will become less common. Technology will persist in transforming the workplace. Health care and insurance, pensions, personal property, education and child support will remain important issues. Disturbing social trends, including youth violence and teen pregnancy, will continue to need attention.

As a planning tool for educators, this article discusses these demographic and social trends in some detail. Like all fields, business education must change to meet the challenges of new demographic and social realities. The time to plan for the 21st century is now.

Demographic Trends

The U.S. population has grown by 13 million people since the 1990 census. On January 1, 1996, residents of the United States numbered 261,638,000. This number represents an increase of 2,471,000 (1 percent) over the Jan. 1, 1995, estimate, and a gain of 12,919,000 (5.2 percent) since the 1990 census. The nation's population growth during 1995 was mostly the result of "natural increase" (3,949,000 births minus 2,294,000 deaths). The United States also experienced a net gain from immigration of 816,000 people. The U.S. population is projected to increase to 392 million by 2050—about 50 percent larger than today's population; and the average age of the population will be older than it is now (U.S. Census Bureau, 1996).

Between 1993 and 2020, states in the South and West should account for 56 million of the 68 million persons added to the nation. Nevada is projected to have the most rapid growth rate. California's Hispanic population is expected to double between 1993 and 2020 (U.S. Census Bureau, 1996).

Immigrants. In 1995, net international immigration accounted for 736,000 of the 2,471,000 (30 percent) total increase of the population. The annual average figure of entering immigrants was 759,000 during the 1990s, well above the annual average of 634,000 for the previous decade. This higher average is partly a result of the provision of the Immigration Act of 1990, which reduced the limiting effect of quotas on family reunifications. See Table 1.

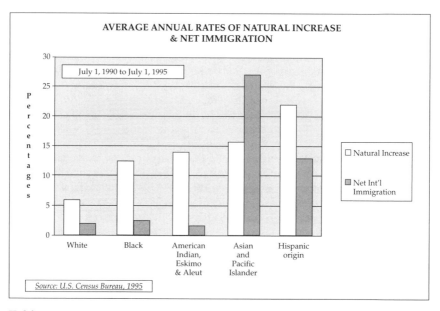

Table 1

	Natural Increase (%)	Net Int'l Immigration (%)
White	6	2.1
Black	12.8	2.6
Amerian Indian, Eskimo & Aleut	14.2	1.6
Asian and Pacific Islander	15.7	27.7
Hispanic origin	22.6	13.4

Baby boomers. In 1996, the Baby Boomers (those persons born from 1946 to 1964) accounted for 79,352,000 people or 30.3 percent of the total population (Farley, 1996). In that same year, the first phalanx of Baby Boomers crossed over into their 50s and entered the general realm of older age. Today, one baby boomer turns 50 years of age every seven seconds. By the time the Baby Boomers are all in their 50s and 60s, they will be running most of the country's institutions and will continue to infuse the culture with their ideas, ideals and temperaments.

Elderly. Although 1995 evidenced the highest annual number of deaths (2,294,000) ever recorded, the number of elderly people is increasing. The number of Americans 65 years old and over on Jan. 1, 1996, was 33,361,000, an increase of 359,000 (1.1 percent) from the previous year and of 2,281,000 (7.3 percent) from the 1990 census. A more pronounced percentage increase occurs in the oldest segment of the elderly population, those 85 years old and over. The number of persons in this category was 3,580,000 on Jan. 1, 1996, an increase of 103,000 (3 percent) from one year ago and an increase of 559,000 from the 1990 census. This differential increase in the population 85 years old and over is the result of advanced medical care, high levels of births during the first decade of the century, and very high immigration figures. The elderly will become increasingly diverse, racially and ethnically. Occupational trends also will be driven by the everyday activities of the elderly.

Employment of Ethnic Groups

Between 1980 and 1995 unemployment in the United States hit two peaks, in 1982, and then a decade later in 1992. Table 2 shows the unemployment rates for blacks, Hispanics and whites in those years, and illustrates that blacks had the highest unemployment rate, followed by Hispanics and then whites. The unemployment rate has been falling since 1992, and another trend is emerging; the gap between the unemployment rates of blacks and Hispanics is narrowing.

Population growth rates are highest for Hispanics. During 1995, the Hispanic population grew by 897,000 people (3.5 percent). At the same time, the white, non-Hispanic population added 813,000 people, an increase of 0.4 percent. This growth marks the first time that the yearly growth in the Hispanic population was numerically larger than the growth in other populations.

If current employment trends continue, the growing Hispanic population will encounter employment difficulties. In the past several years, the unemployment rate among Hispanics has declined more slowly than for either whites or blacks. Traditionally, Hispanics had a higher unemployment rate than whites, but a significantly lower rate than blacks. As Table 2 indicates, this gap is narrowing. Economists say the national recession that began in 1990 hit Hispanics especially hard. During the downturn, Hispanics were twice as likely as blacks or whites to lose jobs, and less likely to get new ones.

Education is a factor in this trend. On average, Hispanics have less education than blacks or white. According to the U.S. Census Bureau, roughly 80 percent of whites and 70 percent of black adults are high school graduates,

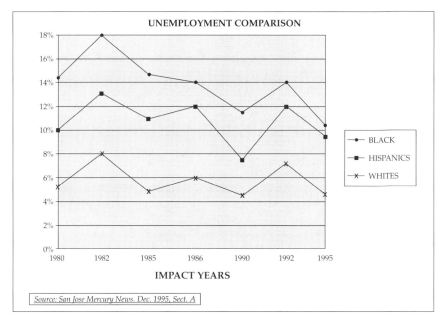

UNEMPLOYMENT COMPARISON

IMPACT YEARS

Source: San Jose Mercury News. Dec. 1995, Sect. A

Table 2

	BLACK	HISPANICS	WHITES
1980	14%	10.10%	5.30%
1982	18%	13%	8%
1985	15%	11%	4.90%
1986	14%	12%	6%
1990	12%	7.50%	4.80%
1992	14%	12%	7%
1995	11%	9.30%	4.80%

whereas only 53 percent of adult Hispanics and 46 percent of Mexican-Americans are graduates. Blacks also graduate from college at roughly twice the rate of Mexican-Americans, and the gap is widening every year.

Hispanics are, on average, much younger than other Americans. Almost 40 percent of the nation's Hispanics are younger than 20, compared to 26 percent of whites. Roughly one-third of the U.S. Hispanics live in California.

Because Hispanics tend to be among the last-hired and first-fired, they have always been more sensitive to the cyclical swings in the economy than most Americans. Some analysts think Hispanics are losing ground because of a surge of immigrants, who tend to have less schooling and speak less English than U.S.-born Hispanics. Many Hispanics contend that a backlash against immigrants has contributed to increasing discrimination against all Hispanics and shrinking job prospects.

Customized Life Styles

The timing of the life stages of people today are very different from those living just one generation ago. Paradoxically, children seem to both be taking longer to grow up and reach financial independence and to be leaving the innocent pleasure of childhood at an earlier age. Adults are experiencing both increased life expectancy and shifting social roles, and so they have more time in which to accomplish their life goals.

A new human frontier beckons all, women and men alike. Consider these statements:

- 9-year-old boys carry guns to school.
- 16-year-old children can "divorce" their parents.
- 30-year-old men live at home with their mothers.
- 40-year-old women are experiencing first pregnancies.
- 50-year-old men are forced into early retirement.
- 50-year-old women who are free of cancer and heart disease can expect to see their 92nd birthdays.
- 55-year-old women can have egg-donor babies.
- 65-year-old men in good health can expect to live until 81.
- 70-year-old men may be able to at least temporarily reverse aging by 20 years with human growth hormones.
- 80-year-old men and women run marathons.
- 90-year-old men and women marry and enjoy sex.
- More 100-year-old people are wished "Happy Birthday" by Willard Scott on the "Today" show (Klieman, 1995).

Household composition. The timing of life stages is not the only thing that is changing. Americans also have altered the composition of their households as shown in Table 3. Since 1970, the percentage of households containing married couples, especially married couples with children, has declined. At the same time, the percentage of households containing persons living alone, non-married individuals with children and non-married people without children has increased.

Just a few decades ago, many family households included relatives who did not work, such as a grandmother, unmarried aunt, or even a brother-in-law. A large assortment of family members lived on the same block or close together where they could depend upon one another in an emergency. Today, most adults work; and more often than not, unmarried adult relatives do not live together nor live nearby. Mothers who live with other adults generally are more likely to work outside the home. A study comparing mothers who did not live in extended families with those who did found a 53 percent increase in labor force participation among Dominican mothers who lived with other adults; a 17 percent increase for Asian mothers; and a 16 percent increase for Puerto Rican mothers. For many of the women, an extended

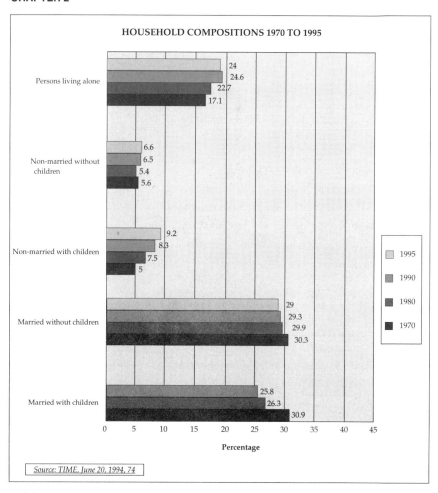

HOUSEHOLD COMPOSITIONS 1970 TO 1995

Source: TIME, June 20, 1994, 74

Table 3

	1970	1980	1990	1995
Married with children	40	30.9	26.3	25.8
Married without children	30.3	29.9	29.3	29
Non-married with children	5	7.5	8.3	9.2
Non-married without children	5.6	5.4 ·	6.5	6.6
Persons living alone	17.1	22.7	24.6	24

household was a way out of poverty (Rosenbaum, 1994). Of course, family arrangements are not the only factors determining whether a woman works; education, training, skills, age, social networks, birthplace and marital status also play roles.

The absentee father. At some point in their lives, nearly half of American children will live in homes with no father. No longer the exception, father-absent families make up nearly half of all households. In 1960, 5.8 million children lived in single-parent homes. Today, that figure is 18 million. Violent criminals are overwhelmingly males who grow up without fathers. Nearly 75 percent of American children living in single-parent families will experience poverty before they turn 11. Only 20 percent in two-parent families will experience poverty. Girls growing up in fatherless homes are far more likely to become teen mothers. Fatherless children are twice as likely to drop out of school. The fatherless-home trend is impacting the school curriculum and lifestyle of America. (Bird, 1994).

24-Hour Work Days

The United States is moving steadily toward a 24-hour-day, seven-day-a-week economy, with no such thing as "standard" 9-to-5 work hours. These non-traditional hours meet the needs of industry and the market, not the workers. The trend is driven by the growth of the service industry, a global marketplace, the influx of women into the labor market who need access to evening and weekend services, and an aging population in need of services, particularly in health care, around the clock.

Only 55 percent of U.S. workers are employed full-time during the day. Job growth to 2005 is projected to be in occupations with high numbers of people working evenings, nights, and weekends, in fields such as retailing, nursing and food service. People who work non-standard hours have higher rates of marital instability, and these hours may even affect fertility.

The rapid advances in electronic communication are changing not only how but also where and when people work. About 9 million employees, not including business owners or independent contractors, did some or all of their work from home in 1995, up from 7.6 million telecommuters in 1994, according to Link Resources. Link projects that by 1998 13 million workers will telecommute (Dykman, 1994).

Until now, both factory and office workers traveled to the workplace where the tools, information, work-in-progress, files, and other employees were located. Today, as the ability to electronically move the work to the person grows, some travel is becoming unnecessary. Personal computers, faxes, on-line services, teleconferencing, and car phones have made tele-commuting possible. Telecommuting is also the result of pressure from people with family responsibilities and those who want to work off hours, even while on vacation.

Studies show that an employee's telecommuting only one or two days a week can save the company from $6,000 to $12,000 a year. New terms such as "virtual office" and "flextime" have been coined. "Hot-desking" and "hoteling" refer to employees who are not assigned to a desk or office but who sign up for space as needed.

Employment Projections

During the 1994-2005 period, total employment is projected to increase by 14 percent or by 17.7 million, from 127.0 million in 1994 to 144.7 million in 2005. Today, about 67 percent of Americans 16 years and over are in the labor force: almost 76 percent of men and nearly 58 percent of women. More than 8 million working-age Americans are prevented from working because of a disability. The top three occupation groups are administrative support, including clerical; professional specialty; and executive, administrative, and managerial. In the retail industry 19.6 million persons are employed. The 1995 median annual earnings of selected ethnic groups is reported in Table 4.

Of the more than 115 million employed workers, 73 percent drive to work alone and 13 percent are in carpools. About 76 percent work in the county in which they live, and the commuting time averages about 22 minutes.

Workers are well-represented among mothers: almost 58 percent of mothers with children under 6, and 75.9 percent of mothers with children 6 to 17, are in the labor force. The number of women-owned businesses (sole proprietorship, partnership, subchapter S companies) increased by a dramatic 57 percent in the 1990s. Minority-owned firms also dramatically increased in number: Asian-Pacific Islander by 89 percent, Hispanic by 81 percent, American Indian/Eskimo/Aleut by 58 percent, and black by 38 percent (Lawrence Hall of Science, 1996).

Professional specialty occupations are projected to increase fastest between 1994 and 2005, and to add the most jobs—more than 5 million. Other groups that are projected to grow faster than the average are executive, administrative, and managerial occupations; technicians and related support occupations; and marketing and sales occupations.

Employment will increase in occupations requiring various amounts of education and training. Growth rates over the 1994-2005 period will range from 5 percent for occupations generally requiring moderate term on-the-job training to 29 percent for occupations requiring a master's degree. All categories that generally require an associate's degree or more education are projected to grow faster than the 14 percent average of all occupations.

According to the U.S. Bureau of Labor Statistics (BLS), the number of Americans age 55 and older holding jobs will climb 42 percent to 22.1 million between 1995 and 2005. That ratio is double the 20 percent projected growth in the 55-plus population.

Geographic Growth Areas

More than half of the U.S. population (55.6 percent), lives in the South and West regions of the country. Between 1980 and 1990, the West grew by 22.3 percent, and the South grew by 13.4 percent. This dramatic growth rate caused a shift of 19 seats in the House of Representatives. Eight states gained seats: California (+7), Florida (+4), Texas (+3), and Arizona, Georgia, North Carolina, Virginia, and Washington (+1 each). Thirteen states lost seats: New York (-3); Illinois, Michigan, Ohio, and Pennsylvania (-2 each); and Iowa, Kansas, Kentucky, Louisiana, Massachusetts, Montana, New Jersey, and West Virginia (-1 each).

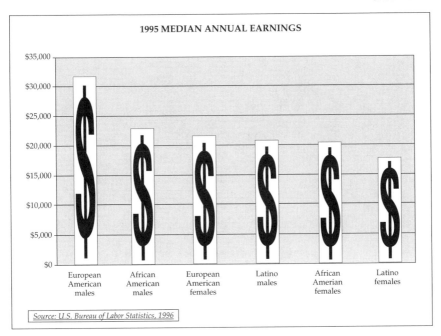

1995 MEDIAN ANNUAL EARNINGS

Source: U.S. Bureau of Labor Statistics, 1996

Table 4

European American Males	$31,737
African American males	$22,942
European American females	$22,423
Latino males	$20,312
African American females	$20,299
Latina females	$17,743

Most Americans—79.5 percent—live in metropolitan areas, and 53.7 percent live in one of the 41 metropolitan areas with populations of at least 1 million. The five largest metropolitan areas are scattered across the map: New York/New Jersey/Long Island (19.4 million), Los Angeles/Riverside/Orange County (14.8 million), Chicago/Gary/Kenosha Counties (8.3 million), Washington/Baltimore (6.8 million), and San Francisco/Oakland/San Jose (6.3 million). Although the New York area remains in first position, the Los Angeles area is growing at a much faster rate—2 versus 0.2 percent since 1990 (U.S. Census Bureau, 1996).

Quality of Life

The powerful forces transforming the world have particular potency in measuring the quality of life in the United States. The U.S. economy is widely seen as the prototype of an economy on the cutting edge of change. The changes demand more effective education, not only to meet new demands by the economy, but for meeting the needs of our democratic society as well. Greater intellectual skills, knowledge, and capacity are important to a person's role as both worker and citizen. The complex issues facing individuals as voters, as parents, as users of the health-care or legal systems, etc., demand a more sophisticated and better-educated individual. Where does the United States rank in the quality of life?

Education. Today, America has a higher proportion of high school graduates than at any other time in U.S. history: more than 79 percent of all Americans age 25 and over. Approximately 27 percent of these graduates also have earned a bachelor's degree or higher.

Educational attainment has a direct impact on many aspects of life, including earnings. Average annual earnings for persons without a high school diploma are $14,078; with a diploma, $19,567; with a bachelor's degree, $32,728; with a doctorate, $53,705; and with a professional degree, $65,648. An average of $4,700 is spent annually per student in the public elementary and secondary schools (Woods and Poole, 1996).

Assets. Home ownership accounts for more than 40 percent of Americans' net worth. Interest-earning assets account for almost 20 percent. About 20 percent of American households hold about 44 percent of our nation's net worth.

Pensions. Two-thirds of the workforce is covered by a pension of some type. Ninety-two percent are covered by Social Security. The great majority of government employees (92 percent) are covered by pensions, while only 36 percent of agricultural and personal service workers are covered by employer-sponsored pensions.

Health insurance. Approximately 86 percent of the workforce has health insurance. Those most likely to be insured are the elderly, the employed, and those with at least a high school diploma.

Child care. Families with working mothers and preschool children spend about 8 percent of their combined income on child care for their children. Most of the care for preschoolers takes place in a home environment, such as with relatives or neighbors (67 percent); about 23 percent of child care for preschoolers is in organized facilities, such as nursery schools and day care centers; nine percent are cared for by the mother while she works; and one percent are involved in a school-based activity.

Child support. Of the 5.7 million women awarded child support, 5 million were supposed to receive payments in 1989. Of those women, about half received the full amount they were due. The average amount of child support received in 1989 was $2,995. The aggregate amount of child support received in 1989 was $11.2 billion, 69 percent of the $16.3 billion due.

Assistance. Approximately 4 percent of our adult population needs assistance with everyday activities. This need increases to 45 percent for persons 85 and over. Most caregivers are female relatives.

Voting. The 1992 presidential election was decided by 61.3 percent of the voting-age population, up 3.3 percent from the 57 percent who determined the outcome of the 1988 presidential election. Voter registration increased for the 1992 election; about 68 percent who were old enough to vote registered to do so in 1992, up slightly from 67 percent in 1988.

Federal aid. In fiscal year 1992, the federal government dispensed nearly $2 trillion to state and local governments and U.S. territories. California received $140 billion of these funds. On a per capita basis, Alaska received the most, with spending of more than $6,800 per person.

Funds were divided this way: $612 billion in payments to individuals, such as Social Security; $162 billion in salaries to military and civilian employees; $200 billion in contracts; $178 billion in grants to state and local governments, for example: Medicaid, Aid to Families with Dependent Children, and highway construction; and $40 billion in other programs, including research grants and agricultural subsidies.

Lotteries. Thirty-two states operate lotteries, which produced $8.8 billion in net revenue in fiscal year 1991. During the same time, state general expenditures amounted to $554.6 billion. State expenditures for highways were up 6.3 percent in 1991 to $47 billion. Expenditures for hospitals rose 8.1 percent to $24.5 billion in 1991 (Scharr, 1996).

Social Trends Affect Curriculum

A new kind of toxicity is seeping into the experience of childhood, putting children on the track toward many problems. According to several psychological studies, highly impulsive grade-school boys tend to be troublemakers with teachers and are three to six times more likely than self-disciplined children to engage in violent behavior by the time they are teens. Girls with similar attributes are three times more likely to become pregnant as teens. Grade-school girls who cannot tell the difference between anger, anxiety, boredom, and hunger are more at risk of developing eating disorders as they grow older (Klieman, 1995).

The present emphasis in schools suggests that Americans are more concerned about how well school children can read and write than whether they'll be alive next week. Yet the sharp drop in children's emotional intelligence is in many ways a more troubling social trend than any dip in SAT scores. Students can learn emotional intelligence when an effort is made to incorporate emotional skills within the curriculum.

A handful of pioneering schools have started courses that teach the basics of emotional intelligence, just as they teach computer skills. In one junior high class in Brooklyn, students think of a single realistic step, no matter how small, that might have helped settle some personal conflict. Third graders in Seattle talk over how it feels to be left out of a game and what they might do in a constructive way to become included. Fourth graders in New Haven have a regular class in key emotional skills such as naming their feelings, distinguishing between them, and recognizing emotions from facial expressions.

These emotional literacy programs show that students become better at:

- Tolerating frustration.
- Managing their anger appropriately.
- Handling stress and anxiety better.
- Becoming less impulsive and better able to concentrate.
- Growing more cooperative and better-behaved.

No one would claim that any such course is enough to transform the economics and culture of neighborhoods. The school curriculum is challenged by some neighborhoods where children are born to unwed teenagers, where dealing drugs is the quickest road to wealth, and where violence is a necessity for survival. These courses make explicit what has always been an implicit role for schools: socializing our young. They teach children how to cope with their feelings and how to take responsibility for themselves. The next century will be a towering challenge for society (Sheehy, 1994).

Summary

The world is constantly changing. The change process is inevitable and can be either disturbing or desirable. Any kind of change, momentarily at least, disturbs the status quo. Even with change that is welcome, adjustments are required. When change is foreseen, decisions to make lifestyle adjustments are more easily understood.

Educational associations and instructors have influenced the changes in society. The business education curriculum is a perfect example of the change process. Business instructors realize the impact of curriculum changes. If teachers cannot immediately adjust the curriculum to the degree they would like, they can take temporary measures to cope with it.

Today's students have many problems in the areas of drug abuse, conflicts, personal rights, the environment, and health issues. The future holds many threats, promises, and challenges for students. How the teacher reacts to and plans for overcoming obstacles will affect the future world, the educational advancement of students, and their sense of purpose. In order to improve this society, the business educator must tackle the job of keeping the student informed about demographic and social changes.

References

Bird, C. (1994). Good years. *Your life in the twenty-first century*. New York: Dutton.

Dykman, A. (1994). Ready for the techno world? *Vocational Education Journal, 69*, 28-40.

Farley, C. J. (1996, July 19). Taking shots at the baby boomers. *Time,* 30.

Jones, V. A. (1993, March). Micrographics. *The Office, 115*, 16-18.

Kimbrell, G., Vineyard, B., & Putnam, M. V. (1994). *Advancing in the world of work.* New York: Glencoe, Macmillan/McGraw-Hill.

Klieman, C. (1995, December 14). Social impacts hit hard. *San Jose Mercury News,* p. A1.

Lawrence Hall of Science. (1996). *Equals.* Berkeley: University of California.

Naisbitt, J. (1992). *Megatrends.* New York: Warner Books.

Rosenbaum, E. (1994, June 20). The war on welfare mothers. *Time,* 74.

Scharr, H. A. (1996). *A typical American as seen through the eyes of the census bureau.* U.S. Department of Commerce. Bureau of the Census.

Sheehy, G. (1994). *New passages.* Reading, MA: Addison Wesley.

U.S. Census Bureau. (1986-1996). Bureau of Labor Statistics. Civilian Labor Force. (internet http://stats.bls.gov/special.requests/lf/cpsbref1.htm or cpsinfo@bls.gov).

Woods, J., & Pooles, C. (1996). 1996 MSA profile. *American Demographics,* 23.

CHAPTER 3

Workplace Environment

Christine M. Haff
Camden High School, Camden, South Carolina

Billie Herrin
University of Montana, Missoula, Montana

No one today can question the impact that information technology has had on the way work is performed in the business organization. The Information Age is still in its infancy, but it is steadily influencing work, play, and life itself. The impact is felt everywhere—in homes, in schools, in businesses, in government, and around the world. The Information Superhighway is talked about in all walks of life, and the Internet is just the transitional technology that will enable anyone to gain access to information needed wherever that information is stored. Everyone needs to be computer literate in order to take advantage of the information and services available.

The use of information technology in business and industry today is a key factor in increasing productivity. Technology does not make employees more productive—employees are more productive when they know how to use technology to carry out their job responsibilities in a more efficient and effective manner. The use of information technology does facilitate work, and employers will continue to seek and recruit prospective employees who can be immediately productive on the job.

Information technology plays a major role in the future workplace environment. The purpose of this chapter is to explore key issues that will have an impact on how and where work will be done. Issues related to technology use, including security and ergonomics, contract staffing and flexible scheduling, changes in organizational structures, and work provisos, will be discussed with respect to how the issues will shape the workplace environment in the 21st century.

Issues Related to Technology Use

At the conclusion of formal education, whether it is the completion of high school or a two- or four-year postsecondary degree program, young people will join the "estimated two-thirds of the technical, managerial, and administrative workforce using computers on their jobs today" (Wooldridge, 1994). While the need to train competent information technology professionals is critical, the majority of the populace will be categorized as end-users— people who use information technology in their jobs and in their personal lives. End-users and the workplace environment are being impacted by the Internet and ergonomics.

Technology use and security. Defined as the global information and electronic communications network, the Internet started with just four computers in 1969 (ARPANET) and has mushroomed into an information infrastructure, comprising an estimated three million host computers linking millions of people in more than 80 countries. End-users, either from home using a commercial on-line service connection or from the office, utilize the Internet to seek information or to communicate with others around the corner or around the world. Discussion groups, newsgroups, audio/video-conferencing, and computer conferencing are current resources that can be utilized in the workplace using the Internet and other communication technologies (Gehris, 1996).

Business and industry firmly believe that in order to gain the competitive edge and compete in global markets, employees must have access to up-to-date information for decision-making and must communicate information to co-workers, customers, and suppliers. The exchange of electronic messages, transmission of documents, retrieval of information from outside sources, and marketing of products and services are among the many uses for which companies utilize the Internet today. Increased Internet usage at work raises issues of business data security, ethical and legal use of information, and privacy of employees.

Security on the Internet is crucial for business and corporate confidentiality. When a workstation on a local network is connected to the Internet, anyone can easily access other Internet sites and download files, open a remote terminal connection to a supercomputer, or browse literature. Significant financial losses are experienced due to the rise in computer break-ins. In a 1994 study of more than 1,000 companies, 20 percent reported a substantial financial loss. Therefore, companies are electronically strengthening security on their local networks through the use of firewalls, wiretaps, cryptography, and surveillance of users, which opens the door to numerous ethical and legal issues (Warren, 1996).

Is "Big Brother" watching you? Could be. With respect to Internet use and e-mail, many privacy issues concerning the sender, receiver, and content remain unresolved, including the monitoring of internal e-mail. What are the guidelines? What are the penalties for violation of guidelines? Who owns the message? Who should have access to the message? What are the rights of the employee or employer with respect to use and content? "No specific federal legislation exists that protects the monitoring of e-mail by employers, and no federal legislation exists that protects the employee's right to privacy in the workplace" (Drexel & Nantz, 1995). As internal and external e-mail use escalates, the need for legislation and institutional policy will be critical to protect the rights of users in the workplace.

Federal legislation authorizing local, state, or federal law enforcement agencies to conduct electronic surveillance to protect networks from un-authorized access and use may be forthcoming. In addition, cryptography can be used to protect the privacy of computerized files as well as voice and data communications. Cryptography is used to guarantee that files and communications have not been altered during transmission. Also government and private-sector censorship efforts guard against offensive speech, dangerous information, and other communications classified as obscene or lewd.

Issues relating to surveillance and censorship of the Internet will receive much debate in Congress due to justified concerns for civil liberties and freedoms of expression and religion. A trade-off between privacy and protection may have to be considered. Users of the Internet on and off the job are concerned about inaccurate information or information taken out of context, the misuse of information, as well as invasion of privacy. Strong privacy policies written collaboratively by employers and employees may be the key line of defense against a "Big Brother" workplace environment.

Ergonomic issues. The increased use of microcomputers has led to an increase in concern about the potential threat to workers' health and productivity. Ergonomics, the integration of the worker into the design of the work, is gaining even more attention as the number of workplace injuries increase. Reports of repetitive stress injury alone have tripled since 1984, rising from 18 percent in 1982 to 55 percent in 1992. The Occupational Safety and Health Administration expects ergonomic hazards in the workplace to be a top priority in the 21st century. As a result, health and safety standards will be developed and implemented to promote safe working conditions for all employees whose job responsibility requires the use of a video display terminal (VDT). Three major areas of concern with respect to VDT use are repetitive stress injuries (musculoskeletal disorders), radiation-related illnesses, and vision impairments (Braganza, 1994).

Repetitive stress injuries (RSIs) are by far the fastest growing workplace injury in the United States and are associated with VDT usage. These injuries account for almost 30 percent of worker compensation claims, and the number is expected to reach 50 percent by 2000. RSIs resulted in an average of 22 days per employee for time lost from work, and the average cost of carpal tunnel syndrome repair surgery averaged $29,000 per wrist (Khalil and Melcher, 1994).

Other musculoskeletal disorders include sprains, strains, inflammation, degeneration, tears, pinched nerves or blood vessels, bone splintering, and stress fractures. Symptoms can range from discomfort, fatigue, swelling, and stiffness to pain, numbness, and tingling. Whenever a worker interacts with tools, equipment, work methods, tasks, and the work environment itself, work-related musculoskeletal disorders may occur.

Radiation-related illnesses linked to the computer screen have been an issue of conflicting research and debate for years. Electromagnetic fields (EMFs), extremely low frequency emissions, and very low frequency emissions are the three common types of radiation associated with VDTs. Research has suggested that radiation emissions may be linked to increased cancer risk, birth defects, and miscarriages; but relevant research has not reached a consensus. Other sources of EMFs include laptop computer screens, wireless local area networks, and cellular telephones (Khalil and Melcher, 1994).

Even though conclusive research on the dangers of electromagnetic fields does not exist, office workers, especially women, should take precautionary measures. In this case, an ounce of prevention is worth a pound of cure until conclusive evidence one way or the other is determined (Khalil and Melcher, 1994).

Vision impairments, which include eye discomfort, strain, burning, itching, irritation, aching, and headaches, are typically reported complaints by workers who use VDTs for more than four hours per day. Improper lighting, brightness and contrast, reflection, background, and glare are the main contributors. Another source of eyestrain results when users proofread work from a screen rather than hard copy. The time needed to proofread from the screen increases 30 percent, thus increasing the time a user stares at the screen. Focusing distance from the screen is also a contributing factor to vision impairment. The American Optometric Association reports that 50 to 75 percent of VDT workers experience eye problems and recommends that users have an eye examination every year (Khalil and Melcher, 1994).

Since the goal of ergonomics is to improve the health, well-being, and performance of workers by making the jobs, equipment, and environment compatible with individual characteristics and needs, numerous studies have been conducted over the years to ensure goal achievement. Information is now readily available on space planning; lighting; selecting office furniture, chairs, accessories, and computer equipment; training workers and supervisors; creating a safe and secure working environment for those employees who use VDTs through task analysis and job design.

To prevent work-related musculoskeletal disorders and eye discomfort, workstation design will receive even more attention in the future as workstations decrease in size. Special considerations will be given to the monitor and keyboard positions, lighting, and seating. Shared workstations will need to be easily adjustable.

Job design and task analysis can make valuable contributions to improving the health and safety of the workplace environment. Work that involves repetitive tasks will eventually cause pain if the same motion is required over long periods of time. Modifying work processes, alternating tasks, and scheduling frequent "mini" breaks have proven to increase productivity and comfort for VDT users.

The Occupational Safety and Health Administration has recently drafted an ergonomics standard that may result in formal regulations to address ergonomic hazards in the workplace (OSHA Draft Ergonomics Standard, 1996). In addition, many organizations are formulating their own ergonomic policies to promote safe working conditions for users of video display terminals in office environments. Topics of policies include the identification of work risk factors, engineering and administrative controls to reduce the risk, and training and education programs for all workers, including management. The goals of training and education programs are to reduce injury, illness, absenteeism, and worker compensation costs, and to improve productivity and work quality. Users of computer workstations have a vested interest in helping to develop programs that will ensure a safe and healthy workplace environment in the future.

Contract Staffing and Flexible Scheduling

Workforce 2000 described the average worker in 1958 as male, age 40, and married with 2.4 children. He had a high school education or less, and worked full time in a factory or in an office support position for industry. He retired at age 65, if he lived that long, and he could count on working with the same company until retirement. Enter the computer and the Information Age. Futurists describe the average worker in the year 2000 to be female, age 39, and working from home as a computer technician. She will be a member of a professional organization (not a union) and her job performance will be based on quality as well as quantity. Women and minorities will dominate the work force and have at least three years of postsecondary education. Workers will possess at least three occupational areas of expertise to increase their job flexibility and cannot be guaranteed employment with any one company for long periods of time. She will be working for a temporary or employee leasing service. (Johnston & Packer, 1987) What a contradiction in eras! What a contrast in life styles! What a drastic change in the environment in which work will be done!

At a time when business and industry is downsizing, rightsizing, restructuring, and reengineering, many companies are using various staffing and scheduling options to meet current employment needs. Two major categories of strategies are currently being utilized: contract staffing and flexible scheduling. Resources cite four reasons from the employers' position why companies are moving toward these employment alternatives—economic and competitive pressures, the need to reduce costs, a decrease in the labor pool, and a more diverse workforce (New Staffing Strategies for the 90s, 1992). From the worker's perspective, the challenge of balancing work and home life requires flexibility in work schedules and locations. These arrangements appear to be mutually rewarding and indicative of future staffing strategies.

Contract staffing. Contract or flexible staffing includes the use of temporary employees, employee leasing, and outsourcing. The use of contract or flexible staffing is typically budget-driven and used in times of either business expansion or downsizing. These staffing strategies involve employment arrangements with workers not employed by the company.

The use of temporary employees is the most prevalent form of contract staffing. Typically a temporary employee is obtained through an outside service firm and is expected to be productive quickly and to work well in new environments. Temporary services, traditionally used for clerical and blue-collar workers, now provide their clients with accountants, lawyers, doctors, nurses, and senior managers. According to the National Association of Temporary and Staffing Services, more than 2 million temporary workers in 1995 constituted 1.8 percent of total U.S. employment. Increases over previous years were said to be caused by downsizing, global competition, and rapidly changing technology. Instead of laying off new hires, companies now use temporary workers as a buffer. Industry reports indicate that temporary employees are growing at such a fast rate that contract staffing is expected to make up 50 percent of the nation's employment by 2000 (Hayes and Solomon, 1995).

The concept of employee leasing is not new. Some employee-leasing companies have been in business for 15 years or more, and the industry is growing at an average rate of 30 percent a year. Estimates indicate that by 2000, between 14 and 20 million Americans will be "leased" employees. Typically, employee leasing involves a contractual agreement with the leasing company in which a business transfers its payroll and human resource responsibilities. The business retains control as the worksite employer. Leased staffing is most frequently used in professional, technical, or medical positions and in the administrative services area. Currently only eight percent of U.S. companies utilize employee leasing, but this figure is expected to increase well into the 21st century (New Staffing Strategies for the 90s, 1992).

Outsourcing is a form of contract staffing that transfers one or more business applications or functions to a third party. Businesses use outsourcing to reduce costs, increase revenues, or improve customer service by transferring non-core business functions to an experienced expert. Outsourcing often delays or eliminates the need to reinvest in new technologies and eases the reengineering of current business processes. Outsourcing is currently used by legal, insurance, accounting, high technology, manufacturing, and banking companies.

In the area of information systems, network outsourcing is a $2.3 billion-a-year industry, growing at a rate of 20 percent yearly (Evans-Correia, 1992). Other common business functions typically outsourced are employee benefits and human resources. Outsourcing allows most companies to reinvest their dollars in their core business function and frees them from many of the costs and aggravations experienced with maintaining the function in-house. A leader in outsourcing is Eastman Kodak, a company that turned over its data processing function to IBM and DEC in the late 1980s, allowing the company to invest in imaging—its core business.

Flexible scheduling. At a time when the number of employees with family responsibilities is increasing, juggling work and family is in the minds of both employees and employers. Dual-income families, single parents, the increase of women in the workforce, and the need for elder care have prompted business organizations to reduce the stress of employees who cope with such family obligations. One strategy has been the adoption of flexible work schedules, and, by 2000, predictions are that almost 80 percent of companies will be offering this employee benefit. The motivation on the business end is to increase morale and productivity and reduce absenteeism and turnover. As American businesses face the effects of changing demographics and a declining labor market, their ability to retain and recruit the best qualified employees will be enhanced if flexible scheduling is offered as an employee benefit (Sachs, 1994).

The most popular flexible scheduling option offered is flextime. Employees work a set number of hours per day with flexible start and finish times and that includes a set of hours when all employees are on the job. Other variations include variable days, variable weeks, and summer hour flextime. While the disadvantages to the employee include a negative impact on one's career, most employees who utilize flextime understand and accept the trade-offs to meet family responsibilities.

Part-time employment, job sharing, compressed work weeks, and tele-commuting are becoming increasingly popular flexible work arrangements. Part-time employment typically means working 35 hours per week or less, the most common forms being 20 hours per week or three days per week. This option is extremely attractive to mothers who need to work but only want to work when their young children are in school. Another form of part-time employment is job sharing in which two employees share a full-time position with either divided responsibilities or unrelated responsibilities. Other job-sharing models include split week, consecutive days (two and a half days each); split week, non-consecutive days; and alternating weeks (Sachs, 1994).

Another popular scheduling alternative available in some businesses is the compressed workweek. The most common option is 40 hours per week over four days; a second option is the three-day, 12-hours-per-day schedule. The use of the compressed workweek scheduling technique allows the organization to extend its business hours, perhaps increasing accessibility to clients and customers. For the employee, a compressed workweek provides a weekday to handle personal obligations. While this form of scheduling is optional in some companies, compressed workweeks are typically mandated for certain jobs.

Once termed the "electronic cottage," telecommuting (working from the home) will be how, when, and where many people will work in the future. More than 7 million Americans are currently working from an office in their homes, and reports estimate that this number will increase at a rate of 11 percent or more over the next five years (Veresprej, 1994). Other estimates indicate that approximately 70 percent of all information workers in the United States (about 50 million workers) could telecommute at least part of the time (Johansen and Swigart, p. 70).

Compliance with the Clean Air Act of 1990, advances in technology, and changes in lifestyle are major forces driving the increase in telecommuting. Concern over air pollution and traffic congestion led to the passage of the Clean Air Act. The act requires companies with 100 or more employees in the country's 10 most polluted urban areas to reduce employees' commuting trips by 25 percent, effective in 1996. Advances in technology, particularly communications technology, have made it easier for home workers to perform job duties and communicate with customers, suppliers, co-workers, supervisors, and executives. Finally, as discussed earlier, flexibility in work scheduling to facilitate the demands of work and family obligations is a necessity for a large part of the American workforce.

As we approach the 21st century, where will people work? When will people work? According to Robert Johansen, director of new technology programs for the Institute for the Future, "The image of work in just a few years will be the ability to work anytime and anyplace and to take care of needs, rather than having to work nine-to-five around a specific work spot" (Veresprej, p. 37).

Jeff Hill, an IBM executive, fits this image. Hill has been working in a virtual office for some time and is conducting research in this area. He defines the virtual office as doing work through electronic means from a variety of locations using a computer, telephone lines, fax systems, pagers, and cellular phones. This concept applied by IBM helped the company survive while in the midst of massive restructuring and downsizing. For IBM, the virtual office has increased worker productivity, decreased costs in facilities, and provided complete flexibility and mobility with respect to when and where work occurs (Hill, 1996).

The word "office" at one time referred to a very specific place in which work was performed from nine-to-five. For years people have tried to define the "Office of the Future." Now a clearer image exists—anytime and any-place people choose to work!

There are drawbacks to telecommuting. While evidence shows that more companies are adopting alternative workplace strategies such as telecom-muting and the virtual office, other companies are reverting to the traditional workplace environment. Connelly (1995) believes that many people will still want to be part of the daily pageant, the drama, and the water cooler community of the office. The office environment gives direction, discipline, structure, and social interaction to many workers. Because of the "social glue" element of the office community, many workers are reluctant to work at home and manage themselves.

Since teams are now the hottest new management tool, the home-based work environment does not allow the worker to have a direct work experi-ence nor to interact as a team member. Another obstacle includes the inability of the home worker to be evaluated effectively. When only the end product is seen, the worker's daily performance goes unnoticed. Yet another hin-drance is that work at home does not provide a way for males and females to interact as equals.

People sometimes believe that working at home can eliminate the need for child care or elder care. The same child and elder care arrangements should exist whether work is done at home or in the office. Flexibility of working at home does not eliminate the need for this assistance.

Since e-mail becomes the primary means of communication, some people believe that e-mail does not fulfill personal communication needs. Tele-commuters cannot substitute the social interaction and informal knowledge gained around the water cooler by communicating solely through their computer. Telecommuting has proven inauspicious for many workers, and they are by choice moving back to the traditional workplace environment. If companies choose to use telecommuting as a means to cut costs and boost productivity, they should also be prepared to help employees through the transition from an office to telecommuting environments.

Organizational Design

The culture of the workplace is changing and transforming organizations in many operational areas. Fundamental changes are found in such areas as male and female roles, womens' role in the workforce, management and support staff roles, the roles and titles of secretaries, workplace culture, man-agement levels, teamwork concepts, and team structure. These changes are all influencing the workplace environment.

Role changes. Because of the change in support personnel, job descriptions, and the work environment, females are assuming more roles formerly dominated by males; and males are assuming more roles formerly dominated by females. Males are found in office manager and assistant-to- the-chief-administrator positions while females are found in team leader, manager, and supervisory positions. The movement of females through glass walls and ceilings into top management, however, is still at a relatively slow pace.

Caudron (1995) stated that workplace gender politics escalated because women want more power and men do not want to share it. If the workplace were to be viewed as a boxing ring, the American male worker would be found in one corner and the female worker in the other. The male worker is tired of all the accusations leveled at him by females while females want more respect, power, money, and understanding from the men who rule corporate America. Many workers believe that the struggle for power, job security, and diversity programs has contributed to increased tension between the genders.

Some companies today offer programs dealing with gender differences. Such workshops as "Men and Women as Colleagues" have been beneficial in some organizations while only exacerbating the conflict in others.

Although the gap between men's and women's salaries has been slowly closing, women still earn 30 percent less than their counterparts. This disparity further fuels the fire that pits the genders against each other in the workplace (Caudron, 1995).

Women in the workforce. In 1960 women made up 32 percent of the workforce as opposed to 44 percent in 1995. Predictions for the next 20 years suggest that women will fill 80 percent of all new jobs. Mahar (1994) stated that even with these current and predicted workforce changes, results of a study conducted by *Working Women* magazine showed that female executives still feel like aliens who are locked out of the good-old-boy network and are unable to shatter the glass ceiling. As women climb the organizational pyramid, the glass walls become thicker making women feel disenfranchised and angry.

Statistics for 1993 showed that women were receiving over half the management and professional jobs created; however, many of those jobs were in the lower-paying public sector. Although women today are increasingly involved in self-employment and own 24 percent of all businesses in America, many of these positions are frequently low paying (Mahar, 1994).

Management and support staff. Executives are finding their work lists too long and are delegating more of their administrative and managerial tasks to their administrative professional (a.k.a. secretary, administrative assistant, executive secretary, administrative secretary, or office professional). A study by Office Team, a staffing service, showed that 93 percent of top managers are giving the administrative professional more authority than was given five years ago (Stone, 1995).

Willingness to delegate is needed in the workplace to increase productivity. Assigned duties for the administrative professional might include managing projects, selecting software, and interacting with vendors. New authority and involvement open doors to greater job satisfaction and promotability.

Although many administrative professionals and managers believe that positive changes are translating into greater opportunities for the worker, others believe that the additional responsibilities and workloads are creating motivational problems. Many believe they are receiving neither training for their new responsibilities nor support and cooperation from peer staff members. Without administrators clearly defining the new authority and role expectations of the administrative professional to all office management and personnel, the administrative professional becomes frustrated with the new challenges and responsibilities (Stone, 1995).

Secretary's role and title. Anita Reed, of Anita Reed Seminars, Dallas, advocates a new name for the office professional—coordinator. Reed believes that the term "secretary" and the work once done by the "secretary" no longer exist. Because managers and administrators are now writing and transmitting their own correspondence with the help of computers and communicating through e-mail and voice mail, secretaries are no longer providing support for these activities. Secretaries are instead being freed to do projects themselves. Project coordinators would plan and manage their own projects, participate regularly in staff and planning meetings, and help set and achieve departmental goals. Other responsibilities might include planning and arranging meetings, supervising others, participating in task forces, making oral and written presentations, and making independent decisions (Stone, 1995).

As project coordinators take on these new responsibilities, management needs to support training programs for the shifting role positions. Coordinators would need to continue to gain the cooperation and respect of those people who would still see them as secretaries.

Ways in which managers could support this new role would include: (a) providing time and tuition to return to the classroom, (b) providing a title and compensation to go along with new responsibilities; (c) serving as mentors who offer advice and counsel when needed; and (d) demonstrating support by invitations to meetings as participants and not as secretaries. This role change would affect all office personnel (Stone, 1995).

Although Reed's suggested name and role change may seem more realistic and applicable to the role of secretary today, many would not agree. Professional Secretaries International, comprising over 40,000 secretaries, has decided to stay with the title "secretary." The association wants to work to change the image of secretary rather than give in to the negative stereotype about the role. A name change for the secretary may be imminent in the 21st century if credibility for the profession is going to be maintained.

Workplace culture. Culture includes the people in the workforce, the staff who makes decisions, how workers are organized, and how trust and respect are developed. Many of the changes in the workplace culture include trends toward a team approach, employee empowerment, global corporate environment awareness, and respect for the worker.

Flynn (1995) stated that people in the United States get a bit smug about multi-ethnicism and refer to the population as a rainbow of different people or the "Great Melting Pot." When looking around many offices today, however, the rainbow found is pale and male-dominated. Results of diversity studies in the United States show that ethnic minorities hold few management or executive positions.

A 1990 survey conducted by New York City-based Catalyst showed that women comprise less than 5 percent of senior managers in Fortune 500 companies. Another survey in 1992 by the American Management Association showed that minorities held only 7.4 percent of senior management positions. Three years later that number had risen to a modest 10.6 percent (Flynn, 1995).

Although diversity programs have emerged throughout corporate America to aid in recruitment, retention, and career development of women and minorities, greater access to management positions has not resulted. To make diversity programs work, support from top-level management, a shift in recruitment goals, a change in management strategies, and additional workforce training are required.

Bank of America Corporation, San Francisco, promotes diversity in its organization. Of their 96,500 employees, 69 percent worldwide are women, and 49 percent are minorities. Bank of America provides 18 diversity network chapters across six states. These networks help employees in their personal and professional development (Flynn, 1995).

To improve and support diversity and feelings of equity in the workplace, company programs should continue which:

- support parenting—provide resources for both parents;
- promote shared responsibility—fair workloads and fair rewards;
- provide economic partnerships—encourage continuing education and retraining of employees;
- promote respect, trust, and support—embrace diversity by not allowing differences to become divisive;
- focus on equity—support solving issues of gender and race differences by shattering the glass walls and ceilings for women, people of color, older, and other differentiated employees.

As the 21st century nears, continued diversity programs will hold even greater importance for workers. Current studies show the following changes in the American culture:

- A 40 percent chance that two randomly selected North Americans today would be from different ethnic or racial backgrounds.
- In 14 percent of American homes a language other than English is spoken.
- Of new entrants into the workforce, 43 percent are immigrants or people of color.
- By 2000, 70 percent of the workforce will be women and people of color (Flynn, 1995).

Management levels. Organizations are at a point of fundamental transformation from the traditional vertical, functional hierarchy to a horizontal, process-based design. This new model includes trenchant elements such as core process teams that provide the foundation of organizational design. Teams are built around a core process instead of departments. Process leaders instead of department managers are the top managers. Another feature of this new model is customer satisfaction. Ford customers are concerned with getting their cars repaired, not with customer service department goals or dealer's sales targets. A support manager at Ford Motor Co. said that this new model represents the kind of company a customer would design (Jacob, 1995).

Many companies are beginning to take the challenge of implementing new ideas in organizational design. Horizontal design experts attest that using a road map for getting from a functional organization to a horizontal organization is important. A company must first determine what core processes will be used and whether a cross-functional, process-based organization will lead the organization to achieve coherent goals. Secondly, CEOs must have a clear strategic direction in which to move before deciding to pursue this new direction (Jacob, 1995).

If companies adopt and move to the 21st century using this horizontal process, predictions are that work will be simplified and technology will move things quickly through an internal superhighway. Use of technology will also improve decision making and quickly move information across the horizontal corporation design. The foundation for this horizontal process model is a derivative of the process emphasis of total quality management.

Teamwork concepts. Teamwork is the rallying cry of business today. Many organizations are replacing hierarchical management structures with self-managed work teams. Team members must accept more responsibility and broaden interpersonal communication skills as well as technological expertise. The elimination of middle management has led to horizontal rather than vertical career movement in many organizations. The creation of work teams is a trend that may signal the end of age-old management methods (Caudron, 1994).

Teamwork takes *work*. Ensuring the success of work teams requires considerable effort. A group of people with different personalities, expectations, experience, and knowledge who are brought together to accomplish a certain task may not easily adjust to the team concept. Americans are taught to value individualism, to respect and accept authority, and to expect pay increases based on seniority. Employees who have worked independently for years do not automatically know how to work in teams; they find that teamwork requires a master plan and takes time, training, team participation, process mapping, benchmarking, bonding, and design planning (Caudron, 1994).

Joan M. Chesterton, associate professor of organizational leadership and supervision at Purdue University, argues that the traditional organization—where managers think, supervisors push, and workers work—is counterproductive in today's business environment. Because of teams and empowerment, employees are learning to manage themselves. Managers must develop such new skills as coaching, facilitating, and resolving conflict, or they will get left behind (*USA Today Magazine*, August, 1995).

Obstacles facing teams include insufficient training, incompatible organization systems, first-line supervisor resistance, lack of planning, lack of management support, and lack of union support. The theory that teams are more productive and will produce a higher quality product functioning as a team is one that traditional managers may find challenging. Managers who will have the most difficult time in the team environment are those who come from supervisory backgrounds. The skills they have been taught apply to managing or supervising individuals—exactly the type of skills that can kill a team project.

Team structure. Three major team structures being used in companies today are collaborative, cross-functional, and global. All three have in common the fact that to be effective in any work environment, planning and effort are necessary ingredients.

A collaborative team's main function is to build ownership of the team's operations and ensure the alignment of its members with the strategic direction of the company. The team works collaboratively to clarify the function of the team, define team members' roles and responsibilities, define operating agreements, create a charter, identify critical success factors, develop an action plan, develop collaborative skills, and establish criteria to measure progress.

A cross-functional team is composed of groups within the organization who take over the previous role of departments or divisions. These teams include people from two or more divisions who work together to complete projects. Instead of work being done in one division and then being sent to another for completion, people from both divisions are team members.

A global team addresses certain problems that may affect the bottom line of productivity in an international operation. Open communication about cultural differences and training to help members develop interpersonal and intercultural skills are necessary for the effective functioning of a global team (Solomon, 1995).

Work Proviso

Work proviso refers to programs that affect the worker and the work environment. Solomon (1995) states that the workplace of the 1990s is a paradox. Although cellular phones, portable faxes, pocket-sized computers with wireless modems, videoconferenceing, and virtual offices allow people to work anywhere at anytime, work/family issues are in the 1980s time warp.

Work and family issues. Many workers today are having difficulty arranging work and family life even with the assistance of company support programs. Concern continues to grow for the physical, financial, and spiritual health of highly skilled, highly paid, knowledgeable workers who are shouldering heavier tax and dependent care burdens.

The 1994 statistics showed that 45.6 percent of the working population were women, 40 percent of all women in the workforce had children under 18, 67.2 percent of women with children under 18 held jobs, and 16 percent had elder care responsibilities. Other studies showed that single fathers were among the fastest growing segments in the workforce; the population in our country was aging, and the average worker lost from seven to nine workdays per year (half of the lost days were due to family problems). In order to provide assistance to workers and to keep them as productive contributors to the company, many organizations are providing benefit packages and programs. Some companies believe that every dollar spent on family resource programs yields more than two dollars in direct cost savings (Solomon, 1994).

Although, some companies are addressing work/family issues with dependent care benefits and family friendly policies, Solomon (1994) believes that work/family issues in most companies are still in a 1980s time warp. United States businesses still fail dismally in taking a long-term, integrated approach to work/family balance.

Compensation packages. Top level executives or CEOs are mirroring the compensation packages paid to movie and sport "superstars," while ordinary working people are languishing in accepting small pay raises and ever slimmer benefit packages. These two trends are widening pay gaps and threatening the country's sense of economic fairness and civility that underpins employee morale in an era of corporate restructuring. The pay gaps are not anomalies that affect only a few workers (McNerney, 1995).

A study by a University of California-Berkeley professor showed that the ratio of CEO compensation (superstars) to the average American worker in 1992 was 145-1, in 1993 170-1, and in 1994 187-1. Second-level earnings (referred to as minor league superstars) of doctors, lawyers, dentists, executives, administrators, sales representatives, accountants, and consultants are not near the ratio of the CEOs. Top level executives or CEOs are also rewarded with long-term incentive packages (i.e., stock, stock options, grants, profit-based bonuses) while ordinary workers do not usually share these incentives.

In this two-tier system, where companies lavish rewards to superstars and remain tight-fisted with others, a message of teamwork importance is not being sent. Employees are getting the message that individual work is what is rewarded. The way in which companies can respond to this trend is to increase stock-based incentives and deferred compensation to the key players in their company and distribute stock and gainsharing awards lower in the organization (McNerney, 1995).

Flex plans. Dependent costs are being absorbed more by the worker in many companies today. Companies cannot afford to pay for full coverage for their employees. They may pay 100 percent of hospital costs but have a shared 80/20 on medical. Costs of dependent coverage are paid more and more by the employee (McNerney, 1995). A Tower and Perrin Survey in 1992 showed that a certain level of employee benefits is now necessary just to remain competitive. A survey of more than 100 employers found that as a group, participants offered more than 100 varieties of worklife initiatives. The baseline for this study was for employers to have more than 20 programs or related benefits, including health coverage. Figure 1 shows the top 12 benefits with the percentage of companies offering each.

Figure 1

WORK-LIFE BENEFITS

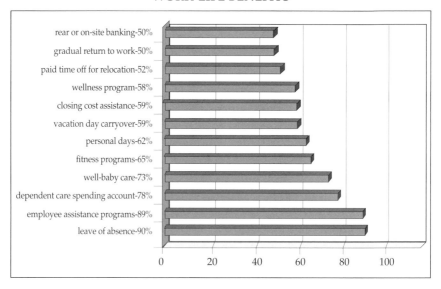

Other services being offered by some corporations today include savings plans, contribution plans, profit sharing, group life insurance, child care benefit plans, elder care, flexible work arrangements, dependent care during holidays, on-site day care, tuition reimbursement or vouchers, elder care education and assistance, family leave, adoption assistance, relocation assistance, and assistance to unconventional families. Studies show that companies that use multiple work-family benefits achieve higher performance ratings than companies that do not offer similar perks (McNerney, 1995).

Impact on Business Education

Peter Drucker, one of this century's most influential management thinkers, believes history's next major transformation, the knowledge age, is here. This transformation is described by Don Tapscott in his new book, *The Digital Economy*, as a knowledge economy. This knowledge economy is based on the application of human know-how, to know what and how everything is produced. Tapscott stated that, already, almost 60 percent of all American workers are knowledge workers and eight of 10 new jobs are in information-intensive sectors of the economy (Tapscott, 1995).

Schools across the nation are becoming involved in School-to-Work programs. These programs are one way in which the linking of learning and work apply to this evolving knowledge economy. Successful School-to-Work programs can help prepare the workforce of tomorrow to meet the challenges of the knowledge age. These programs also allow business teachers to team and interact with other academic teachers, administrators, and counselors in coordinating the School-to-Work program.

Today, a wealth of information is available at the touch of a computer key. The ability to effectively use information technology will be a required skill for productive citizenship in the 21st century. In order to prepare today's students for tomorrow's challenges and the knowledge economy, schools must integrate technology as a tool to enhance and facilitate the learning process. Business educators can look at the strong information systems base in our business curricula and build courses and units that continually update students' knowledge about the changing workplace. Business educators must continue to teach students to live and work productively as technology changes. The efficient utilization of information technology will help schools and students achieve world-class education standards.

Future workforce. Technology provides instant access to detailed information about current employees and previous applicants. Waiting many days to receive information through the mail is unnecessary because transmission through fax machines or information faxed directly from computers is instantaneous.

As we move into the 21st century, techno-literacy will become even more important. Multimedia programs will take over a large portion of employee education, mainly training. Workers will continue to become more proficient in the use of e-mail, voice mail, teleconferencing, videoteleconferencing, and image "zapping." Portable faxes, cellular phones, pocket-sized computers, wireless modems, and other new devices in the traditional office and the virtual office will continue to allow universal information access.

Business education and business educators can continue to lead and prepare students for the 21st century by remaining knowledgeable about the changes in the workplace environment. Continual professional development workshops and updates on future trends and issues will keep business educators and students "fit" for the 21st century.

References

Adapting to a work team concept. (1995, August). *USA Today (Magazine), 124,* 10-11.

Braganza, B. J. (1994, August). Ergonomics in the office. *American Society of Safety Engineers,* 22-27.

Caudron, S. (1994). Teamwork takes work. *Personnel Journal,* 40-48.

Caudron, S. (1995). Sexual politics. *Personnel Journal,* 50-61.

Connelly, J. (1995, March). Let's hear it for the office. *Fortune,* 221-222.

Drexel, C., & Nantz, K. S. (1995) The legal issues of electronic mail. *Office Systems Research Journal, 37*(2), 15-19.

Evans-Correia, K. (1992, June). Outsourcing demands changes in purchasing. *Purchasing,* 42-43.

Flynn, G. (1995). Do you have the right approach to diversity. *Personnel Journal,* 68-75.

Gehris, D. O. (1996) Using the internet in the communications technologies course. *Proceedings of the Fifteenth Annual Office Systems Research Association Conference,* 71-77.

Hayes, C., & Solomon, C. (1996, February). The lure of temping. *Black Enterprise,* 119-122.

Hill, J. (1996, February 29) Life in the Virtual Office. [Speaker at Office Systems Research Association Conference, Orlando, Florida].

Jacob, R. (1995, April). Organization for the 21st century. *Fortune,* 90-99.

Johansen, R.,& Swigart, R. (1996). *Upsizing the individual in the downsized organization,* Reading, MA:Addison Wesley.

Johnston, W.B., & Packer, A.H. (1987). *Workforce 2000.* Indianapolis: Hudson Institute.

Khalil, O. E., & Melcher, J. E. (1994, Summer). Office automation threat to health and productivity: A new management concern. *SAM Advanced Management Journal,* 10-14.

Mahar, M. (1994, March). White-collar wash: for women, more jobs, less $. *Working Women, 19*(2), 16.

McNerney, D. J. (1995, October). Compensation trend: The winner-take-all economy. *HR Focus,* 3-5.

OSHA Draft Ergonomics Standard, http:/www.dir.ca.gov/dir/Bulletin/Jan_Feb_96/OSHSB.html

New staffing strategies for the 90s. (1992). Westbury, NY: Olsten.

Sachs, S. (1994) Balancing work and family through flexible work options. *Education for employment, vocational equity.* Ohio State University, College of Education, (Monographs) 9(1), pp. 3-9.

Solomon, C. M. (1994). Work/family's failing grade: Why today's initiatives aren't enough. *Personnel Journal,* 73-87.

Solomon, C. M. (1995). Global teams: The ultimate collaboration. *Personnel Journal,* pp. 49-58.

Stone, F. (1995). Meet the secretary of the '90s. *HR Focus,* 22-23.

Tapscott, D. (1995). *The digital economy.* (p. 6). New York: McGraw-Hill.

Veresprej, M. (1994, July). The anytime, anyplace workplace. *Industry Week,* pp. 37-39.

Warren, J. Surveillance and Censorship on the Internet, http://www.sims.berkeley.edu/conferences/warren.html (18 November 1995).

Wooldridge, B. (1994) Changing demographics of the workforce: Implications for the use of technology as a productivity strategy. *Public Productivity & Management Review,* 371- 383.

CHAPTER 4

Learning Environment

Marlene Todd Stout

Kokomo High School, Kokomo, Indiana

Schools have been referred to as "learning organizations" (Senge and O'Neill, 1995). This term brings together the "business" and "education" aspects that business education teachers are trained in, function in, and work to coordinate, explain, and promote.

Just as job, economic, and global uncertainties currently exist, the educational environment remains uncertain. The educational community is experiencing change and must react and respond to the myriad of criticisms, recommendations, and support received from all arenas. Mandates, programs, funding, general teacher licensing, and a host of educational philosophies necessitate continual response by teachers and administrators.

Of all the disciplines that exist within a total school curriculum, none has traditionally been impacted or responsive to change as has the business education curriculum. In addition, business teachers are accustomed to and comfortable with curriculum change and the learning environment change.

The learning environment encompasses any and all factors that enhance or impede the learning that does or does not occur. The learning environment is traditionally thought of as the "atmosphere" that exists within a classroom. During the past several years, that environment has been dynamically changing.

The term "learning organizations" reflects a business environment or business organization where "learning" is the product. Figure 1 (Stout and Hamilton, 1996) illustrates the correlation between production in a business/manufacturing environment and in an education environment. The correlation illustrates one main difference: quality control. At each level, uncontrollable variables exist in the educational environment. Educators and those involved directly or indirectly with education are looking (or searching it seems) for ways to produce a more skilled, competent, and knowledgeable product that will meet the requirements or expectations of employers, parents, legislators, and postsecondary institutions.

Much of the current reform movement is directed at the "quality control" element. Methodology and structure are two examples used to manage, curtail, and even eliminate uncontrollable variables in order to produce a better product.

School Climate

The learning environment encompasses all areas of education from the organizational structure of the school to the curriculum, location, and

Figure 1

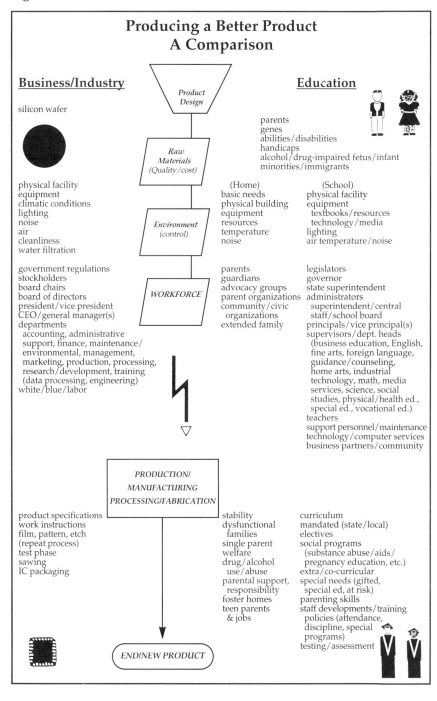

Producing a Better Product
A Comparison

Business/Industry

Product Design

silicon wafer

physical facility
equipment
climatic conditions
lighting
noise
air
cleanliness
water filtration

Raw Materials (Quality/cost)

Environment (control)

government regulations
stockholders
board chairs
board of directors
president/vice president
CEO/general manager(s)
departments
  accounting, administrative
  support, finance, maintenance/
  environmental, management,
  marketing, production, processing,
  research/development, training
  (data processing, engineering)
white/blue/labor

WORKFORCE

PRODUCTION/ MANUFACTURING PROCESSING/FABRICATION

product specifications
work instructions
film, pattern, etch
(repeat process)
test phase
sawing
IC packaging

END/NEW PRODUCT

Education

parents
genes
abilities/disabilities
handicaps
alcohol/drug-impaired fetus/infant
minorities/immigrants

(Home)
basic needs
physical building
equipment
resources
temperature
noise

(School)
physical facility
equipment
textbooks/resources
technology/media
lighting
air temperature/noise

parents
guardians
advocacy groups
parent organizations
community/civic
  organizations
extended family

legislators
governor
state superintendent
administrators
  superintendent/central
  staff/school board
principals/vice principal(s)
supervisors/dept. heads
  (business education, English,
  fine arts, foreign language,
  guidance/counseling,
  home arts, industrial
  technology, math, media
  services, science, social
  studies, physical/health ed.,
  special ed., vocational ed.)
teachers
support personnel/maintenance
technology/computer services
business partners/community

stability
dysfunctional
  families
single parent
welfare
drug/alcohol
  use/abuse
parental support,
  responsibility
foster homes
teen parents
  & jobs

curriculum
mandated (state/local)
electives
social programs
  (substance abuse/aids/
  pregnancy education, etc.)
extra/co-curricular
special needs (gifted,
  special ed, at risk)
parenting skills
staff developments/training
policies (attendance,
  discipline, special
  programs)
testing/assessment

mission. The learning environment, however, is embodied in the school climate. Factors of school climate can address trust, respect, cohesiveness, continuous academic and social growth, and safety. A school climate determinant includes, but is not limited to:

- *Program determinants:* opportunities for learning, varied learning environments, flexible curriculum and extracurricular activities, rules, varied reward systems.
- *Process determinants:* improvements of school goals, effective communications, autonomy with accountability, effective teaching-learning strategies.
- *Materials determinants:* adequate resources, suitability of school plant (Howard, Howell, Brainard, 1987).

The degree to which business education programs and positive learning experiences for students is influenced by school climate is reflected by the attitudes and support of the administration regarding equipment, technology, resources and supplies, curriculum, staffing, recognition of the importance of the discipline, and encouragement of students to take business courses. One of the most critical aspects of business education programs is the continuous growth and aggressive pursuit by business teachers to implement current strategies, to be aware of current business practices including technology, and to promote the discipline.

Curriculum

The business curriculum and the delivery medium are continually changing. Courses are being added and deleted; content is constantly being revised; the resources and equipment used to deliver business courses are forever evolving. Technological advances often determine what is taught.

Business education teachers must take the lead to ensure that the business curriculum reflects current and future needs of the students. The content and skills areas will continue to be critical as new software, equipment, information, business practices, procedures, and protocol become available. Business educators must also infuse global learning, research skills, ethics, cultural perspectives, diversity, collaborative learning environments, and electronic communities of learning while they focus on academic excellence (Cummins & Sayers, 1995).

The National Standards for Business Education (NBEA, 1995) in addition to such documents as SCANS (Secretary's Commission on Achieving Necessary Skills) developed by the U.S. Department of Labor, 1991, and various standardized assessments reflect the need to maintain high standards for business education courses. At the same time, business education teachers must look for ways to affiliate business courses with traditional "academic" or basic courses such as accounting and algebra. Pairing courses and integrating the course contents allows for relevance and greater understanding for students. For example, associating algebraic equations with accounting formulas perpetuates an "academic" image for business courses.

Business educators must promote the business course curriculum in terms of basic skills (core areas), life skills, information technology skills, entrepreneurship skills, international business knowledge, and lifelong learning needed by all students regardless of their career goals. When the business education curriculum is recognized as an essential component in the total school curriculum, the image of the courses changes. This improved image impacts the learning environment by appealing to more students with varying ability levels.

When a discipline is viewed as "essential," a more serious attitude prevails on the part of students and administration, thus creating a more positive environment within the classroom. For example, economics of business may be taken for business or social studies credit in Indiana. Many students who take this course for the required social studies credit appear to be more serious about completing assigned work, participating in class, and improving overall performance. Subject matter, relevancy, requirement, association, career and college preparation, interest, importance, and image also contribute to the learning environment. If a course is required, needed for college entrance, or considered academic, students appear to be more conscientious about their work and a studious environment prevails.

Methodology and Instruction

The business education curriculum has been secure in the validation of instructional methodology based upon years of research. Technology is impacting all curricula and has become a benchmark for school progressiveness and student learning.

Business educators are being challenged to "not hide behind old studies," to show proof that their methods are still "valid," and to be receptive to new or different ways of instructing students. Business educators must not abandon proven methods of instruction that best deliver subject matter but must also continue to be the innovators incorporating applicable new techniques.

Terms like application-oriented, team work, school to work, and cooperative learning embody many of the methods and concepts that have been used for years by business educators. At the same time, business educators must be cognizant of and receptive to instructional techniques that will demonstrate and enhance the learning environment without impeding acquisition and subject matter mastery. If the business curriculum is to be recognized as a vital part of the total curriculum, current practices must be reflected in instruction. Many schools are providing staff development on current instructional techniques and strategies to facilitate instruction.

Empowerment is a term that has surfaced at all levels of education. Administrators, teachers, and students want to be empowered to make decisions. Learner-centered schools are emerging that focus on students making more decisions and assuming more responsibility for managing their learning.

Two techniques used to empower students and facilitate the learning environment are the rubric and t-charts.

The rubric. This evaluation device provides students with an assessment instrument. Students often provide input for the development of the rubric. Performance indicators may be listed on the x-axis and the criteria on the y-axis. Indicators represent the weight or points that a criterion will receive.

A rubric can be developed for almost any area of performance such as a speech, a job interview, or a final exam. Table 1 illustrates a rubric for a business plan.

Table 1

Business Plan Rubric Cube

CRITERIA	1 (5 POINTS)	2 (10 POINTS)	3 (15 POINTS)	4 (20 POINTS)
Organization	Poor - lacks order/confusing	Average- major points included	Good sequence - all parts included	Excellent - extra points included
Content	Poor - information missing	Average - most information included	Good - all included	Excellent - above and beyond requirements
Correctness	Many errors - spelling, grammar, incorrect format	Average - a few mistakes	Good - correct format almost no errors	Excellent - error free
Neatness - Presentation	Sloppy folder, no folder	Average quality - poor folder	Good quality - neat, good folder	Excellent - very professional

T-chart. T-accounts or charts are used within a classroom for establishing rules of classroom performance, behavior, or a task-specific activity. When establishing classroom behavior rules, the teacher draws a T-chart on the board, and together the students and the teacher list acceptable behavior on the left side with corresponding "looks like" or consequences on the right side (Johnson, Johnson, Holuybec, 1994). One benefit of utilizing these charts is improved behavior/performance because the students have a voice in establishing the rules or criteria for their expected behavior. Table 2 is an abbreviated T-chart for class rules.

Table 2

Classroom Behavior Rules

Rule	Looks Like
1. Participates	1. Volunteers; answers when called upon.
2. Remains on task	2. Completes activity assigned; does not stop to visit; does not do other work; does not sleep
3. Displays courtesy	3. Raises hand to be called upon; does not disrupt.

Cooperative learning. Teachers use cooperative learning as a classroom management tool. Cooperative learning has gained popularity as an instructional method to help students learn teamwork and to reach a higher degree of knowledge. The fact that many employees lose their jobs from their inability to work in teams and cooperate with co-workers validates the need for cooperative learning. Cooperative learning provides opportunites to work in teams and to reinforce learning as students teach other students.

According to Johnson and Johnson (1983), cooperative learning promotes:

- Higher achievement.
- Increased retention.
- Greater use of higher level reasoning.
- Increased perspective taking.
- Greater intrinsic motivation.
- More positive heterogeneous relationships.
- Better attitudes toward school.
- Better attitudes toward teachers.
- Higher self-esteem.
- Greater social support.
- Improved psychological adjustment.
- More on-task behavior.
- Greater collaborative skills.

Basic elements of cooperative learning include positive interdependence, face-to-face interaction, individual accountability, interpersonal and small group skills, and group processing. (Johnson, Johnson, and Holuybec, 1986). Students are divided into groups; are assigned roles such as reader, recorder, and checker; are given clear expectations; and then issued a problem or task to solve as a group or team.

Many business education courses lend themselves to cooperative learning activities. Utilizing the team concept presents opportunities to discuss management and production techniques in different countries and to solve problems.

T.E.S.A. Teacher Expectations and Student Achievement is teacher-oriented and directed toward improving teacher performance in order to improve student performance. T.E.S.A. is based upon expectation theory.

T.E.S.A. offers five units of teacher instruction in each of the three interactions: response opportunities, feedback, and person regard. Units include equitable distribution, individual help, latency, delving, higher-level questioning, affirm/correct, praise, proximity, and courtesy (T.E.S.A., Los Angeles County Office of Education, 1993). During T.E.S.A. training, teachers are grouped and spend time observing and coding each other based on the units studied. T.E.S.A. provides teachers an opportunity to evaluate their teaching methods and techniques and creates a greater awareness of the teacher's role in learning.

4-Mat learning, learning styles, and multiple intelligences. Determining a student's learning style and developing lesson plans to facilitate that style is indicative of an emphasis on individualized learning and an increased effort to accommodate all students within a classroom. In the business education classroom, teachers have been adjusting and accommodating these various styles for many years. A formalized assessment of students is often undertaken using a learning-style grid. A completed grid helps determine a student's learning style.

A learning-style inventory describes the way a person learns and how the person deals with ideas and day-to-day situations. Styles are divided into: concrete experience (feelings), reflective observation (watching), abstract conceptualization (thinking), and active experimentation (doing) (Kolb, 1985). Learning-style tests may be given to determine whether a student is a visual, manual, audio, or multisensory learner. Learning-style test results assist the teacher in recognizing learning difficulties, developing lesson plans, and planning student activities.

To implement the 4-Mat system, the teachers may determine their own learning and teaching styles (Excel, Inc., 1993). The teacher's learning and teaching styles often dictates the methodology used, because teachers often use the instructional methods that reflect their own learning styles.

Multiple intelligences. This is the theory that emphasizes the highly varied capacities of human beings. The MI theory proposes that people use at least seven relatively autonomous intellectual capacities—each with its own distinctive mode of thinking—to approach problems and create products. These seven intelligences are:

- Linguistic intelligence.
- Logical - mathematical intelligence.
- Spatial intelligence.
- Bodily kinesthetic intelligence.
- Musical intelligence.
- Interpersonal intelligence.
- Intrapersonal intelligence (Gardner, 1983).

Right- and left-brain approaches to learning can be determined by completing a hemispheric mode indicator (HMI). HMI provides right/left mode characteristics that aid the teacher in determining why students are or are not acquiring certain skills and knowledge. Left mode learners are classified as being rational and sequential. They prefer multiple choice tests and talking/writing activities. Right-mode learners are intuitive; they respond to demonstrations and illustrations (Excel, Inc. 1993).

The degree to which these methods or theories are utilized in the classroom varies. The learning environment is impacted when educators become aware that students and teachers have different learning styles, dominant intelligences, and preferences. This information becomes more important than ever before because the student population for many business courses appears to be changing. The business education curriculum serves all learners with varying abilities. Implementation of learning-style assessments and the development of materials to accommodate these styles reflect an academic image.

As business education advocates strive to change the perception or image of business education, an awareness of the necessity and benefits of integrating "academic"and "elective" courses is emerging. An increased emphasis on "life skills," such as those acquired by taking business courses, is gaining support.

The benefits of skill- and technology-driven courses are gaining popularity and support and are viewed as essential for college-bound students. However, low-ability, unmotivated, and uninterested students may also enroll in the courses. Often the term "elective" equals "easy" to many students.

Incorporating techniques beyond lectures, discussions, videos, and questions at the end of the chapter with the presentation of various learning style activities reaches out to a varied student population. These techniques can enhance the learning environment and thus increase the success of students.

Teacher, Coach Facilitator

Through instructional methods such as cooperative learning, the concept of the teacher as "coach" or "facilitator of learning" has emerged. The objective is to empower learners to make more decisions and assume more responsibility for their own learning.

Learner-centered schools create an environment in which the teacher functions as a facilitator. Instructional support teams are established and case managers identified. This approach supports the "learning organizations" concept. Students become more responsible for their own learning. Students work to complete various projects, activities, and compile portfolios in an open, unstructured environment (Indiana University, 1994).

Instructors often present the lesson, topic, or problem and then set up teams or individual stations. The next step is to let the students solve the problem or complete the assigned work. The teacher as coach supervises, coordinates, referees (if necessary), and assists when needed, but leaves the problem-solving and completion of the problem/task to the students.

To some degree, business educators have been applying these concepts for years in application-oriented courses. However, this concept has been expanding across the curriculum through all grade levels. Many college courses use the team approach where the professor provides essential information but serves as a facilitator as students work to complete their projects. The business curriculum is ideally suited to this concept of transferring time management, coordination, human relations, communications and technology skills, and business management techniques from the school environment to the work environment.

Acting as coach or facilitator allows the teacher to work with students on an individual basis, to encourage and interact with students, and to assess student progress and potential. Students and teachers are freed from the philosophy of "keeping the entire class together no matter what" and "a classroom must be quiet for learning to take place." Business educators have always been managers of learning but now they have increased "license" to implement true business management techniques in their classroom.

Design

As schools are challenged to deliver quality programs and to produce quality graduates, designing the school day, the semester, and the year are recognized as relevant factors. Principals and superintendents who are committed to the task of ensuring students time to acquire skills and subject matter beyond the "core" or basic requirements for college are developing structures that enable students to take more courses.

Block schedules. This method of scheduling varies in design. Many of these block schedules extend the number of class periods from six to seven or eight. Incorporated within the block may be a student resource period. This resource period provides time for activities, especially for make-up time and teacher-student assistance. Some schools have shortened the class periods to 45 minutes and offer eight periods within one day. Other schedules offer four 90-minute classes one day (periods 1 - 4) and another four (periods 5 - 8) on the second day. Students may be required to take at least seven classes. The school may restrict the number of academic classes a student can take to ensure exploration in other curricular areas and to prevent an overloaded schedule. Thus students will then have career exposures they might not otherwise have during their high school experience. Classes that meet every other day allow students more time to prepare for each course.

Other schedules offer one-semester courses in a nine-week period. Classes meet 90 minutes every day for the nine weeks. This schedule is also viewed as a way to provide students with more choices; however, this pattern may also be a way of utilizing current staff to teach more sections as enrollments increase in elective areas. Some schools on a block schedule offer an embedded curriculum which may be one or more courses that meet each day during the semester or year. Vocational cooperative education courses that require students to work each day are examples.

Teachers who are accustomed to and have developed curriculum on a daily schedule of classes that meet for between 45 and 60 minutes must adjust their curriculum and strategies for block scheduling. A block schedule with classes that meet every other day (this means that one week they meet three times and the next week two times) presents some problems, especially for the skill areas. Daily practice and lecture information are lost; if a student is absent one day during the week that the class meets two times, the student will only have one day's instruction for the week.

The *positives* for block scheduling include:

- Increased enrollments.
- Extended lab time.
- More time to complete homework assignments.
- Fewer classes to prepare homework for each day.
- Extended time for in-depth experimentation, demonstration, research, etc.

The *negatives* for block scheduling include:

- Less instruction time.
- Less material covered in one semester for many courses (especially the skills areas).
- A loss of daily practice for skill building.
- Loss of opportunity to help students who miss a class. Missing 90 minutes of class work can be difficult to make up, especially if the work needs to be done at school.

Business teachers must evaluate the pros and cons of block schedules and recognize that many arrangements and variations exist that will alter or change "business as usual."

Year-round school. The year-round school plan is currently employed by some schools and being investigated by others. Students may or may not attend the entire year and teachers may not work all year. The school may also be divided into at least three semesters. This schedule allows for full utilization of the facility as well as increased opportunities for teacher income and student remediation. Many proponents of the year-round school concept believe that a higher student knowledge retention rate occurs from year to year without a long summer break.

Integrated or paired courses. Proper designing and scheduling are required for integrated or paired courses that are curriculum driven. Students can be scheduled in paired classes back-to-back to allow for extended time together. Teachers may prefer to have common preparation (prep) time to facilitate planning or opposite periods to allow for classroom visitations during the time the other teacher has the students. Table 3 illustrates two schedules with the same students in accounting and algebra classes:

Table 3

Integrated Course Teacher Schedule

	Opposite Period Preps				Same Period Prep		
	Period 1	Period 2	*OR*		Period 1	Period 2	Period 3
Teacher A	Accounting*	Prep			Accounting*	Business Law	Prep
Teacher B	Prep	Algebra*			Geometry	Algebra*	Prep

*Denotes same students in each class.

Physical facility. When new schools are built or renovations are made to existing buildings, business education classrooms can easily incorporate arrangements, designs, size, colors, furniture, and technology that are conducive to current and futuristic needs. Renovating older facilities to accommodate technology is, however, difficult.

As school corporations or districts and business teachers strive to provide students with relevant learning experiences that prepare them for work environments and postsecondary training, classroom design is crucial to instruction. Facilities should accommodate cooperative/team activities, project-oriented assignments, portfolio storage and access, fiber optics, computer technology and storage, and ergonomic design including handicap access.

The goal of every business educator is to remain current in knowledge and skill; however, securing the funding and ongoing commitment to upgrade and remodel becomes one of the greatest frustrations for most business teachers. The task, therefore, becomes one of providing the most realistic, beneficial experiences possible with available resources while continuing to "lobby" for improvements.

Location and Delivery System

One of the most exciting components of the business education curriculum is diversity. Within one discipline, students have many opportunities for a wide range of experiences including where and how the curriculum is delivered. The impact of technology in the workplace, workforce development legislation, business partnerships, and increased global competition have created new concepts, opportunities, and expectations. In addition, technology has virtually increased the number and types of learning experiences and changed the environment in which the learning occurs.

Preparing students for the workforce of tomorrow is the challenge. This includes better preparation, more experiences, and higher academic standards. To improve curriculum delivery or enhance skill and subject matter acquisition, initiatives such as Tech Prep and School-to-Work have been legislated. Apprenticeships, mentoring, and job shadowing have regained popularity. These programs are designed to prepare students for greater academic success and to provide employers with highly skilled employees. These initiatives may provide an improved, more realistic delivery mode for both skills and content mastery.

Tech Prep. This initiative reflects a contextual approach to learning (Hull, 1995). "Application oriented," "hands-on," " applied academics," and "real world" are terms that define Tech Prep. Of course, business education courses such as keyboarding, computer applications, and computerized accounting have always incorporated these concepts.

School-to-Work (STW). Another initiative that brings many programs together is School-to-Work. One of the main thrusts is to integrate academic and vocational programs. This initiative includes work-based learning, school-based learning, and connecting activities. Through the integration of business classes such as accounting and algebra, students see relevance and approach traditional academic subjects in a realistic manner.

Distance learning/education. A vehicle that provides instruction for students in schools that do not have the student enrollments or a certified teacher for a particular course is distance learning. When distance learning is used to present a course, schools must consider and determine the following:

- What course(s) will be offered?
- Where will the class be given or taken?
- What supervision is necessary?
- How many students will be in the class at the host and sending sites?
- What time of day will the course be offered?
- What is the length of the course?
- What grading techniques will be used?
- What peripheral tehnology will be needed?
- Will an assistant or aide with technical knowledge be employed?

Distance-learning technology can also be used for video teleconferences to provide students with opportunities for questions and interaction with various people.

The Internet. One of the most innovative ways to deliver instruction is through the Internet. As classrooms and entire school buildings are upgraded with fiber optics, internet usage will increase. The Internet may dramatically change the learning environment as students "surf the net" to explore information or take courses. A school with a home page may provide information about course offerings, pictures of students and staff, and even a copy of the school song.

Entire courses such as economics or entrepreneurship may be taught on the Internet. Business plans, business formation, and ownership information can be found on the Internet.

Without question, technology impacts the learning environment and changes the way students learn. One can only imagine the impact virtual reality will make on courses like international business and career exploration. The need to address funding, access, censorship, and other issues will require business educators to evaluate the curriculum, delivery, methodology, and assessment plans.

Summary

Business education will continue to be a viable discipline in the school curriculum. The discipline and the learning environment will constantly change. New methods, new theories, new equipment, unbelievable advances in technology, continued business and government involvement and mandates, and a continually changing "raw product" with uncontrollable variables will be the norm. Today, students appear less capable of listening to lectures or of tolerating the "chalk and talk" concept. Students want action, direct involvement, hands-on experiences, and computer access. Students seem to enjoy something different, yet they also want stability.

A continuing need for business educators is securing the support of lawmakers, businesses, school officials, students, and parents. To gain support, business educators must share the virtues of business education including: development of essential life skills, preparation for college, and reinforcement of workplace skills and knowledge. The future of business education is dependent upon the initiatives of business educators and supporters of business education. Business educators must be the leaders and managers of change.

References

Blythe, T., & Gardner, H. (1990, April). A school for all intelligences. *Educational Leadership, 47*(7), 33-37.

Cummins, J. & Sayers, D. (1995). *Brave new schools, challenging cultural illiteracy through global learning networks.* New York: St. Martin's Press.

Excel, Inc. (1993). *Hemispheric mode indicator (HMI), Right and left brain approaches to learning, 4-mat.* 200 W. Station St., Barrington, IL 60010.

Gardner, H. (1983). *Frames of mind.* New York: Basic Books.

Indiana University (Producer). (1994). *Gathering the dreamers, the transformation process to learner-centered school* (Video). Indiana University, Bloomington, IN: Department of Radio and Television).

Hull, D. (1995). *Who are you calling stupid?* Waco, TX: Cord Communications.

Howard, E., Howell, B., & Brainard, E. (1987). *Handbook for conducting school climate improvement projects.* Bloomington, IN: Phi Delta Kappa Educational Foundation.

Johnson, D. W., & Johnson, R. T. (1984). *Circles of learning,* Alexandria, VA: The Association for Supervision and Curriculum Development.

Johnson, D. W., Johnson, R. T., & Holuybec, E. J. (1986). *Circles of learning: Cooperation in the classroom (rev. ed.).* Englewood Cliffs, NJ: Prentice-Hall.

Johnson, D. W., Johnson, R. T., and Holuybec, E. J. (1994). *The new circles of learning: Cooperation in the classroom and school.* Alexandria, VA: Association for Supervision and Curriculum Development.

Kolb, D. A., (1985). *LSI: Learning-style inventory, (rev. ed.).* McBer & Company, Training Resources Group.

LeMeres, C. (1991). *The winner's circle: Yes, I can!* Newport Beach, CA: LaMeres Lifestyles Unlimited.

Los Angeles County Office of Education. (1993). Teacher expectations and student achievement (T.E.S.A.). Downey, CA.

National Business Education Association. (1995). *National standards for business education.* Reston, Virginia.

Senge, P., & O'Neill, J. (1995). On schools as learning organizations: A conversation with Peter Senge. *Educational Leadership, 52,(7),* 20-23.

Stout, M. T., & Hamilton, D. (Eds.). (1996). *Producing a better product.* (Available from Marlene Todd Stout, Kokokmo High School, 2501 S. Berkley, Kokomo, IN 46902 and Doug Hamilton, Delco Electronics, Kokomo, IN 46903).

CHAPTER 5
Globalization

Les R. Dlabay
Lake Forest College, Lake Forest, Ilinois

Most people in industrialized economies take for granted that they can purchase a suit made of wool from Argentina, designed by Italians, sewn by people in Romania, moved across the ocean by people from Spain, and sold in a store with Japanese owners by retail workers from Nigeria. However, this economic interdependence, while very common, involves a complex system of global business activities.

International influences on business and personal lives are not something that will happen in the future. These global forces are happening now, both around the world and around the corner. In education, for example, more than 80 different languages are taught in the Los Angeles school system. In business, AT&T in the United States employs staff members capable of contacing prospective customers in 140 languages. These observations, along with many others, recognize the movement of societies from a national reference to a global existence.

What is Globalization?

In Mexico, they are *Zucharitas*. In Latvia and Poland, they are called *Frosties*. And in the United States they are *Frosted Flakes*. Products previously sold only in a small region of the world may now be found almost anywhere. For a package of Wrigley's Doublemint gum to get to a customer in China, several transportation modes may be required, including a thousand-mile trip by truck, a rusting freighter, a tricycle cart, and a bicycle.

Globalization is the process of expanding business activities and operations in order to gain a world-wide perspective of customers, products, and operating procedures. While the terms *global*, *international*, and *multinational* are frequently used interchangeably, slight distinctions exist. Many view *global* companies as those that offer a product in a standardized form in all world markets. In contrast, the *international* and *multinational* companies give their foreign operating divisions autonomy to adapt and customize products and operations to local cultures.

Global companies. Coca-Cola products are sold in more than 190 countries. Coca-Cola's global strategy of direct investment in bottling facilities allows the company to oversee better production and distribution. The company is able to take action when new markets open. As described by Farrell (1993), well before East Germans were able to buy Coke, strong brand awareness existed as a result of seeing commercials on West German television. More than 90 percent of East Germans knew exactly what Coca-Cola was, even though they could not purchase it for 40 years. With a massive investment of more than $400 million in bottling plants and distribution centers in Germany, Coke was able to deliver quickly this world-famous brand once the Berlin Wall collapsed.

Generally, companies with global perspectives have certain characteristics. These organizations:

- View the entire world as their potential market.
- Seek product ideas through foreign subsidiaries.
- Look for similarities among markets in an effort to offer a standardized product whenever possible.
- Use consistent hiring policies throughout the world but also are culturally sensitive to host countries.
- Recruit managers internationally rather than just from the organization's countries of operation.
- Analyze competitor actions and obtain raw materials on a world-wide basis.
- Establish distribution systems, production methods, pricing techniques, and promotional strategies that reflect both an international outlook and a local perspective.

Global products. *Global products* refer to items sold in a standardized form in several markets. Industrial and technical products including cameras, motor vehicles, computers, production equipment, and agricultural goods are the items most likely to be sold on a standardized basis. Monsanto's herbicide, "Roundup," has been on the market since 1974. As reported by Fritsch (1996), the continued success of the product has been partially the result of sales growth in emerging markets such as Brazil and Indonesia that use no-till techniques (tilling their fields chemically). This process saves water, creates less soil erosion and, in some situations, saves so much time that an extra crop can be planted.

Services are also offered on a global basis. Travel services (airlines, credit cards, hotels) and specialized assistance (financial services, package delivery, health care) can meet common market needs in various cultures. However, other types of services (restaurants, hair styling, local transportation) require adaptation to a nation's economic and cultural situation.

Some business enterprises try to fit a product to a country with slight modifications. Others assess the cultural needs and social desires of a society and develop goods and services that are sensitive to the situation. For the Chinese market, Frito-Lay developed a version of *Chee-tos* snack puffs eliminating the cheese. This seemingly essential ingredient was omitted because dairy products are not a major part of Chinese diets. After testing 600 different flavors, the company selected a popcorn-like "Savory American Cream" and teriyaki-style "Zesty Japanese Steak." Similarly, in India, Kellogg introduced corn, wheat, and basmati flakes breakfast cereals.

Global brands. Standardized product names are also increasing in worldwide visibility. American Express and McDonald's (United States), Green Giant and Lipton (Britain), Mercedes-Benz (Germany), Nestle (Switzerland), and

Sony (Japan) are some of the brand names recognized throughout the world. Companies attempt to create a global identity for their products. This strategy allows an enterprise to move selling efforts quickly across national borders into new markets.

Global markets. Many companies are attempting to evolve from multi-national companies to global ones, eliminating the distinction between domestic and international operations. This strategy allows ideas and people to move across borders in all directions. For example, Gillette recently introduced a new product in Europe before introducing it in the United States. This approach communicated that the organization does not have just one "home market" and allowed Gillette to take advantage of its larger sales staff in Europe.

Global promotions. During the 1992 Winter Olympics, Coca-Cola used a standardized advertising campaign. As Wells (1992) reported, identical television commercial visuals, presented in 12 languages, were used to reach 3.8 billion television viewers in 131 countries. While a global approach for promotion can be efficient, many foreign governments place restrictions on advertising. For example, Britain requires that viewers be told the price of toys advertised on television for items costing more than 15 pounds. The Province of Quebec prohibits television advertising aimed at children. In certain European countries, food ads aimed at young consumers must include a toothbrush.

What Drives Globalization?

Each day, our homes, mailboxes, and televisions are filled with products, promotions, and images from around the world. Communication technology, modern transportation, political reforms along with the exporting of managerial skills are escalating the impact of globalization.

Communication technology. Technology allows information and cultural influences to travel around the world at an unprecedented speed. The Cable News Network (CNN) is available in more than 140 countries. The Internet and the World Wide Web make access possible within seconds to libraries, museums, and databases anywhere in the world. The World Wide Web is the basis of an electronic marketplace that is already in operation. Transmission of data along with real-time audio and video allows business transactions to occur in a setting only dreamed of a generation ago.

Electronic communication also results in a transfer of values along with the transfer of information. An awareness of various products and behaviors creates demand previously limited to one geographic region. World-wide sports coverage has made the National Basketball Association very popular in France and Greece as well as other areas of the world.

Transportation systems. Faster and less expensive commercial jet travel makes it easier to bring people together for business. Efficient movement of goods is also crucial in a global marketplace. Containerization allows shipments to be easily transferred from one transportation mode to another. Products that once took weeks to receive from foreign suppliers are now obtained in days.

Political reform. As eastern European countries evolved from central planning to market economies, foreign investment and entrepreneurial efforts spurred expansion. These political reforms opened business opportunities not available previously. However, at the same time, shortages of supplies and skilled workers limited the speed of economic growth.

The deregulation of customs and paperwork at European Community (EC) borders has reduced distribution costs and time for many manufacturers. A single EC market enables producers to reach and satisfy cross-border demand for products. This increased competition accentuated each nation's comparative advantage. As less expensive, small business products from Italy and Spain poured into France, small shopkeepers often converted their stores into alcohol-tobacco shops. This conversion responded to the influx of British consumers avoiding higher taxes in England.

Entrepreneurial infrastructure. Physical infrastructure, such as highways, roads, bridges, and communication systems, facilitate business activities. Also necessary is a *managerial* and/or an *entrepreneurial* infrastructure that supplies skills needed to acquire, coordinate, and implement productive resources. When McDonald's first opened in Moscow, efforts were needed to coordinate people, capital, and equipment. The fast-food company helped local businesses grow better crops, improve building construction, and train employees. These endeavors not only benefited McDonald's but also resulted in higher productivity and increased employment for other Russian companies.

Russia is also a booming market for retail cosmetics. Mary Kay Cosmetics, Inc., allows many Russian women to gain unprecedented financial freedom as the country economy evolves from a common economy to a free enterprise economy. The country moved to No. 4 among Mary Kay's 25 international affiliates.

Where Will Globalization Take Us?

Globalization means changes in the way business is conducted. No longer will obtaining employees, funds, and raw materials be limited to one geographic region. Organizations will continue to view the effects of economic interdependence, expanded product innovation sources, commercialism, and cultural homogeneity.

Expanded economic interdependence. People who think they are buying American cars are often buying just American names. The Ford Festiva, for example, is built in Korea. Ford's Crown Victoria is assembled with 26 percent foreign parts. Kiley (1991) estimates that by 2000, less than 50 percent of new cars in the United States—and perhaps less than 30 percent— will deserve the label "Made in the U.S.A." No completely American-made car exists; except for Saab or BMW, no national car from any one country exists.

Interdependence is further seen with a joint venture between General Mills and Nestle to sell various cereals. In Europe, products such as Cheerios, Golden Grahams, and Lucky Charms are sold under the Nestle name rather than the General Mills name familiar to U.S shoppers.

Interdependence can benefit less-developed economies. In India, Sundram Fasteners Ltd. is the largest supplier of metal radiator caps to General Motors. As of the mid-1990s, as noted by Jordan (1996), the company was exporting more than 300,000 caps each month. Caterpillar also buys radiator caps, and Ford purchases nuts and bolts from Sundram. The number of joint ventures between Indian enterprises and other U.S. companies continues to increase. These agreements take advantage of India's low labor costs, strong basic skills among workers, and a large pool of talented engineers willing to learn.

Increased product innovation. Europe, Asia, and other areas of the world are becoming a major source of new product ideas for U.S. companies. While what works overseas doesn't always work here, many companies have been able to adapt foreign products for domestic success. In recent years, companies have attempted to expand international marketing of food in tubes for products such as tomato paste and mayonnaise and to use edible food wrappers.

Intensified commercialism. Higher levels of economic development are commonly accompanied by strong marketing endeavors that result in changed demand within a society. Extensive media efforts project images of beauty, material resources, and financial success. This increased emphasis on profit tends to create a preoccupation with individual consumption and materialism. Time, effort, and money are used for material items rather than for intellectual or spiritual endeavors. People place an emphasis on accumulating things rather than nurturing relationships.

Expanded commercialism by global retailers in Europe, such as Costco, Toys "R" Us, Kmart, and factory outlet malls, has met resistance. Some British consumers do not embrace discount shopping; they suspect that low prices mean low quality. In Germany and France, merchants opposed proposals to legalize late-evening and seven-day-a-week retailing. Small retailers tried to persuade the government to limit the spread of big discounters.

Escalated cultural homogeneity. International business efforts frequently influence a nation's ethnic identity and behaviors. With the dissolving of the Soviet Union, a vast market hungry for consumer goods opened, especially for foreign products previously banned under communism. Mars, Inc., has succeeded in Russia by arousing curiosity with ads before products were on shelves, by maintaining a stable distribution system in spite of the run-down infrastructure, and by accepting payments in rubles. The company's success resulted in *Sneekerz* becoming a Russian word.

While this may not seem like a significant influence on a nation's cultural identity, over the years global business activities have changed the emphases in a society. Countries that once emphasized family values or religious beliefs find their culture is being defined in terms of pop music, brand names, and food products available throughout the world.

What Do Business Educators Need To Do?

Every business employee works for an organization that either imports, exports, or competes against other companies that import or export. As a result, business educators face the task of preparing students of all ages for the global workplace. Economic, cultural, political-legal, technological, and human relations skills are the foundation of global business instruction.

Expand awareness of economic and social-cultural factors. The level of economic development persists as a driving force and/or barrier of a country's ability and willingness to participate in the global marketplace. Travel and distribution difficulties continue to be present in less-developed economies. Low bridges and tunnels along with limited highway systems impede movement of raw materials and finished goods.

From a cultural perspective, companies must blend organizational goals with a nation's social environment. For example, Colgate-Palmolive attempted to expand its toothpaste business in the countryside of India. With 70 percent of the country's population in these rural areas, the company wanted to increase sales among these people. To achieve this goal, the company could not rely on conventional marketing tactics. More than half of all Indian villagers are illiterate, and only one-third live in households with television sets. The focus of Colgate's promotional effort involved using a video van to present a half-hour infomercial to people in rural areas. These dramas explained the uses and benefits of toothpaste and shampoo.

When United Parcel Service spent $1 billion to buy delivery businesses in Europe, the company faced various obstacles due to cultural differences. French drivers were indignant when told they could not have wine with lunch. Protests occurred in Britain when drivers' dogs were banned from delivery trucks. Apprehension reigned in Spain because the brown UPS trucks resembled the local hearses.

Examine political-legal influences on business. The emerging middle class in China provides new opportunities for movie studios, television production companies, consumer products divisions, and theme park developers. However, these media enterprises face political and legal barriers. For example, the Chinese Film Ministry, which decides how many foreign films may be shown, only allowed 10 from the United States in a recent year. In addition, the state board may ask that certain scenes be cut that can hurt the popularity of a film.

In the transition to a unified market, the nations of the European Union had nine different value-added taxes. These levies ranged from 15 to 25 percent, each in a different currency. The result was that global companies had to price products to take into account these complex tax circumstances.

Develop technical and human relations skills. The need for business skills was very clear as eastern Europe evolved from state-run companies to a market economy. Companies faced problems such as training a sales staff that was used to only calling on one buyer—the state wholesaler. Managers had to be taught that a market economy involves customers who can actually refuse to buy your products because someone else's products are better. Thus, preparation of students with a global perspective will require: (1) an ability to work with individuals from varied cultures, and (2) the competence to deal with potential tensions that may occur when balancing global strategies with local customs and values.

Evaluate both financial gains and social contributions. Increased profits, expanded market shares, and higher return rates are common measures of business success. However, as companies gain greater economic influence in foreign markets, global enterprises also must assess performance other than financial factors. Improved schools, new highways, better health care, adequate housing, and a safe food supply are just a few of the criteria global companies can use to evaluate their contributions as partners in the global economy.

Globalization is both the foundation of business activity and the basis for curriculum planning. Through integration of international business content into existing courses along with the creation of innovative courses and programs, teachers will provide students with needed skills and experiences. Business students will also need academic training in foreign language, history, political science, cross-cultural communications, and technology to ensure success in the global workplace, the global marketplace, and the global economy.

References

Farrell, G. (1993, January 18). We got the achtung, baby! *Brandweek.*

Fritsch, P. (1996, January 2). Top-selling Monsanto herbicide won't die on the vine. *The Wall Street Journal*, p. A1.

Kiley, D. (1991, March 4). The end of the 'American' car. *Adweek's marketing week.*

Jordan, M. (1996, February 1). Small-parts firms in India win U.S. fans. *The Wall Street Journal*, p. A14.

Wells, K. (1992, August 27). Global ad campaigns, after many missteps, finally pays dividends. *The Wall Street Journal*, p. A1.

Reform and Regulations

Joyce P. Logan
University of Kentucky, Lexington, Kentucky

A. C. "Buddy" Krizan
Murray State University, Murray, Kentucky

Educational reform and regulation have been ongoing processes since the introduction of public education. The purpose of this chapter is to address current ideas and practices in modern educational reform and regulation. Emphasis is placed on high school restructuring, accountability, curriculum, reform, and equity. The effects on business education are discussed in each of these sections.

High School Restructuring

The kind of learning necessary to achieve national education goals requires major reorganization of the educational system. Early reform movements emphasized spending more time on tasks by reducing noninstructional activities and extending the school day and school year. Current educational reform movements emphasize more effective use of instructional time and active learning that applies knowledge. School reform empowers individuals at the local level to make curriculum-related decisions and to try alternative scheduling of the school day and school year.

Local empowerment. Historically, state and federal regulations determined, in large measure, how schools were operated and what curricula were offered. Under educational reform, state and national directives are less prescriptive. States define a curriculum framework along with expectations and standards for student achievement. Within this framework, schools have a high level of autonomy to develop educational programs that meet student needs and interests, address community educational issues, and determine resource allocation.

Placing power at the local level embraces the philosophy that education is not only educators' responsibility but that responsibility is shared with parents, business, industry, and other community groups. Schools must design programs that build on community strengths and needs (Rutherford & Billig, 1995). Business and industry involvement with schools adds relevance to the curriculum. In addition, parent participation on school councils gives community stakeholders a real voice in setting direction for the educational process.

Parents and teachers become empowered when decisions are school-based and when school councils function. Local power resides in the collective force of parents, teachers, and principal (Bryk, Easton, Kerbow, Rollow, & Sebring, 1994). School council responsibilities relate to curriculum, instructional materials, extracurricular programs, personnel, and numerous other school management issues. Expectations are that school leadership for educational change and student achievement will emerge from these councils.

Time scheduling. Another restructuring strategy deals with time allocations and alternative schedules. When active learning becomes integral to instruction, 40-minute periods are inadequate for students to complete their work. Knowledge application activities take more time, and necessary resources may be available in the community or through telecommunication networks rather than within the school (Sheingold, 1991).

More intensive instructional time for subject mastery may come through scheduling classes in larger time blocks. The purposes of block scheduling are to give more focused time on task, allow time for independent or group-learning experiences and demonstration of knowledge, and provide teacher planning time for curriculum integration. Although block scheduling in and of itself does not improve performance, block scheduling does afford students a better chance to do so (Edwards, 1993). Courses scheduled in a four-period day for half a year reduce the likelihood of students falling behind their classmates. Also, alternative time schedules may enable students to earn as many as 32 credits during high school. These additional credits allow curriculum expansion. With a four-period schedule, a student may complete foundation courses during the freshman and sophomore year and devote the last two years to a concentrated course of study related to the student's career choice. Opportunity to take additional courses may enable students to complete an intensive college preparatory program or gain advanced standing in a two-year technical or associate degree program.

In addition to block scheduling, school restructuring may involve implementation of an alternative school year (year-round scheduling). Spreading the school term over 12 months instead of nine or 10 months permits scheduling flexibility.

An alternative school year may be scheduled in a variety of time segments. Common scheduling patterns are the 45-15 plan, 60-20 plan, 60-15 plan, and 90-30 plan. In these plans, the first number represents the days for instruction, and the smaller number is the length of the intersessions (days out of school). Thus, with the 45-15 plan, students attend four 45-day sessions (nine weeks) and have four 15-day sessions (three weeks) with no required classes. This pattern is repeated a total of four times during the year (48 weeks), and the remaining four weeks may be used for holidays and breaks.

Schools using year-round schedules identify the following benefits:

- Reduction of student and teacher stress.
- Fewer discipline referrals.
- Improved attendance.
- Makeup time for inclement weather.
- More efficient use of buildings.

- Flexibility of family vacation time.
- Better opportunities for continuous learning.
- Less time needed for review.

Time intervals between instructional sessions (intersessions) present multiple opportunities for educational enrichment opportunities. Intersession time may be used for activities such as the following:

- Remediation.
- Out-of-school academic experiences.
- Educational travel.
- Extracurricular activities.
- Special interest classes.
- Teacher revitalization.

Restructuring implications for business education. What does restructuring mean to secondary business education programs? With school councils making decisions on instructional resources and curriculum, business educator involvement in the work of these councils becomes essential. Business educators must make sure that school council members understand how business education programs meet student needs and interests. Business education plays a vital role in meeting the challenge to prepare all students for an increasingly technological and interdependent world (Nebraska State Department of Education, 1994). Established business program linkages with the business community contribute significantly to school and community partnerships.

Innovative high school scheduling permits business teachers to try different curricular approaches. Block scheduling extends concentrated instructional or laboratory time. In addition, time is available for in-depth business projects requiring community experiences or research. Block scheduling enables students to take more classes, and intersessions establish time periods for innovative elective course offerings. Business education programs can use this time effectively for activities such as community service, field trips to business organizations, international business travel, mentorships, or special interest classes such as desktop publishing or presentation software. Opportunities for remediation occur more frequently through intersessions; therefore, business students needing remediation do not have the long delay currently experienced when students must wait for remedial classes during summer sessions. In addition, business teachers can take advantage of flexible scheduling and use intersessions for professional development or flexible vacation time.

Accountability

"All constituents must realize that accountability is both the key and the lock to the door of school reform" (Funk & Brown, 1994, p. 769). Schools exist for student learning. In order to receive funding, schools must be accountable for assuring that learning takes place. Accountability ties funding to student performance, sets higher standards for teaching and learning, and requires valid assessment measures.

Decentralized funding. America 2000 gives little attention to the funding needed to turn educational reforms into reality (Clinchy, 1991). The federal government's movement to balance the budget will result in fewer federal dollars for education. Also, federal emphasis on decentralized funding places more responsibility at the state and local level. However, states have experienced budget restraints that limit their ability to absorb educational costs. Since approximately one-fourth of America's households have a child in public school, local bond issues will become more difficult to pass in the future (Hodgkinson, 1991).

Proposed workforce-development federal legislation consolidates funding for education, employment, and economic development into block grants to states. States will be given more programming flexibility using federal funds; however, most of the funds (80-90 percent) must be spent at the local level.

Public support of education expects and demands high standards and accountability for performance. Limited budgets result in the public wanting to know what its money buys and what results are achieved.

Assessment. Assessment, the most difficult piece of educational reform, must be based on clearly stated standards that describe what students know and are able to do. Educational assessment has two major functions: (1) classroom assessment to guide instruction and (2) school-wide assessment to determine whether reforms in that school are achieving desirable results.

Educational reform has increased the variety of assessment measures and has placed more emphasis on higher-order thinking skills and knowledge application. Portfolios, performance tasks, and open-ended questions have been advocated as replacements or additions to the traditional standardized tests. The emphasis is on student performance measured against performance standards instead of traditional standardized norm-referenced tests. For example, Kentucky's educational reform legislation requires a student assessment system that uses performance measures and a school accountability system based on the student assessment results. School assessment is linked to financial rewards and sanctions. Student assessment data can become a high-stakes measure of school success. Performance measures are part of a national reform of educational assessment.

Portfolios have emerged as a common measure of individual student accomplishment of standards. Portfolios typically include samples of work that demonstrate achievement of each standard. In some states, high school restructuring requires students to submit an academic portfolio as part of graduation requirements.

Performance tasks require students to produce a quality product or performance. A performance task should have a meaningful context that involves an issue, problem, or theme observed in a real-world situation. The task should be authentic; that is, have a meaningful purpose. Tasks may be designed for individual students or for completion by a small group of 3 to 5 students. Group tasks may include both individual work and group work. The content and performance expectations to be assessed must be selected carefully; the estimated time for task completion should correlate with content relevance and significance. Task developers decide what evidence will be needed to show student learning; this evidence becomes the basis for a scoring guide.

The scoring guide is completed before writing the task. The task should provide students with a description of what students are expected to do, outlining the responsibilities of the group and the responsibilities of individual students. Students must also develop a tangible demonstration or product of their learning. For example, with a group project, the group may design a product with each student preparing a written statement explaining the design merits.

Open-ended questions may have more than one correct answer. Open-ended questions allow responses with sufficient scope for discrimination at various scoring levels (from satisfactory or novice level through outstanding or distinguished). Questions are written to require analysis, synthesis, and evaluative skills. The issues that make up the question content must be of interest and appropriate for the age group, as well as realistic in terms of the students' knowledge, background, and experiences. Critical elements of open-response questions include the following:

- Content selection that assesses student achievement of academic expectations—what students should know and be able to do.

- Question development that is authentic, challenging, clear, concise, focused, appropriate, and meaningful.

- Question development that allows flexibility in the methods and strategies students may use in responding and/or allows for response variety for the maximum points.

- Scoring guide development that identifies criteria for assessing responses within each performance level.

Educational reform has not eliminated use of multiple-choice tests. Instead, multiple-choice tests are used primarily to assess subject content knowledge and are used in conjunction with other assessment instruments that measure knowledge application. A strength of multiple-choice design is that it efficiently and clearly assesses specific content.

Teacher standards. Another reform effort to improve teaching and learning involves establishment of pedagogical standards for various subject areas and teacher assessment to verify attainment of these standards. Teachers are at the heart of classroom instruction. Because of the close association of teaching and learning, accountability for student learning includes verification that teachers possess skills necessary for delivery of high quality instruction.

Public school K-12 teacher certification is a state function. In many states, educational reform incorporated portfolios, internships, and teacher testing into teacher certification. In addition to new state certification requirements, a National Board for Professional Teaching Standards was created to establish rigorous standards for what outstanding teachers should know and be able to do. This national teacher standards effort is designed as a voluntary system to assess and certify teachers who meet these high standards. Teachers eligible for certification under the national standards must validate state licensing, have at least a baccalaureate degree, and have three years of teaching experience. Assessment will cover decision-making abilities, collaboration with colleagues, teacher reflection and insight, and subject mastery. The assessment process will include a portfolio, student work samples, in-basket exercises, and oral interviews.

Business education accountability. What can business teachers do to demonstrate public accountability consistent with reform efforts? With public education financing moving away from categorical funding and moving toward block grants and programming decisions at the local level, business teachers must become an integral part of the decision-making team at the local level. Business students' achievements of both academic and occupational skills and their successful transition to higher education or the workforce must be documented and shared widely.

Student achievement performance measures must be embedded in the instructional process. Performance tasks are not new to business education. The production of letters, research papers, accounting records, and other tangible products has always been a part of business classes. However, more attention may be needed to help students reflect on their work products and to refine their analysis and evaluative skills. Open-ended questions resemble well-written essay questions that address higher-order thinking skills. Open-ended questions, as such, have not been used to any degree prior to the current educational reform. These questions may assume a variety of formats:

- Description. Letters, product comparisons, directions, and procedures challenge students to observe, describe, record, and report data.

- Comparison. Sequencing events and ideas, making predictions, and comparing products help students make linkages to previous knowledge.

- Analysis. Data analysis, explanations, directions, and multiple perspectives may be used to help students visualize the whole idea, examine its parts, and explain sequential relationships.

- Problem solving. Challenging students to describe, analyze, and propose solutions for given situations builds problem-solving skills.

- Evaluation. Evaluating issues, making a decision, and using supporting evidence (facts, figures, expert opinions, and research) give students experience with decision making based on relevant data.

New teacher standards for teacher certification affect business teachers the same as other teachers in the school. However, business teachers need to build more recognition of their academic and their business professional skills. The National Standards Board certificate should be a goal for all business teachers. State licensure sets entry-level standards whereas the credentialing proposed by the national board establishes high standards for experienced teachers. The national certificate available for business teachers is for early adolescence through young adulthood. Teachers who achieve this high honor will be role models and spokespersons who can help build and strengthen the teaching profession.

Curriculum

Curriculum reforms are extensive, complex, and connected to all aspects of teaching and learning (Anderson, 1995). New orientations to the curriculum call for a different kind of teaching, demand new roles of students, and require different types of student work.

Curriculum is a process of thinking through, facilitating, and assessing the learning of intended educational ends (Komoski, 1990). Schools have learning expectations that incorporate how to think, how to learn, and what subject content to include. These expectations can be achieved only through integration of learning. The use of technology and business/industry resources supports teaching and learning.

Learning expectations. Specific learner expectations for all students are often developed at the state level. Schools are held accountable for student achievement of these expectations. Learning must be more than fact- or skill-based. Students are asked to apply skills and knowledge across traditional subject areas. This knowledge integration requires business teacher collaboration with other teachers and with students (Newmann, 1994). Collaboration does not mean ignoring skills specific to each area (Beck, Copa, & Pease, 1991). Rather, teachers work with colleagues and students to determine curricula that are important for students' futures. This collaboration creates richer learning processes and higher educational aims.

Cooperative learning. One component in a systematic approach to reform is cooperative learning (Bryk, Easton, Kerbow, Rollow, & Sebring, 1994). Research shows that cooperative methods can and usually do have a positive effect on student achievement (Slavin, 1989/90). Students work with one another through cooperative learning. Cooperative learning achievement depends on group goal accomplishment through positive interdependence as well as individual accountability.

Technology. Another key curricular element in educational reform is technology implementation. Technology helps motivate students, prepares them for an ever-changing technological society, and provides meaningful applications of academic concepts. Also, Internet access provides students with an international knowledge base.

Technology implementation increases educational costs and requires continuous teacher training. Teachers must receive formal training or be given time for independent study. Instructional material development for classroom use takes additional teacher time. Inherent with technology is the need to use current hardware and software and yet to avoid simply adopting the latest fad. Computer technology use determines the level required for instruction. The most current equipment may not be essential for computer-assisted instruction; however, skill development for the workplace requires hardware and software comparable to that found in businesses.

School-to-Work and Tech Prep. Educational reform emphasizes realistic learning experiences. School-based and work-based learning experiences are planned and supervised by the school and employers to contribute to students' educational and career objectives. School-to-Work and Tech Prep legislation encourages workplace and school experiences such as cooperative education, mentoring, pre-apprenticeship programs, school-based enterprises, and community service. No single path is right for all students. The true test of School-to-Work programs is whether the context, information, and resources help students make choices and support their career goals (Charner, Fraser, Hubbard, Rogers, & Horne, 1995).

Life-long learning. Students of today will also be students of tomorrow because rapid changes will require continuous upgrading of knowledge and skills. The school curriculum must teach students to be independent learners. How to learn and how to locate learning resources become as much a part of the school curriculum as content that is learned. Problem solving and critical thinking skill development help prepare students for life-long learning. The curriculum should provide tasks that require students to generate new ways of viewing situations outside the boundaries of standard conventions and to engage in tasks when answers or solutions are not apparent (Marzano, Pickering, & Brandt, 1990). A curriculum that promotes critical thinking pushes the limits of students' knowledge and abilities.

Business education curricular implications. How does the business education curriculum need to change to contribute to attainment of educational reform goals? Business education teachers have experience in providing relevant learning applications. With reform emphases on academic expectations and knowledge applications, all teachers are searching for appropriate hands-on learning. Business teachers are trying to incorporate more academic content into their business curriculum. Business education teachers who take the initiative to form partnerships with other teachers can gain ideas for including basic subject content into business subjects while assisting English, mathematics, and other subject area teachers with incorporating real-world experiences into all courses. The following activities have been used in successful integrated subject content partnerships:

- All courses emphasize writing and reading skills.
- Business teachers use more basic skill terminology; for example, referring to the accounting equation as solving for the unknown.
- Business teachers work with science teachers to develop joint student research projects. The research experiments may be designed in a science class with the report format and final research reports completed in a business class.
- Teachers from all subject areas meet together to share curricula and to prepare matrices of specific competencies. Business teachers support integrated learning when they can discuss with students how the skill or knowledge studied relates to what is being learned in other classes.
- Team teaching with English, science, or mathematics teachers uses each teacher's special expertise and also helps students to experience unified learning rather than segmented knowledge.

Teamwork is critical in the business work environment. Preparing students to be team players contributes to employability and promotability of business graduates. Collaboration on projects in and out of the classrooms enables students to practice teamwork skills. In addition, teaching the process of productive team membership is an essential collaborative skill development component. Students must learn to be productive team members and work with others to accomplish specific tasks.

Business teachers need to provide leadership in technology instruction. Most students will receive their first formal computer instruction from business teachers. Although students may use computers at the primary level, formal instruction on computer skill development is generally delayed until middle school. In their leadership role for technology, business teachers often serve as technology resource persons for their school systems. Business educators are expected to assist other teachers with computer training, to provide information on hardware and software purchases, and to suggest ways of incorporating computer instruction into classroom activities.

Business teachers, along with other vocational teachers, provide leadership for Tech Prep and School-to-Work programs. Securing work-site experiences for business students can be facilitated through Tech Prep and School-to-Work community partnerships. Tech Prep and School-to-Work programs also help business students see a linkage to postsecondary education and focus on a smooth transition to associate degrees or other two-year postsecondary business programs.

Life-long learning skills developed in the business education curriculum may result from incorporating the following techniques:

- Asking open-ended questions.
- Assigning tasks that use a variety of resources.
- Solving problems creatively.
- Exhibiting a spirit of inquiry.
- Designing activities that promote critical thinking.

School-reform proposals reflect a common theme: Students must become active learners who can solve complex problems and construct meanings based on real-world experiences. Authentic achievement represents significant, worthwhile, and meaningful accomplishments that prepare students for continued learning. Authentic achievement has three criteria (Newmann, Marks, & Gamoran, 1995, p. 4):

- Construction of knowledge. The teacher provides tasks that require organization of information and consideration of alternatives. Students are taught to analyze alternatives by examining limitations, relevancy, and effects.

- Disciplined inquiry. Teachers abandon the primary role as knowledge dispensers and become coaches, guides, and mentors who inspire students for the work of learning. Through substantive conversation and elaborated written communication, students demonstrate in-depth understanding supported by authoritative knowledge from the field.

- Value beyond school. Learning becomes more powerful when students see meaningful connections between school work and their own experiences and situations.

To encourage students to use critical and creative thinking skills, teachers may ask questions such as these: What would happen if. . .? What else do you need to know? What are the choices to solve the problem? Is there another possibility? What can you add that makes the situation unique? What is unusual about. . .?

Reform and Equity

In many states the funding for schools did not support children's rights to an equal education (Alexander, 1991). Inequalities in the amount spent for education in different sections of the same state resulted in unequal educational opportunities.

Reform legislation. From 1973 to 1989, litigation pertaining to inequalities in school finance occurred in numerous states. School finance cases in most states resulted in judgments related to the unconstitutionality of state finance formulae, taxation methods, or other causes of disparities in school revenues. For example, the Supreme Court in Kentucky held that Kentucky had failed to establish an efficient system of common schools as required by the state constitution; therefore, the entire school system was unconstitutional. This court ruling resulted in legislation that abolished the state's educational system and established Kentucky's educational reform and a new formula for school funding (Kentucky Education Reform Act, 1990).

Equal access. Reform in financing public schools attempts to ensure that equal educational opportunities are available for all children regardless of where they live. More than one-third of American children have the deck stacked against them before they enter school (Hodgkinson, 1991). Almost one-fourth live in poverty. Educational opportunities that are limited by race, social class, gender, or cultural background violate the democratic principle of educational equality. Educational reform seeks to find new terms of unity based on respect and equitable resources to meet the needs of all students (Howe, 1991).

Concern for the plight of children and youth resulted in school reform initiatives for educational excellence that were framed in an inclusive manner. The Paideia program, a reform movement of the 1980s, held as a basic principle that all children are educable and deserve the same quality of schooling (Weissbourd, 1994). America's Goals 2000 called for all children to start school ready to learn and proposed to increase the graduation rate to a minimum of 90 percent by the year 2000 (U.S. Department of Education, 1991 revised).

Equity influences on business education. What do funding equity and high expectations for all students mean to business education programs? The increasing diversity of students mandates that teachers learn how to address different cultural and experiential backgrounds. Group activities that mix students from different backgrounds to accomplish a task help build mutual understanding and respect. Using the international business world as a basis for studying different cultures also helps students acquire an appreciation for diversity. The key to remember is that standards are not lowered—all students work to achieve high standards. The path to standard achievement may differ in terms of activities and in terms of time. Business students, as well as other students, have a better chance for successful program completion because of support services initiated from educational reform. Extended school hours, peer tutoring, career counseling, in-school or work-site mentoring, and flexible time schedules assist students with standards mastery.

Summary

Education reform legislation has similar characteristics across states. Establishing learning expectations or student performance standards; using assessment measures for application of knowledge; moving decision making to the local level; incorporating cooperative learning, work-based learning, and community services; restructuring instructional time; involving parents; and empowering teachers are familiar reform themes. A changing global environment, an increasingly diverse society, and a growing need for educational equity contributed to the educational reform movement.

Business education has a viable role in the preparation of students for business environments that foster teamwork, technological advances, and international markets. As partners with academic teachers and parents, business education can be a vital link in achieving state and national goals for education and in preparing students to become part of a world-class workforce.

References

Alexander, K. (1991). The common school ideal and the limits of legislative authority: The Kentucky case. *Harvard Journal on Legislation, 28*(2), 341-366.

Anderson, R. D. (1995). Curriculum reform: Dilemmas and promise. *Kappan, 77*(1), 33-36.

Beck, R. H., Copa, G. H., & Pease, V. H. (1991). Vocational and academic teachers work together, (Reprint Series). Berkeley: National Center for Research in Vocational Education.

Bryk, A. S., Easton, J. Q., Kerbow, D., Rollow, S. G., & Sebring, P.A. (1994). The state of Chicago school reform. *Kappan, 76*(1), 74-78.

Charner, I., Fraser, B.S., Hubbard, S., Rogers, A., & Horne, R. (1995). Reforms of the school-to-work transition: Findings, implications, and challenges. *Kappan, 77*(1), 40, 58-60.

Clinchy, E. (November 1991). America 2000: Reform, revolution, or just more smoke and mirrors? *Kappan, 73*(3), 210-218.

Edwards, C. M., Jr. (1993). Restructuring to improve student performance. *National Association of Secondary School Principals Bulletin, 77-88.*

Funk, G., & Brown, D. (1994). From dissonance to harmony: Reaching a business/education equilibrium. *Kappan, 75*(10), 766-769.

Hodgkinson, H. (1991). Reform versus reality. *Kappan, 73*(1), 8-16.

Howe, Harold II. (1991, November). America 2000: A bumpy ride on four trains. *Kappan, 73*(3), 192-203.

Kentucky Education Reform Act, Kentucky Acts of 1990, c. 476.

Komoski, P. K. (1990). Needed: A whole-curriculum approach. *Educational Leadership, 47*(5), 72-78.

Marzano, R.J., Pickering, D.J., & Brandt, R.S. (1990). Integrating instructional programs through dimensions of learning. *Educational Leadership, 47*(5), 17-24.

Nebraska State Department of Education. (1994). *Business education framework for Nebraska schools.* Lincoln: Department of Education. (ERIC Document Reproduction Service No. ED 381 619).

Newmann, F. M. (1994). School-wide professional community. *Issues in Restructuring Schools,* (No. 6). Madison, WI: University of Wisconsin, Center on Organization and Restructuring of Schools.

Newmann, F. M., Marks, H.M., & Gamoran, A. (1995). Authentic pedagogy: Standards that boost student performance. *Issues in Restructuring Schools,* (No. 8). Madison, WI: University of Wisconsin, Center on Organization and Restructuring of Schools.

Rutherford, B., & Billig, S. H. (1995). Eight lessons of parent, family, and community involvement in the middle grades. *Kappan, 77*(1), 64-68.

Sheingold, K. (1991). Restructuring for learning with technology: The potential for synergy. *Kappan, 73*(1), 17-27.

Slavin, R. E. (1990). Research on cooperative learning: Consensus and controversy. *Educational Leadership, 47*(4), 52-54.

U.S. Department of Education. (1991). *America 2000: An educational strategy.* (Rev. Ed.) Washington, DC: U.S. Department of Education.

Weissbourd, B. (1994). The evolution of the family resource movement. In S. L. Kagan & B. Weissbourd (Eds.). *Putting families first* (pp. 28-47). San Francisco: Jossey-Bass.

PART III

TECHNOLOGIES THAT ENABLE CHANGES IN BUSINESS EDUCATION

CHAPTER 7

Emerging Technology

Pamela Ramey
Kent State University, Tuscarawas Campus
New Philadelphia, Ohio

Shirley Barton
Kent State University, Regional Campuses
Kent, Ohio

Following several hectic days of working in her office at home, **Ms. Nan O'Second** comes into the office on Friday for her **in-office hours**. She obtains access to the building via **thermal zone recognition**. **Artificial intelligence** sets the room temperature for her preferences. **Fuzzy logic** controls lighting to an even level regardless of the amount of sunlight coming through the windows. Via the computer, her **electronic whiteboard wall panels** become adorned with her personal photos, calendar, and favorite artwork.

Nan works as an **administrative associate**. Many tasks are on her agenda today. When she connects her laptop to the office network this morning, her Internet computer maintenance service provider detects a problem with her computer and makes the repair before she notices that anything went wrong.

As Ms. O'Second's **virtual secretary** scans her e-mail and sorts messages in categories, the **electronic calendar** reminds her of a 1 p.m. meeting. First, she must spend the morning reviewing all **digital documents** created during the past week by employees in her company. Nan prefers to use the **whiteboard** wall panel to view the documents because they contain film clips, graphics, photographs, and **authenticated signatures**.

Because of the superior security and the multimedia nature of the documents, Nan does not make paper copies. She conducts **drill-down searches** to locate documents for today's meeting with an international firm.

It is almost 1 o'clock, and one of the attorneys has not arrived for the meeting. Nan uses the **global positioning system** to determine his location en route. She recommends that the attorney use the third alternate route on his **smart car's map control panel** to get around a traffic jam.

Nan's presence is critical at this meeting because it involves a teleconference that will focus on questions that she has thoroughly researched. At this meeting, she assumes the role of **information manager** by presenting her research, finding answers to attendees' queries, using **neural networks** to draw conclusions, and performing **data mining** to make predictions.

Technology has made Nan more productive, but her skills as a communicator are just as important to the company because face-to-face meetings and person-to-person conversations are paramount to the company's image.

Before she leaves, Nan reviews work assignments for the upcoming week with her work team colleagues who also report to the office on Friday.

Soon it will be time to decide whether to have her computer make those **automated dinner reservations** or program the **smart stove** at home!

This scenario illustrates the tremendous potential of existing and emerging technologies. These technologies will be integrated into the business office and even the business classroom within the next two decades. The attitude with which business educators approach changes in technology is critical for the continued vitality of business education.

Based on the data available today and projections for 2000, the quantity of information on this planet will possibly double every 70 minutes, compared with every 100 years in 1900. In the world of technology, more is to be gained by studying the future than the present because the present becomes history all too quickly. Business educators have little time to get prepared for the next wave of innovations.

Technological changes will impact how and where business people communicate, approach work, conduct business, and advance their careers. This chapter takes the reader on a tour of technological innovations that are on the horizon and analyzes the resulting impact on business and business education.

Emerging Technologies

Current technologies involved in the administration of most office functions—computer hardware and software, telecommunications, and work design—will fuse into one supertechnology. Explosive changes are imminent for the office. These changes, driven by consumer needs and demands, will result in new appliances and products. Many of the most promising emerging technologies discussed in this chapter presently are not known to most office workers but eventually will have a major impact on their working lives.

Digital means compatibility. One of the critical obstacles in the emergence of the Information Age has been the incompatibility of hardware and software. Conversion of all data to pure digital form will be the first step in removing the barriers posed by incompatible computer platforms or software programs. Gone will be the days of inflating software programs' bulk by writing line after line of compatibility codes. Instead, incompatible computers will be sent instructions embedded in the software to tell them to think they are identical machines. Digital information will be compressed, stored, transmitted, and returned to its original form.

Digital data is not limited to facts and figures crunched at a computer terminal. When the television set, telephone, newspaper, videocassette recorder, and other tools of telecomputing become 100 percent digital, the separate worlds of cable, phone, and computer will become one.

Data compression to integrate both audio and video will become necessary and commonplace in the continuing enhancement of telecomputing. Competition will be severe as the telecommunications industry strives to meet bandwidth demands to transmit emerging technology applications with great speed (Negroponte, 1995).

If all communication to a home or business (telephone messages, cable television programming, and telecomputing data) is to be provided over a single wire, then the broadband line of today will have to be remanufactured using new materials that are capable of carrying the heavy traffic. According to Microsoft's Bill Gates, the last mile of the Information Superhighway may be the most difficult one because it means building a compatible and coordinated infrastructure of heavy-traffic lines that are available to people around the world (Gates, 1995).

Computer IQs skyrocket. The capabilities of the computer to surpass human thinking is depicted in this paraphrase of a witticism by business expert Warren Bennis (Pritchett, 1994):

> The business of the future will have only two employees, a human being and a dog. The human being will be there to feed the dog. The dog will be there to keep the human from touching the computer.

The power of the computer is impressive if not frightening. Computing will enter new plateaus when 3-D, interactive capability, and virtual reality are no longer just novel ideas. In fact, computers will become multifunctional telecommunication appliances that select telephone routing, manage voice mail, and establish video conference calls. Already marketed are 31-inch-screen computers that also serve as televisions.

Although software gives the computer its intelligence, computers will provide almost-human or even better-than-human reasoning (Port, 1995). With **silicon brains** already growing in research labs, the next decade or two will usher in new generations of the manufactured brains. Early versions of silicon brains will have the ability to regenerate and pass along their power to design themselves. Unsuccessful attempts in new generations will be cast off, thus leading to "survival-of-the-fittest" functions. Human beings will not take kindly to the risk that a computer might design itself to be superior to human thinking.

A less threatening form of superior computer intelligence is **fuzzy logic**. Fuzzy logic, not confined to black and white considerations, recognizes shades of gray when decisions must be made. Business decisions of the future based on fuzzy logic will appear to be more humanistic or natural. For example, an insurance agent will use a computer to analyze multiple factors that, in combination or in isolation, provide a unique profile of the insured. Based on those factors, a personalized rate will be determined for the insured's coverage.

Expert systems learn by running an initial set of rules, making inferences, generating new information, and either changing or writing new rules. As a result, computers running with the assistance of expert systems learn from experiences. The computers only get smarter and smarter, as their intelligence continues to evolve. Once the computer is shown how to do something once, it will remember the process and will improve the process if given the latitude to do so. One such example is the **virtual assistant** that will one day perform the laborious task of classifying one's electronic, voice, and video mail messages.

Neural networks emulate the brain's processing capability by performing parallel processing. Unlike expert systems that function through deductive reasoning, neural networks rely on inductive reasoning. Once fed volumes of data, neural networks will look for what causes the data to perform as it has. One day neural networks will identify unusual long-distance calling activity and intervene even before customers are aware that their calling card numbers have been hijacked.

Knowledge discovery or **data mining** also takes existing data and analyzes it thoroughly but differs from neural networks because it makes predictions rather than drawing conclusions. Although predictions involve statistical and visualization procedures, they are presented in a common-sense form for humans. With vast storehouses of databases, companies will be able to identify successful products, plan future production, and balance inventories based on predictions.

Genetic algorithms may provide solutions superior to human thinking. Similar to mathematical brainstorming techniques, all possibilities and options are initially considered, leaving out human bias that a procedure may not work. Problems are broken apart into building blocks and are arranged into thousands of configurations. Multiple models are constructed to find a successful result, and each trial retains successful attempts and abandons failed ones. As an example, financial markets will benefit greatly as portfolios are assembled and tested in virtual reality before the actual money is invested.

Each form of computer intelligence has its advantages and disadvantages. The integration of two or more computing techniques can counterbalance limitations with strengths. The outcome is impressive computing that is more efficient or capable of producing better results.

The Information Superhighway cruises ahead. The Information Superhighway is under construction and will be for some time to come. Just as some four-lane highways were converted to links on the interstate highway system three decades ago, the present telecommunication system, already dubbed the information highway, will have major thoroughfares added to the network to carry voice, data, and video simultaneously.

Stumbling blocks will be removed as ultra-clear fiber optic cable carries communication lines over land. The best of telephone industry technology in providing fiber optic installations for voice and data will be augmented with the best of the cable industry in transmitting full-motion video. Eventually, the two providers will merge.

Several travel modes on the present information highway are considered forerunners to the true Information Superhighway. **Digital simultaneous voice data** (DSVD) provides conversation and image transmission. **Integrated systems digital network** (ISDN) transmits faster than DSVD and offers a somewhat choppy form of motion video. Broadband lines carry voice and data as well as full-motion video, and cable modems connect computers to cable networks. Demands for high-speed voice and data transmission as well as full-motion video will spawn new technologies to increase efficiency.

The view from the Internet will literally take shape as objects move from two dimensional to three-dimensional. This transformation will be possible due to virtual reality modeling language (VRML). VMRL will permit Internet users to visually walk through an office displayed on the screen or examine it from any angle by manipulating the image. So realistic is the view that people working in VRML environments may experience motion sickness symptoms. VRML has the potential to redefine cyberspace and is expected to be used on a regular basis.

Cellular companies have a looming commitment to provide interference-free wireless technology capable of carrying voice, data, and video. Much of the wireless capability will be improved with the use of low earth-orbiting satellites. Distance will be a non-issue as signals will be beamed interference-free to satellites and back to earth. Because the direct distance upward to a satellite and down to an earth location is the same whether it is to the next city or halfway around the world, remote access without costly cable infrastructure will grow. The cellular companies' greatest challenge will be in increasing their bandwidth and transmission speed to become providers for the future Information Superhighway.

Applications for the Information Superhighway will evolve out of the personal computer and the Internet. Specialized Internet cruising appliances will be so inexpensive that they may be given away for customers and clients to use as vehicles to communicate with companies via the Internet.

Business is virtually different. Large and small companies will gain new perspectives as they use the future Information Superhighway to conduct transactions. The market area will be both next door *and* global as communication technology makes possible differentiation and specialization not viable in smaller markets.

In the computer industry and with related providers, the cost of doing business will be no more than a download of software. For instance, instead of going to the nearest computer store to purchase software, customers may simply request it over the Information Superhighway. Buyers may obtain a permit to download the software as needed for a given duration, much like a magazine subscription.

Software will become modular as customers select only the options they need, and the price will be adjusted accordingly. Then, if a need develops later, options can be downloaded for an additional fee. If a software package is required for a period of short duration, leasing may be more feasible. At the expiration of the lease, the software download will no longer be permitted.

The Information Superhighway will provide customers the ability to obtain software upgrades or fixes automatically. This new delivery vehicle will also allow customers to have their computer equipment repaired. Sensors will detect imminent problems and make repairs before they materialize.

Because software will be sent over the Information Superhighway, developers will need to write only one version for all platforms. The communication standards of the Internet allow computers to speak to one another via a common language. Tiny virtual machines created from software code and embedded in the application software will allow any computer to think and act as if it were an Internet computer, sharing a common language. Decreased development costs may result in lower software prices.

Documents get a new view. The static view of documents traditionally held by individuals will change to a dynamic one. Content will be the focal point and not the software program that produced the document. Currently, a document is useless without an associated software application. In **object programming**, such applications run in the background of a document, almost invisible.

Object programming will also spell success for what are known as **active documents**. By linking parts of documents to other programs, object programming permits changes to occur automatically as they develop, which is characteristic of today's object linking and embedding. Teamed with artificial intelligence, the documents will customize themselves for different audiences such as in interactive training manuals.

The word *document* brings up visions of text on paper. In the near future, however, **digital documents** will become more popular with low cost, simple storage and retrieval, and ease of movement from one location to the next. Some parts of future documents will not lend themselves to printing on paper because they will include video clips, audio, programming code, and images, often in three dimensions. A memo may contain a video clip of a company president explaining the rationale behind new procedures for employees and will also have a text version of the procedures. An e-mail tear-off form for employees to digitally sign if they agree to the procedures may appear at the end of the document. The **authenticated digital signature** will become an acceptable substitute for today's handwritten signature.

The transmission of digital documents via e-mail will reach new heights. The documents being sent will contain, among other things, forms and the ability to branch to other options.

Groupware will become more sophisticated, and **interactive documents** will be created by individuals or groups working simultaneously on a common item. Each contributor's changes and annotations will be initialed and dated.

Smaller is better ... sometimes. Concerning hardware, **miniaturization** is a major design factor for emerging information appliances. Users will continue to push for smaller products to fulfill their portability needs without having to sacrifice computing power. With miniaturization, ease of operation will be compromised when the tradeoff is readily available access to information. The Dick Tracy watches will no longer be folklore, and subscriber fees will be charged to obtain downloaded information to the tiny appliances.

As information appliances get smaller, they also will become more specialized in their capability to perform distinctive functions. The **wallet computer** may contain a single **smart card**, much like a credit card with a microchip, to perform a designated function. A multifunctional wallet computer may contain multiple smart cards working simultaneously to perform orchestrated functions when not working alone. Smarter smart cards will read and write data. Future developments of the smart card will include sophisticated identification data about its owner as well as the storage of **digital money**, tickets, and business transactions.

Microsoft's Bill Gates (Gates, 1995) envisions that the essentials of a wallet PC will include a small screen, a microphone, and reading and storage capability. Accompanying gadgetry may include a camera, a scanner that reads print or handwriting, a panic button to signal emergency help, a thermometer, a barometer, or a heart-rate sensor.

As mentioned earlier, the **Internet appliance** is another specialty product. Already on the drawing boards of several television and game manufacturers, a set-top unit allows Web pages to be displayed on an ordinary television screen. The need for an expensive and bulky multimedia PC is eliminated, space is saved, and the television is serving a dual purpose.

Network **personal digital assistants** (PDAs) are also Internet appliances. These portable hand-held devices, a combination cellular phone, pager, fax machine, personal organizer, and pen-based notepad/notetaker, will eventually provide low-cost mobile access to the Internet. Still, these devices will probably work in tandem with full-function **personal communication systems** (PCSs) because most people want to download a large quantity of the information they see on the Internet.

Palmtop computers featuring full keyboards or **pen-based input devices** are the intermediate step between true miniature and notebook size. When wireless is available everywhere, is dependable at all locations (primarily due to satellite connections instead of land-based connections), and is provided at a reasonable cost, the power of the palmtop will be appreciated by all who value size as a virtue.

Even today's notebook computers will become tablet computers as display panels are made slimmer with existing re-engineered LCD and gas plasma technologies. Tablet computers will demand much less power and will obtain what little power they need from solar panels instead of from bulky batteries.

Displays reflect new technologies. The slimmer version of the notebook display will also appear in flat-panel displays of varying sizes, ranging from wrist size to full-wall size. **Electro-luminescent panels** will offer paper-thin display devices in brilliant color with light 25 percent brighter than today's computer monitors.

Within the next decade, people will read newspapers, books, files, and other written materials with tablet-sized, hand-held wireless viewers, called **e-books**, linked to a computer. Flat-panel screens on these viewers will have the appearance of paper with pages that change using touch-screen control. The viewers will be used at home, at the office, or on the road. Such paperless reading is another application made possible by new liquid crystal flat panel technology. Inch-thick **digital whiteboards** mounted on the wall of a conference room will change as needed. The computer controlling the whiteboard will display a photograph, a movie, text, or other finely detailed images. Handwriting on the whiteboard will be recognized by the computer and converted into typefaces. The conference table will have handwriting input screens through which the conference participants may communicate visually with others. Video projectors, visualizers, and electronic information display boards will be additional tools that may be used to make a meeting truly a multimedia experience.

Input technologies gain sophistication. The long-awaited **voice recognition** technology will become more sophisticated as it adapts to a variety of accents, dialects, and languages. Voice transfer on the Internet will be perfected and popular. **Desktop broadcasting** will become the next buzzword as users rush to create the voice equivalent of a World Wide Web page.

The refinements of handwriting recognition technology have been just as difficult to achieve as those in voice recognition technology. Existing pen-based computers use a pointer and other restricted input procedures. Nevertheless, because of the convenience of handwritten input, pen-based computers capable of reading legible handwriting will be marketed extensively.

Pen-based and voice recognition input, however, will not be the input method of choice by many individuals for the same reason that people prefer writing rather than dictating messages. Using the hands allows one to keep the brain in manageable control and to choose words carefully. Current users of the keyboard for text input are expected to continue to favor that method for a long time. However, the next generation, growing up with voice recognition and handwritten input, may have a different perspective.

The **EyeMouse**, a smart instrument that controls a computer with eye movements, was initially developed to help the disabled control home appliances or be more effective in the workplace. This device will have application for mainstream users. By controlling the cursor with "active looking," a user can click on icons and menus and draw pictures with slight head motions. In the future, all users will have the option of continuous, unattended, and fully automatic operation of computers with their eyes. Thus, sending computer fax messages or turning on the copier will be done literally at the blink of an eye. In summary, a variety of input alternatives, whether activated by keyboard, voice, pen, or eye, will be available to users in this decade at affordable prices and with reliable results (Myers, 1992).

Mobility and portability are driving forces. Telecommuters working out of remote offices will introduce a whole new set of needs for the business world. Among these needs will be appliances and technologies that are mobile and portable.

To keep up with incoming calls, telecommuters will use more sophisticated voice mail features. A forwarding feature will connect the caller with a pager or will ring the cellular phone number. Technologies of the future will take the present **one-number-follow-me-anywhere** technology one step further. As a telecommuter pulls into the driveway of the home or office, the cellular phone will automatically switch to a cordless telephone or a **handyphone** within a building.

The portable handyphone is part of an internal telecommunications network. This device has a short range of less than two miles but is perfect within buildings or between adjacent buildings. Handyphones operate on very low battery power, are wireless, and are characterized by the presence of stick-on antennas throughout the building(s). Sometime in the future, cellular phones will serve dual functions as handyphones for internal communications and as cordless phones for external communications from offices and homes.

Road warriors will hold face-to-face meetings using desktop video-conferencing with microchip cameras built into a PC. At the same time that images are being transmitted, data will appear on the remaining part of the screen. Small **active pixel camera chips** will also grace video telephones to provide two-way video telecommunication. The video telephone will appear hardly different from today's telephone, but internally it will be a complex telecommunication appliance.

The concern over privacy in wireless communication will diminish as encryption and filtering devices are perfected. However, the challenge to break into yet another computer system will continue to torment the cybercrook no matter how sophisticated the system.

Security is still a critical factor. Cybercrimes perpetrated by cyber-criminals will open up a totally new area of investigation for cybercops. Virtual crimes will occur with no footprints and no trails of evidence. Already, cellular phone fraud and stock scams are frequent. The seriousness of the crimes will increase as society builds a dependence on its access to data. At the extreme, entire cities or companies run the risk of being held hostage by cyberterrorists. Rather than outsiders trying to get inside a system to perpetrate their crimes, employees with access to inside information will be the leading culprits.

Passwords to provide access to computer systems will be replaced with better safeguards. For example, **handprint recognition** is an alternative. Potential computer users will place their hand upon a designated sensor and will wait to have the handprint matched with stored data. When the handprint matches, access will be permitted.

Visual imaging will scrutinize access by photographing a potential computer user, identifying significant facial landmarks, matching them against a stored template, and providing access within a couple of seconds. Other comparisons using DNA identification, voice spectrographs, and encryption will control access to computer systems.

The most promising computer security technology to scrutinize access, **thermal image mapping,** however, cannot be fooled even by identical twins trying to access a system. Imaging that maps heat zones will scan the head and will develop a heat zone pattern that is compared against a template. Even twins have different heat zones that do not change. This type of access appears to be unmanipulable, even by surgery.

The volume of information floating in cyberspace continues to increase and is fair game for unscrupulous use. Database mines that offer limitless potential to improve business efficiency can be turned into a cybernightmare if used for the wrong purpose. E-mail sent and subsequently deleted may be unearthed and used in litigation. Ethical standards will be developed to protect individuals whose personal information is misused.

Impact on Business

The entire concept of the office will change from a fixed place to more of a process. As telecommuters take to the road, the office will be identified as wherever business is conducted. This may be in a person's home or it may be on the road where the employee is close to the customer. Due to miniaturization and portability, the **office-in-a-briefcase** concept will allow the telecommuter to keep all the essential work tools in a briefcase: a palmtop computer, a cellular phone, and a printer/copier/scanner/fax combination unit.

By 1998, 13 million people are expected to be part of the telecommuter work force (Baig, 1995). Many of these telecommuters will choose to live in rural areas, creating a new shift in population and a drain on rural resources. They will do this because technology allows them to stay completely in touch with the home office using faxes, laptops, modems, videoconferencing, voice mail, and e-mail.

Because road warriors occasionally have to return to the base of operations to hold meetings or to get materials, a new office concept called **hoteling** will emerge. Telecommuters will reserve office space in advance, and a work area at office headquarters will be readied by rearranging modular panels to fit individual needs.

Individuals who have already chosen the telecommuting route are quick to point out the advantages: no commuting time, fewer interruptions, casual dress, and a flexible schedule. Although the benefits usually outweigh the shortcomings, telecommuting married couples may be too close for comfort if both have to perform their work in a confining home office and see each other 24 hours a day. Workers who thrive on interaction with co-workers will find this work style lonely and unstimulating. The traditional rewarding of individual accomplishments will be replaced with team recognition.

Technology changes office roles. For those who are left at the office headquarters, a job shift will occur. Some forecasters believe that the secretary will take on more responsibilities and will be elevated to a middle-management position. This person will virtually be the glue of the organization, coordinating projects, scheduling meetings, posting appointments on interactive electronic calendars, planning facilities and linkups, and working without supervision. *Administrative associate* might be a better term than administrative assistant.

In a sense, the home office may be a lonely place. With no co-workers present with whom to interact, a lone office worker may feel isolated from human contact and thus lack **psychic reward**. To counter this phenomenon, managers will need to develop new reward systems. Stimulating assignments that involve external interaction will also help to maintain employee morale. Professional association connections will grow in popularity because of their therapeutic value and opportunity for personal interaction.

The work style revolution continues. Companies that have been accustomed to a controlling climate will not adapt easily to the virtual office, which is characterized by employee empowerment, trust, and teamwork. Neither will individuals adapt well to the virtual office if they have thrived on office politics in the past.

Technology alone cannot make an inefficient company efficient. Even the most productive companies must change the way they do business if the technology is to make them more productive.

Skills and transfer of skills will be more important than company loyalty. Most people will be hired to come to a company, tackle a project, and then leave. Temporaries will be hired as consultants. Job seekers will hire a personal agent to market skills to potential employers much like people in the movie industry do today. Thus the way individuals obtain and maintain employment will be altered.

Implications for Business Education

Emerging technologies are forcing businesses to re-engineer themselves based on the flexibility of information technology. Education will find itself having to do the same.

Although commitment to provide schools with state-of-the-art technology exists, sometimes the implementation lags far behind. For example, about one-third of the nation's schools have access to the Internet, but only five percent of the classrooms participate in this valuable link (O'Neil, 1995). Teachers may appear to be less than enthusiastic until they have access to the new technology in their classrooms, receive appropriate training, and are comfortable using the technology.

Change is the expectation. Do business educators have an edge as a result of working with technology in preparation for their careers? Perhaps not. A common pitfall of many teachers, including business teachers, is to use technology simply to accomplish teaching goals *faster*. Because they value the expeditious accomplishment of goals, faculty have a tendency to cling to traditional teaching approaches when using technology. Pedagogically, however, the real challenge is to teach students how to use technology to study subject matter in greater breadth and depth.

Business teachers have always prided themselves on being some of the first teachers to integrate subjects and to provide realistic preparation for students entering business careers. The multifunctional nature of emerging technologies affords business teachers the perfect opportunity to integrate technology with subject matter. The ideal integrated teaching model will bring single business subjects together under one comprehensive umbrella that emphasizes interrelatedness with new content areas such as information management, facilities coordination, and multimedia communication.

Business teachers will find creating scenarios and simulations reflective of virtual office operations particularly difficult. Nonetheless, students must be able to address concepts such as working alone, self-talk and self-reinforcement, problem solving, and decision making. Business students must understand that re-engineering can involve an organizational chart change or a change in job responsibilities that aligns better with emerging technologies.

Teaching students to function within a workgroup also requires a different instructional approach. Students must be asked to work in groups as they collectively create and share information. The business teacher will be challenged to encourage group work yet must assess individual effort within the group to comply with an educational system that requires individual measures.

Many of the devices and applications that are suitable for the business world can be used as teaching tools in the classroom. By maintaining contacts with members of the business community who are using cutting-edge technologies, business teachers can gain more first-hand information about new technologies. Teachers must comfortably use technologies in the classroom so that students will feel confident using the same technologies later in a business setting.

Technology *is* the method. The Information Superhighway will afford teachers and students an opportunity to learn collaboratively, perhaps through a global strategy such as international learning circles. For individualized instruction, **mediated learning** via interactive multimedia programs will provide students with specialized assessment and personalized lesson plans, notifying the teacher when individual assistance is needed. Another individualized approach to learning uses **artificial intelligence** that provides students the opportunity to learn independently through training materials that adapt to their individual responses to questions. Business teachers will be given an additional role of preparing students to be self-taught. This valuable skill will be introduced to students during their formal classroom education in a nurturing environment. Students will use self-teaching skills for a lifetime of learning.

As teachers' roles move from being information disseminators to becoming **technology coaches** and **information facilitators**, the ongoing battle to keep up will not only continue but also accelerate. Proficiency and innovation in teaching and technology will be taken for granted. Business teachers increasingly will feel pressure to fulfill the implied contract to provide students with a means of earning a living in a fast-changing technological world.

Business-teacher educators play a pivotal role in moving current and future business teachers into new methods of teaching *with* and *about* the emerging technologies. Of equal importance, business teacher educators must offer professional development programs that have as a goal the integration of technology with methodology.

Survival Kit for the Future

Business teachers must help students develop a survival kit to succeed in the workplace of emerging technologies. These basics are often found embedded in other business courses.

Communication skills persist. Students' communication skills will be even more important and will take on new dimensions. Consequently, students will need to select the correct communication medium for the objectives to be achieved.

Because of the growing importance of e-mail and digital documents, composition at the computer will be an essential communication skill. Writing standards that emphasize organization and development of topic sentences will be no less important in the electronic world than in the paper-and-pencil days.

Oral communication skills in presentations, videoconferences, and in ordinary videotelephone conversations will be important. No longer can people do other things while talking on the telephone and appear as though they are hanging on every word a person is saying. They will be seen and will have to appear interested. Thus, active listening and reading body language will take on even more importance in this environment.

E-mail will advance a set of acceptable behaviors called **netiquette** that emphasizes messages that are appropriately brief and meaningful, convey a positive tone, and demonstrate restraint in copying recipients. The rush to create must not get in the way of quality communication.

The unscrupulous will set traps on the Information Superhighway, and students will need to be highway smart. Students should be taught to recognize and encouraged to avoid possible threats to their well being on the Superhighway, such as the following:

- Behavior or actions appearing to be unethical or inappropriate.
- Actions that may compromise privacy.
- Activities that could pose a threat.

Workplace skills expand. Technology is causing more and more people to work at home. The work-at-home trend is growing among many Fortune 500 companies and will filter to smaller companies as well (Baig, 1995). This growing work style, made possible by the computer, saves money for both the employer and employee, is flexible, and adapts well to individual workers' personal needs. Students must be prepared for these variations in how people have traditionally gone to work. They will need instruction on how to manage interruptions or distractions when working at home.

Working at home will require the ability to work both independently and interdependently. Students must be taught how to be independent in exercising judgment, organizing work flow, being self-starters, and assessing their own performance. The overwhelming volume of electronic information bombarding the workers of the future will cause them to become more interdependent. Students will need to know, in interaction with others, how to access, evaluate, and disseminate electronic information.

Teachers must prepare students to become pivotal information sources who hold more power than ever before in the organization. Students must be taught how to share correctly, interpret, communicate, organize, and learn from information. Research savvy will be a key component for success as workers sift through volumes of data and extract the essential information upon which companies base decisions.

Workplace coping skills to deal with stress, isolation, and rapid change will be required of office employees of the future. They will communicate with supervisors and co-workers daily but may see them only intermittently.

Technical skills predominate. With their multiple technical skills based on oral and written communication, technofiles will characterize the future office force. Students must be forewarned that in order to succeed, their education will not be ending anytime soon. Grow or die will be the guiding principle for maintaining employability.

Essential technological skills that should be part of a future office employee's survival kit are primarily concentrated in computers and telecommunications. These skills must be integrated with oral and written communication skills. The nature of each business's operations will dictate the variety of technical skills needed. Students should be expected to exhibit information management skills and the ability to execute simple to multidimensional queries. In the area of computer applications, students must know which application works best in a given situation. They must also know how to transfer skills between different applications.

Job search skills compete. For persons conducting a job search in the business world of the future, job skills will be the focus, not job descriptions. The structure of a resume will be significantly different. Work experience and classroom experience will be organized by project or task rather than by job title. A list of skills will replace course titles because of the use of computer searches that rely on key words appearing on the resume. Students need to know how to develop two resumes: one that uses a variety of fonts and layouts for presentation at the time of an interview and another one that functions electronically for easy transmission over the Internet.

Teachers need to let students experience how to use the Internet for a job search. Current electronic job listing services will soon be augmented by on-line interviews via the Internet and integrated software packages that match applicants with appropriate jobs.

Interview preparation should include development of a portfolio that depicts technical skills, abilities, and strengths. The interviewee who effectively uses a laptop computer to present an electronic portfolio has a competitive advantage. Such a presentation demonstrates the applicant's communication, technical, organizational, and job-search skills, all of which will assist the interviewer in deciding upon the applicant's potential for success in the workplace.

The Challenge Ahead

Business teachers are on a knowledge journey for all of their professional lives and must replace dated knowledge with emerging telecomputing learning tools required on today's information highway. Since today's information highway will soon become tomorrow's information superhighway, business educators must commit to pursuing the expertise needed to prepare students for a job like Nan's.

The "grow or die" creed is a mandate, not a choice, for all business educators.

References

Baig, E. (1995). Welcome to the wireless office. *Business Week, 34(30)*, 104-106.

Gates, B. (1995). *The road ahead.* New York: Viking Penguin.

Myers, G. A. (1992). The eyemouse. *T.H.E. Journal, 19,* 13-15.

Negroponte, N. (1995). *Being digital.* New York: Alfred A. Knopf.

O'Neil, J. (1995). Teachers and technology: Potential and pitfalls. *Educational Leadership, 53(2),* 10-11.

Port, O. (1995). Computers that think are almost here. *Business Week, 34(33),* 68-73.

Pritchett, P. (1994). *New work habits for a radically changing world.* Dallas: Pritchett and Associates.

CHAPTER 8

Integrated Software Applications

Sharon Fisher-Larson

Elgin Community College, Elgin, Illinois

The role of the office professional has changed and continues to change. Although many businesses still use *secretary* within job titles, many businesses are changing to more global titles that adequately reflect the scope of the evolving position. As an indication of support for this change, Professional Secretaries International voted recently to add a tag line to the association's name, *Professional Secretaries International, The Association for Office Professionals*. As a worker in the information age, this new breed of office professional must deal with a great explosion of knowledge. Organizational structures are flattening and office professionals are taking on more and more responsibility. Students will be able to meet these additional challenges with the help of computers, specifically with Windows technology.

Decisions were once made daily; now decisions are made from minute to minute with changes occurring every second. Office professionals now make decisions based on information accessed from the computer. One used to wait for printouts supplied by data processing, read and study pages of hard copy, formulate a proposal or report, and finally make a decision. But turnaround time was inadequate. Today the office professional must gather information from a variety of sources through the computer. While reading information on a computer screen, the office worker simultaneously collects data and compiles statistics that will help the individual make an intelligent decision. That decision may need to be communicated through electronic mail rather than a formal memo, letter, or report. And, even more importantly, this decision will not be arrived at by one individual. Communications will occur locally, regionally, nationally, and internationally, all within minutes.

To cope successfully, office professionals need to learn to contribute to the team using integrated software applications efficiently. One individual may be responsible for checking financial data, another may be checking databases for related information, while yet another individual may be pulling scattered information together into a report. Office professionals will all work together through electronic communications. Office professionals will be able to transfer information to one another, view one another's work, brainstorm, and finalize decisions together over a network.

Although DOS (Disk Operating System) has been the predominate operating system for personal computer users, DOS has always been somewhat cumbersome and time consuming to learn and use. With the introduction of Microsoft Windows, the need for office professionals to learn complex DOS commands was eliminated. In addition, office professionals were required to become "mouse" proficient! Although Windows 3.1 continues to need DOS, Windows 95 no longer needs DOS since Windows 95 is its own operating system. Although Windows was once thought to be a fad, one can no longer believe that Windows will disappear and that the computer user will once again only have to be proficient on the keyboard. Where DOS was once the standard, Windows is now the standard. As Windows 95 and Windows NT become more common, users will be required to "click" even more to get work done. However, the overall system will be easier to use as the interface becomes more and more user-friendly.

The Windows environment is a graphical user interface (GUI) that provides visual cues for working with applications software. Additionally, Windows also provides an environment that allows users to transfer knowledge learned in one application to another application. For example, the shortcut keystrokes, Ctrl + C, Ctrl + X, and Ctrl + V for Copy, Cut, and Paste, are used universally in all Windows software applications. Windows allows for multitasking that enables the user to run more than one software application at a time as well as transfer information among the open applications. Visual cues, universal procedures, and multi-tasking all open new doors for both the instructors preparing their students for the 21st century office as well as students preparing for work in the 21st century office.

Application software is designed to help individuals accomplish a specific task using the computer. Today many businesses purchase suites or integrated software that include a variety of applications. These suites enable the business to have a variety of applications for users such as word processing, spreadsheets, presentation graphics, electronic mail, etc. Each component has a specific purpose even though the features available may overlap from one component to another. Presently, the major suites include Corel, Microsoft, and Lotus. The Microsoft suite, which includes Word, Excel, PowerPoint, Access, Scheduler, and Bookshelf, appears to be the most popular. However, the introduction of the Corel suite, with WordPerfect, Quattro Pro, Presentation, SideKick, Netscape Navigator, Dashboard, and Envoy, may challenge Microsoft's domination. Lotus by IBM and the Smartsuite, which includes Lotus 1-2-3, WordPro, Approach, Freelance Graphics, and Organizer, are also found on many computers.

Teaching the Applications

At one time, business instructors were able to keep up-to-date by returning to the classroom every few years, working in industry, and reading current periodicals. Now the business instructor must think about learning new computer procedures and new software every few months. In addition, the classroom instructor's role is changing. Many times the instructor becomes more of a facilitator while leading students through the many options available for completing activities in the various applications. Flexibility is more important than ever; teachers and students have no guarantee that the computer setup will remain the same from day to day or from session to session.

Operating systems/environments. An operating system controls the workings of the computer and may be compared to an air traffic controller. Rather than coordinating planes taking off and landing, however, the controller coordinates the activities within the computer. It makes the keyboard, microprocessor, disk drives, mouse, and other peripherals perform properly. DOS, MS-DOS, PC-DOS, OS/2, and UNIX are just a few of the operating systems available. Windows 3.1 or lower is an operating environment that works under DOS. Windows 95 has its own operating system and does not need DOS or a supporting operating system to function. With the ability to multi-task, users can have multiple applications opened at the same time. Windows also provides the user with the ability to transfer information easily from one application to another.

Students should be instructed in the operation of these systems as the systems apply to the integrated software being used. When using DOS, students need to learn when and how to use DOS rather than the application for specific job tasks. In addition, students should learn how to customize the environment for the specific needs of the integrated software applications. Windows students should be introduced to the desktop feature and instructed how to modify the desktop for the best ergonomic conditions, thus preventing unnecessary eye strain. And, more importantly, students should know how to work in multiple applications and transfer information from one application to another.

Word processing. Word processing is the most common applications software used by office professionals. Although many packages are available, the most frequently used packages are WordPerfect for Windows and Word for Windows. Each of these is also part of a suite. Word processing enables the user to create, edit, format, store, and print documents. Features such as a spelling checker, thesaurus, and a grammar checker are common. Most word-processing software also includes graphics and other desktop-publishing features.

Students need to learn basic word-processing features for completing routine office documents. Templates, macros, and styles are the future in word processing. Students need to learn how to use these features to complete everyday activities. Rather than create a memo, students should access a memo template. If the memo template does not meet their format needs, students should modify the template and create their own memo template. Windows word processing applications provide many time-efficient features. In Windows, the students should use both the mouse and the keyboard so that users can complete documents quickly and accurately. Using just the mouse is really not any better than using just the keyboard.

Because one word-processing software program no longer dominates the industry, users need to know how to import and export from one word-processing software program to another as well as to other applications.

Spreadsheet. Although simple spreadsheets are similar in appearance to tabbed columns, complex mathematical calculations are also easily handled by spreadsheet software. Spreadsheet software allows the individual to create, calculate, edit, retrieve, modify, and print graphs, charts, reports, and spreadsheets.

Users must know how to create, edit, and analyze the data in spreadsheets. Students must learn spreadsheet terminology and be comfortable with the "what if" feature. Just as in word processing, students must know how to import and export spreadsheets into other spreadsheet software as well as other applications. Students should be instructed how to create graphs and other statistical data from spreadsheets.

Desktop publishing. Most word-processing software can now produce many desktop publishing documents. However, specific desktop-publishing software usually includes more graphics and more features, resulting in a higher-resolution product. Copy is easily prepared as camera ready, saving businesses considerable sums of money for printing costs. Recently one of the state educational associations in Illinois needed to cut costs. In evaluating the cost for the publication, office personnel realized that typesetting fees were exorbitant. As an alternative, their office professional took desktop publishing training, created camera-ready copy, and saved the organization thousands of dollars. Although the differences between Macintosh and IBM compatible equipment have all but disappeared, most desktop publishing users still prefer using the Macintosh.

Students must know how to use the desktop-publishing features of a word-processing application or specific desktop-publishing software. In addition, students must learn the principles of basic design and be able to apply these principles to completed documents. Students must know how to scan documents. Also, students must know how to import information from other applications to create professional desktop-publishing documents. Students should be introduced to the procedures for sending published documents electronically.

Presentations graphics. Presentation graphics software increases the impact of a presentation through words, numbers, and data in picture form. Graphics make the information being presented visually appealing. High-quality graphics have been shown to increase both the reader's ability to learn and the length of time that the information is retained.

Students must learn how to develop presentations using presentations-graphics software. Design principles and sound will also play an important part as more and more individuals use multimedia notebook and laptop computers to make presentations. Students must know how to import documents from other applications to develop presentations (e.g., spreadsheets for graphs, charts for summaries).

Personal information management. Although PIM software differs in its capabilities, most PIM software offer calendars, appointment schedulers, to-do lists, tickler files, calculators, phone and address lists, and other organizational tasks. On a network, PIM software would normally also include electronic mail. PIM software would enable individuals to search an individual's calendar, schedule an appointment, and cut down on the infamous telephone tag.

Students need to use PIM software for their own scheduling as well as scheduling others and should have an opportunity to use all aspects of PIM software.

Communications. Communications software allows individuals to communicate with one another with the computer as a tool. E-mail, voice mail, and fax can all be transmitted over the computer using communications software.

Students should know how to communicate with others locally as well as globally using e-mail and other telecommunications devices. Each student should be using the Internet and be responsible for communicating daily with others via electronic media.

These various aspects no longer work independently of one another. Therefore, students must be able to schedule a project using the calendaring application, create a document using a word-processing application, enhance the same document with desktop publishing, import a spreadsheet into a document from a spreadsheet application and possibly create a chart for a document from the spreadsheet. Students must also create or access a database that will enable a user to distribute final documents as needed, and then distribute a document to individuals in the database electronically. Students can have the opportunity to experience all of this in an office procedures course or similar technology course.

Using Office Procedures To Apply Integrated Software Skills

As students are educated for the office of the 21st century, business education professionals must introduce the students to all aspects of computer applications. The office professional no longer just keyboards letters and memos. The office professional is expected to know word-processing, spreadsheet, database, presentation, scheduling, and communications software. Therefore, students should be able to schedule a project using the calendaring application; create that document using the word-processing application; enhance the same document with a desktop-publishing application; import a spreadsheet into the document from a spreadsheet application; and possibly create a chart for the document from the spreadsheet; create or access a database that will enable the user to distribute the final document as needed; and then distribute that document to the individuals in the database electronically.

The ideal office-procedures classroom. The perfect office-procedures classroom would include the following: a classroom of networked, state-of-the-art computers with an up-to-date suite of applications software, personal information management software that enables the students to schedule and communicate electronically, and individual logins for the network so that students can totally customize the software to their needs.

The applications. With this type of classroom setup, all assigned work would be completed using one of the software applications. Students would use word processing and spreadsheet software for financial activities, desktop publishing to create camera-ready copy, presentation graphics to design presentations, and database software to input records for textbook assignments and information about the class. Students would use PIM software to schedule their own appointments, send e-mail to one another, and use e-mail to receive all their assignments from their instructor. Students would use PIM software to manage their to-do lists and set priorities.

E-Mail. E-mail must continue to be emphasized and used frequently in class since e-mail will continue to increase in actual use. Therefore, students must be efficient using e-mail, must know etiquette rules for e-mail, and must learn to send a correct e-mail message. Frequently, an e-mail message is criticized for not being well-thought out or even proofread. E-mail messages may contain incomplete sentences, incorrect word usage, and poor grammar. Having students complete assignments using e-mail messages forces them to both compose and proofread at the computer. Students truly become responsible for their e-mail messages.

Syllabus and course outline. In an ideal office-procedures course, the course outline would be included as an attachment to an e-mail message. After reading the message, the students would have an opportunity to print the course outline for their records. During the semester, activities on the syllabus would be transmitted as reminders about appointments and tasks for the students. Students would be required to accept the various appointments and tasks. Accepting these tasks places additional responsibility on the students for follow through.

Session updates. As additional activities are included, students will again be notified by e-mail. All students will need to add these activities to their calendars as well as update the task list.

Case studies. Most office-procedures textbooks include case studies at the end of each unit. These case studies can be used to encourage students to communicate with one another via e-mail and formulate a group consensus. For each case, one student would be put in charge of the case study and be responsible for communicating the final e-mail message to the instructor.

In-class assignments. For each class session students would be given e-mail instructions for assignments that need to be completed during the class session. The instructions will sometimes be complete, needing no further clarification. Other times, the instructions will be purposely vague requiring the students to follow up with e-mail messages to the instructor. All hard-copy assignments would require the students to use the various applications software.

Out-of-class assignments. Students will also be assigned out-of-class work. Instructions for these assignments will also be given through e-mail that will require students to print their e-mail, messages. The students may refer to the assignments outside of class or communicate with their instructor via the Internet.

Technology update. For each session, students would be required to e-mail the instructor with a technology update that has been learned about by reading a newspaper, magazine, or other trade publication. Again, each student would have an opportunity to compose at the computer and utilize good language skills.

A sample session. In this ideal class, students would enter class, sit down at their workstations, and login at a computer. Each student would immediately check for e-mail. While students look at returned assignments, they would also read e-mail messages from the instructor relating to those assignments turned in at the previous session. New assignments would be waiting as e-mail messages. One assignment is requesting that the students create a report. The students are given specific instructions. The students will need to use word processing to create the report; however, they will also need to use spreadsheet software to create a graph for the report as well as the database software to create a listing of individuals related to the project. In addition, each student has been given an individual assignment to complete. The individual assignment will become part of the final report. In order to compile the report, the students must communicate with one another electronically as well as transfer files electronically that will all be used in the final draft of the report. Once previously assigned activities are finalized and material is reviewed, time is spent instructing students on the various procedures that will be used to complete the new assignments. In this case, creating a report with a template, creating a spreadsheet, and converting information to a graph will be reviewed. Once students have been "briefed" on procedures, the process will begin by gathering information from a variety of sources. In addition to the report, students will work on the individual project that will become part of the overall report. Students will use the different applications software for their individual projects; one student might use word processing, another a spreadsheet, and another desktop publishing. As students complete the work, files will be saved to a project directory that all students share. Sharing a directory will enable the students to access each others' files and make the necessary changes or possibly communicate comments or questions via e-mail. Working as a team to complete a report is just one of many possible scenarios for using Windows applications in office procedures. Completing a report as a group is just one activity that helps the office procedures class to become a more realistic setting for using the features of Windows, applications suites, and e-mail.

Advantages for the Future Office Professional

Students who complete office procedures where they are introduced to software integration and electronic communications will be prepared for the future workforce. Students will enter the workforce better prepared to find a position, be more flexible, and be more successful in working as part of a team.

Students develop a portfolio. Students will be able to easily develop a portfolio of their work that represents a wide range of activities since the many applications available in various suites will have been mastered. With desktop publishing, graphing, and the many features of word processing, the student's portfolio can demonstrate up-to-date skills using current technology. Student evaluations of completed projects will also demonstrate the ability of the student to work as a team player on the many projects.

Students learn to work in a flexible environment. Sometimes instructors refer to the flexible environment in the classroom as *controlled chaos*. However, students do learn to be flexible as equipment fails to work, as information is not ready, and as a syllabus is changed because a key player is not available. Technology forces individuals to be flexible. Inadequate flexibility will only result in failure for the individuals involved; therefore, students must learn to roll with the punches.

Students learn to work as a team. Multi-tasking and e-mail enable the students to truly work as a team on classroom projects. Students learn to depend on each other; and more importantly, they learn to be responsible to one another. Students quickly learn they must all work together to earn the evaluation they desire.

The Future is the Present

As instructors teach computer skills in today's classroom, they cannot teach just today's skills; they must teach the computer skills of the future. Both the present and the future include the various Windows applications that must be reinforced through a variety of repetitive activities. Just as business educators once used practice sets and simulations to imitate the real office world, business educators need to continue to create simulations that will enable students to apply e-mail skills and truly integrate the various Windows applications.

CHAPTER 9

Technology and Accounting Methodology

William B. Hoyt

Wilton High School, Wilton, Connecticut

Over the past decade technology has had a dramatic impact on the way business records, summarizes, reports, and analyzes financial information. With the introduction of the microcomputer, the manner in which accounting documents and reports are processed and prepared has significantly changed. Recent advancements in hardware and software have provided opportunities to integrate automated procedures into the smallest of business operations at reasonable costs.

As technology continues to impact and enhance the accounting process, the knowledge, skills, and experiences needed by accounting students is being assessed. Students should not only master the concepts and principles of accounting but also should acquire the skills and experiences necessary to utilize modern technology. The accounting curriculum must address both of these issues.

Everyone would agree that accounting methodology is not the same as it was only a few years ago. Technology is having a tremendous influence on accounting procedures and accounting education.

Automating Accounting Procedures

The concepts and principles of accounting used by business date back to more than 500 years ago. Business transactions were recorded, and financial statements were prepared manually. The introduction of any real type of automation to assist in preparing financial records only began approximately 40 years ago.

Early technology. During the 1950s and 1960s, various types of automated equipment were developed that allowed certain aspects of the accounting process to be completed in a more efficient manner. Hardware, such as unit record equipment and accounting machines, provided opportunities to take several error-prone, time-consuming tasks and process the same information with increased productivity and efficiency.

Unfortunately, most automated equipment was generally available only to larger business operations. The lack of access was primarily due to the high cost of purchasing or leasing the equipment, space availability, and the need for highly trained personnel to program, operate, and maintain computers. Technology was making contributions to the accounting process, but few business operations would have been referred to as fully automated.

Although automated equipment was providing increased efficiency to some accounting procedures, the majority of accounting documents and reports were still being created manually. People involved with accounting had very limited contact with computers and were generally dealing with computer printouts generated by other individuals. The majority of people working with computers were trained in the area of computer programming or data processing. Accountants did not operate the computers, and computer operators did not perform accounting functions.

Because of this lack of "hands-on" usage and limited data-processing capabilities of this early technology, accounting methodology changed very little from 1950 through 1980. Automated procedures were seldom included in accounting methodology during this period. Due to the size, cost, and accessibility of the hardware, accounting students seldom, if ever, experienced any computer application in their study of accounting.

Microcomputers. With the introduction of the microcomputer in the late 1970s, the manner in which most business operations recorded, analyzed, and reported financial information changed dramatically. Automated accounting became available to all levels of management and business operations. For the first time, businesses of all sizes and financial status could afford to automate many aspects of their business operations. Efficient, cost-saving alternatives were available that could replace time-consuming, manual accounting procedures. The long-awaited road to efficient financial recording, analyzing, and reporting for all business operations was underway by the early 1980s.

As more automated procedures were being integrated into various aspects of the accounting cycle, some individuals became concerned that fundamental accounting principles and concepts were being abandoned. However, the microcomputer did not challenge the fundamental concepts of accounting but rather provided opportunities to replace most manual procedures with more efficient automated alternatives. More time could now be spent interpreting and analyzing financial data rather than recording and processing information in a mundane and often inaccurate manner. Up-to-date financial information, needed for sound decision-making, could now be made available to management in a timely manner.

However, when integrating microcomputer applications into accounting systems, most accounting and management personnel were dealing for the first time with automation in a "hands-on" situation. They were no longer relying on computer specialists to program and process financial data but rather were sitting at a desk with a microprocessor under their direct control. In order for people involved in the accounting process to successfully utilize modern technology, they had to become knowledgeable in the applications and capabilities of accounting software. This new technology did not limit automation capabilities to selected accounting procedures but provided the opportunity to automate all aspects of the accounting cycle. Now, business operations of all sizes had the ability to totally automate all accounting functions.

Initial Technology Integration Efforts

During the early 1980s, microcomputers were beginning to influence the accounting procedures of many businesses. Accounting teachers also realized that this new technology must be integrated into the accounting curriculum. Without a clear vision as to the ultimate influence technology would have on the accounting process, teachers expressed varying views on what accounting students needed to know regarding automated accounting. Acknowledging numerous concerns and questions, the unique challenge of integrating technology into the accounting curriculum began.

Early computer integration. Teachers made efforts to bring some computer activities into the accounting classroom by modifying software designed for small business operations. These efforts, although courageous, proved to be frustrating for both teachers and students. These accounting programs allowed students to experience some automated procedures but required considerable modifications and data preparation by teachers. Software was poorly written and difficult to use; memory capacity was extremely limited; software documentation and explanations were poor; and data storage was clumsy and unreliable.

During the early 1980s, no organized effort to recommend specific modifications or revisions in accounting methodology was evident. Teachers were experimenting with improving computer applications and assessing the role of computers. During this period, computers began to be used as both a learning and thinking tool (Kizzier,1995).

For accounting teachers, this new technology provided an exciting challenge to revise and stimulate a curriculum that had experienced very little change over the years. No matter how successful or unsuccessful various attempts at technology integration turned out to be, all accounting teachers realized that automation certainly should play an intricate role in accounting education.

Throughout the 1980s, the quality of accounting software continued to improve with several software companies designing user-friendly software for the smaller business operation. The development of more sophisticated hardware and more powerful microprocessor chips caused rapid improvements in operating speed and memory capacity.

Educational software. During this same period, educational accounting software was developed by educational publishers that addressed identified needs of students and teachers. This software simulated the accounting software designed for small business operations and provided many of the educational characteristics, capabilities, and resources as well as supplementary materials needed for instruction. This software eased efforts in bringing automated activities into the accounting classroom. Accounting teachers no longer had to be knowledgeable in programming or program modification but now could concentrate their efforts on becoming familiar with the functions and capabilities of selected software packages.

Assumptions Regarding Technology

By the end of the 1980s, educators and business leaders had been learning more about the role technology would play in accounting procedures and in accounting education. With the quality of hardware and software improving at a staggering pace, what seemed appropriate and timely for classroom use in one year became dated only a year or two later. Since accounting methodology had changed so little over the years, technology-based modifications now developed faster than teachers could adequately implement or assess the educational value.

In this period of dramatic change, certain curriculum assumptions regarding technology within the accounting curriculum evolved. These assumptions were based on the success or failure of existing computer activities and applications in the classroom; the impact of computers on accounting procedures in the business environment; the expansion of knowledge and skills needed by students; initial attempts to define the role of computers in the accounting curriculum; and an assessment of the importance of automated accounting in education. These assumptions form the basis for current changes in accounting methodology and create the framework for future curriculum modifications as accounting education continues to integrate with emerging technology.

Entering the 1990s, secondary accounting courses and postsecondary financial accounting courses were modified based on the assumptions that follow.

Assumption 1. The primary objective of the accounting curriculum in an introductory course is for students to develop and demonstrate knowledge of the concepts, procedures, and applications of accounting.

Assumption 2. Analyzing financial information must be an integral component of the accounting curriculum. Activities involving analysis of financial data develop critical thinking skills, involve students in problem-solving activities, and integrate decision-making activities into the curriculum.

Assumption 3. Students must first prepare documents and complete the accounting cycle using manual methods in order to understand and demonstrate mastery of the concepts, principles, and procedures in accounting. Computers provide vast opportunities for higher-level activities, but students must understand the accounting procedures in the cycle before they generate documents in an automated system. Accounting teachers have always tried to emphasize the *why* in accounting procedures, not just the *how*. With the introduction of many computer programs, students unfortunately do not need to know the *why* or the *how* of a procedure for it to be successfully executed. For example, once journal entries are entered, the posting function is completed by a command in the program. Students will not understand the significance or purpose of the general or subsidiary ledgers or a trial balance without understanding the posting process. To understand posting, students must first experience activities involving posting using manual procedures.

Assumption 4. The computer is a valuable learning tool that enhances the study of accounting. By integrating activities involving technology, students become more active participants as inquisitors and problem solvers. Modern technology provides opportunities to experience a vast array of creative applications that previously had been impossible to provide.

Assumption 5. All accounting students should experience automated applications involving the input of financial data and the preparation of documents and reports. Technology is an integral aspect of accounting and should be an integral aspect of accounting education.

Assumption 6. The use of computers reduces the mundane bookkeeping activities and provides time for alternative, higher-level intellectual and communication applications. The study of accounting principles and procedures becomes an active rather than a passive experience when appropriate activities involve technology.

Assumption 7. The skills, knowledge, and experiences needed by students in today's higher education and work environments have dramatically changed due to technology. The accounting curriculum must address these issues and provide opportunities for the development of these skills and experiences.

Assumption 8. Computers can provide a variety of automated activities and should not be viewed as equipment that only provides automated bookkeeping applications.

Throughout the early 1990s, accounting methodology addressed and integrated into the curriculum the emerging technological advancements.

Current Accounting Technology

Advancements in software and hardware design have created an array of educational experiences appropriate for the introductory accounting course. From the early days of providing only simulated business experiences, modern technology can provide activities that incorporate the latest advancements in hardware along with innovative, state-of-the-art, quality software. Technology currently influences present accounting methodology and will probably initiate constant change in methodology over the next several years. As more sophisticated hardware and software become available, accounting teachers will learn, evaluate, and react.

Simulated business applications. The most essential computer activities provide realistic automated procedures. These procedures provide students opportunities to input, process, and analyze data and to produce a variety of financial documents and reports. Activities include end-of-chapter problems, textbook mini-practice sets, business simulations, or teacher-generated problems. These types of computer applications provide students with the knowledge and hands-on experiences needed to secure entry-level jobs and a solid foundation for further study in accounting.

The learning process for students is enhanced and supported by clearly defined functions and a pop-up calculator. Software programs also offer extensive help capabilities that provide explanations of accounting procedures along with referrals to textbook pages for further explanation or review. Recent advancements in software design have expanded programs to include:

- More extensive report capabilities.
- Ability to generate graphs based on the financial data.
- Opportunities for financial analysis.
- Integration of depreciation and inventory systems into the program.
- Export capabilities to expand problems for additional analysis or report writing.

These activities also accommodate teachers by providing clear guidelines for successful integration, teaching suggestions to assist students, and automated review and correction capabilities. Application activities have proven to be essential for all students and should take top priority when teachers select automated accounting activities.

Spreadsheets. Spreadsheets provide opportunities for students to create documents, change variables, interpret results, analyze data, and make recommendations. Spreadsheet software takes accounting education to a higher level. As students advance in their study of accounting, numerous activities can be integrated into the classroom using this type of software. These activities offer opportunities for individual and group activities and develop students' interpretive, analytical, and communication skills.

Since spreadsheet software has become the major analytic tool of the accounting process, a working knowledge of spreadsheet software is essential for accounting students. Using this software, students become decision makers rather than merely processors of data.

Electronic study guides. Using electronic study guides, students answer a variety of questions involving specific accounting principles or procedures, obtain immediate feedback, and get additional explanations along with page references in the textbook. Electronic study guides assist in assessing students' mastery of a particular procedure or concept but most often do not simulate actual accounting functions.

Study-guide activities are not new to accounting classes, but advancements in software and innovative educational designs have produced quality programs that are easy to use, hold the interest of students, and reinforce learned accounting principles and procedures. Electronic study guides are of value for all students but are especially helpful to students who could be having difficulty with a particular topic or procedure and may need additional assistance or reinforcement.

Multimedia accounting. Advancements in technology have created opportunities for accounting activities involving the use of CD-ROM and laserdiscs. Through integrated activities, students can experience multimedia lessons on chapter material and procedures or take on-site electronic field trips to a variety of businesses. When CD-ROM and laserdiscs are combined, students can experience interactive multimedia activities.

Using CD-ROM, student understanding of chapter material is enhanced by accessing instructional and accounting activities. Audio segment integration into learning activities usually adds to the attention level of students. CD-ROM technology also provides access to templates for accounting simulations as well as export applications that could involve other commercial software.

Laserdiscs provide opportunities to access a variety of businesses by using video segments that explain both accounting procedures and applications in various forms of business operations. Students can relate chapter material to actual business practices by seeing both graphics and video examples of businesses using modern accounting procedures and/or documents. Opportunities for students to develop communication and critical thinking skills are provided by end-of-segment questions related to the selected presentations. These classroom activities serve an additional dimension by providing opportunities for students to engage in higher-level activities such as problem solving, decision making, group interacting, and verbal and written communicating. Using sophisticated technology enables students to become active participants in the learning process, not merely absorbers and regurgitators of information.

Current Impact on Accounting Methodology

Modern technology has created tremendous opportunities to integrate activities and applications that were not previously possible. At the same time, technology has redefined and expanded the skills and knowledge needed by accounting students. Individuals involved in accounting functions are no longer merely processors of financial data but now must have the ability to analyze and interpret the financial information, draw conclusions, and communicate the recommendations in a concise, articulate manner. Thus, students must achieve a higher level of learning.

Revising objectives. Clearly defined objectives must be developed as business leaders and teachers assess the role of technology in the accounting curriculum. As objectives become better defined, technology can be utilized to maximize students' understanding and learning (Gueldenzoph and Hyslop, 1995). Although these objectives will vary from school to school, district to district, and state to state, certain characteristics will remain consistent in all curriculums. Accounting instructors are addressing the framework of these objectives by considering the following influences:

- The capabilities of current technologies and possible future applications.
- The continued commitment that students demonstrate a mastery of accounting principles and procedures.
- The rapidly changing work environment and the need to prepare students with the skills and knowledge they need to be successful in a competitive job market (McNulty, 1995).
- The identified need to integrate higher-level learning activities into the accounting curriculum.

Revised curriculum objectives must reflect the fact that students will not master accounting concepts and procedures by merely completing automated accounting applications. Rather, technology should be viewed as a vital tool that teachers may utilize to enhance the core accounting curriculum.

In developing objectives for accounting courses, the following observations involving technology should be addressed:

- The ability to automate almost all accounting procedures is having a tremendous impact on small business operations.
- Recent publications by the Accounting Education Change Commission (AECC), the Secretary's Commission on Achieving Necessary Skills (SCANS Report), the National Center on Education and the Economy, and publications by national accounting firms have all emphasized the important role of technology in the accounting curriculum.
- The Policies Commission for Business and Economic Education (1993) stressed the impact of technology on every aspect of our society.

- The Accounting Standards established in *National Standards for Business Education-What America's Students Should Know And Be Able To Do In Business* (NBEA, 1995), emphasized the important role technology plays in business education and included the need for computer experiences in numerous accounting procedures.

- A demonstrated understanding of procedures involving the preparation of accounting documents and reports using computer programs is essential for all students.

- Modern technology can provide a wide variety of computer activities that provide educationally sound experiences that enhance the accounting curriculum. In addition to simulating business practices, technology stimulates student interests, expands their knowledge of accounting, and prepares them for the work environment.

- The time allocated in the curriculum for technology activities must be balanced with the need for students to demonstrate a mastery of accounting procedures. Sufficient computer activities must be included in order to provide the learning experiences needed by students, yet the curriculum must not become an environment where menu selection takes priority over mastery of concepts and procedures. The time allocated to the preparation of manual documents should be reduced, but not reduced to the extent that students cannot demonstrate their ability to understand basic concepts and procedures.

- Demonstrated mastery of concepts and procedures should come before automated applications involving those procedures. Students cannot analyze, interpret, or make recommendations on financial data if they do not understand how and why this data functions within the accounting cycle.

- The knowledge and skills needed by students to secure jobs or to successfully continue to higher educational levels in accounting are rapidly changing. Technology activities in accounting classes should integrate vital critical thinking, analytical, and communication skills (Hogan, 1994).

- Technology should change the role of the students from passive learners to active learners and change the role of teachers from disseminators of information to directors of applied knowledge.

The secondary level. Secondary accounting classes are primarily utilizing software developed by textbook publishers. The software simulates business software and also provides CD-ROM and laserdisc applications and experiences. Publisher software has allowed accounting teachers to integrate a wide variety of computer activities into their classes.

The degree to which computer activities are used in the classroom should be determined by teachers or departments. The type of computer activities and the time allocated to these experiences should be contingent on the following criteria:

- Amount of hardware available to students on a daily or periodic basis.
- Adequacy of funds allocation for hardware and software.
- Level of confidence and training that teachers have in integrating the activities.
- Time allocated to assure that students master the chapter content by completing activities manually.

Chapter methodology without integration of technology. Before technology was used in a classroom, a typical presentation of a chapter topic in first-year accounting progressed in the following manner:

(1) Teachers explained the chapter topic and its relationship to the accounting cycle and gave an overview of what students would learn.

(2) Teachers presented the chapter information and responded to questions.

(3) Students completed between four and six end-of-chapter problems.

(4) A test was administered to students. Tests most often recreated the same documents and/or procedures presented in end-of-chapter problems.

In this style presentation, students were passive learners who absorbed information, applied this information to problems, and repeated the information to the teacher in the form of tests. Although an assessment of students' mastery of concepts and procedures is important and necessary, the higher-level skills were often not addressed. Students were not challenged to take the chapter material beyond the repetitive level.

Chapter methodology with integration of technology. A variety of classroom activities based on chapter material surfaced with the integration of technology.The initial presentation by the teacher involving chapter content, the relationship of the content with the accounting cycle, and the answering of students' questions may be quite similar to what has been done in the past. Students must still complete some problems manually to understand the accounting procedure being presented. However, students do not need to prepare any more end-of-chapter activities or problems than the teacher feels is necessary to achieve understanding. The amount of manual work will vary from chapter to chapter due to the complexity of the topic and the ability of students to demonstrate an understanding of the material.

Once a demonstrated mastery has been achieved, a variety of additional activities can be integrated. The type of activities may vary from chapter to chapter, and the time allocated to each chapter may also vary. Some possible applications may include the following student activities:

- Complete end-of-chapter activities on the computer.
- Complete electronic study guide activities.
- Complete additional teacher-generated problems on the computer.
- Work independently or in groups to create and enter financial data from problems to complete "what if" activities.
- Discuss CD-ROM or laserdisc activities and write individual or group reports.
- Arrange data using spreadsheets or similar software, address variables that could be considered, reach conclusions, and make recommendations.
- Transport financial information to other software packages, prepare written reports, prepare graphic displays, and possibly make oral presentations on the topic.
- Conduct research with on-line systems by accessing data bases provided by corporate, governmental, or post-secondary sources.
- Use networks, scanners, and facsimile equipment to obtain and complete additional activities.

By integrating these activities in the classroom, accounting teachers are also elevated to a higher level of challenge. Teachers are no longer merely presenters of chapter material and administers of chapter and unit tests but now become initiators and advocates of activities that apply the learned accounting knowledge to challenging, skill-building applications.

Alternative forms of assessment. Due to changes in learning activities, students should be evaluated on criteria other than merely test scores. In addition to tests, homework, and completion of computer applications, additional measurements of success may include observations of students involved in individual or group projects; oral presentations; written reports; portfolios and journals; individual and group research projects; supplemental activities and presentations involving technology. All these assessment forms should involve subjective judgment in evaluating each student's performance in mastering the skills and knowledge needed for today's workforce.

The post secondary level. Postsecondary curricula are not only addressing these changes but are also placing greater emphasis on commercial software. A working knowledge of leading commercial software packages is essential because students will seek employment upon course completion. Unfortunately, classroom time is limited so other types of computer activities, such as electronic study guides and simulations, are often assigned to students to complete out of class, or are presently not utilized.

Articulation of curriculum. Education reforms such as the Tech Prep/ Applied Academics Reform Initiative have had a profound effect on the accounting curriculum on both the secondary and post secondary levels. These efforts reinforce the integration of academics with vocational knowledge and skills to ensure a smooth transition between educational levels and eventually into the work force. The need to address the role of technology in education on both levels will assist in further articulation of accounting curriculums.

The Future: Technology and the Curriculum

Technology will continue to influence business accounting procedures, and the methodology used in accounting classes will continue to respond to changes. However, the impact on business and the impact on instruction may not be as dramatic as business and teachers have experienced over the past few years.

The automation of the accounting cycle has been initially addressed and significant changes in the process over the next two or three years are not expected. Areas that can anticipate improvement are processing speed, storage capability, and data input. Demonstrated mastery of commercial software will continue to be an important aspect of the curriculum.

Technology affecting accounting education will continue to improve with greater emphasis placed on CD-ROM and laserdisc applications, graphics, external data bases, on-line information research, videotex, and presentation software. Technology will continue to enhance the learning process, and the role technology should play in accounting education will continue to be assessed.

The principle objective of the accounting course will remain the same: Students must demonstrate mastery of accounting principles and concepts. This mastery is essential for successfully integrating technological activities. Only by completing documents and reports manually will students understand the function and purpose of all steps in the accounting cycle. A solid foundation in the basics is essential to enable students to process financial data in a meaningful manner.

Summary

Technology has had a significant impact on accounting methodology and will continue to be an important component of the curriculum. Computers will continue to change the ways businesses do business and the ways schools teach accounting. Technology brings a dimension to the accounting curriculum that provides opportunities for students to engage in higher-level learning activities. Through technology usage, students learn to analyze, synthesize, and apply financial data and not merely record data. Advanced technologies such as CD-ROM and laserdiscs are the forerunners of the next wave of technological advancements. These technologies will continue to enable students to become more active participants in their education and to attain higher achievement levels. The role of technology in accounting classes will continue to increase, and the educational value of the applications and activities will continue to be assessed.

References

Committee on the Future Structure, Content and Scope of Accounting Education (Bedford Committee) of the American Accounting Association. (1986). *Future accounting education: Preparing for the expanding profession.*

Gueldenzoph, L.E., & Hyslop, D. J. (1995). Evaluating instructional technology for classroom application. In N. J. Groneman & K. C. Kaser (Eds.), *Technology in the classroom* (pp. 95-105). Reston, VA: National Business Education Association.

Hogan, D. (1994). Applied academics in accounting. *Business Education Forum, 49 (4),* 35-37.

Kizzier, D. (1995). Teaching technology vs. technology as a teaching tool. In N. J. Groneman & K. C. Kaser (Eds.), *Technology in the classroom* (pp. 10-24). Reston, VA: National Business Education Association.

McNulty, B. (1995). Educating students for the demands of the workplace. *Business Education Forum, 50 (2),* 35-37.

National Business Education Association. (1995). *Standards for business education—What America's students should know and be able to do in business.* Reston, VA: National Business Education Association.

Policies Commission for Business and Economic Education. (1993). This we believe about the role of business education in technology, *Business Education Forum, 48,* 11-12.

U.S. Government Printing Office. (1992). *Skills and tasks for jobs: A SCANS report for America 2000.* Washington, DC: U.S. Department of Labor.

CHAPTER 10

Communication in a Changing Environment

Betty S. Johnson

Stephen F. Austin State University, Nacogdoches, Texas

Today's rapidly changing global business environment presents many challenges to its participants. One of the most significant of these challenges is effective communication. Recent advancements in technology have expanded greatly the options for preparing and transmitting messages. Traditional means have been supplemented through—or perhaps replaced by—technology. Current technology, however, cannot ensure communication success.

To communicate successfully, one must convey a message in the most accurate, efficient, and effective manner. The challenge, therefore, is to identify the most appropriate avenues available to produce accurate, efficient, and effective messages. Today's marketplace challenges business people to expand their knowledge of communication to include not only the principles of effective writing and speaking but also to identify the most appropriate channel to use in expressing their messages.

Factors Influencing Communication

The changing business environment is a result of many factors. Among those factors, technology, diversity, and globalization appear to have the greatest impact on communication.

Technology revolutionizes communication. Rapid advances in technology enable today's business people to communicate more easily, accurately, and quickly than they could even a few years ago. Since the introduction of personal computers, technology has continued to advance, providing increasingly sophisticated systems that today enable the user to not only generate written documents easily but also to communicate with people around the globe. The traditional software programs for word processing, spreadsheets, and databases have been joined by presentation graphics, multimedia authoring packages, executive management programs, electronic mail, and communication packages for connecting individual workstations with other local workstations and to the Internet for expanded communication options.

Electronic mail has become extremely popular as a communication alternative "because it is more efficient than using the telephone, less formal than writing a letter, and much faster than the mail" (Stipp, 1996). E-mail also eliminates the communication barriers of distance and time because messages may be sent at the sender's convenience to receivers around the world without regard for time zones, working hours, etc. (Nelson & Luse, 1994).

The World Wide Web (WWW) has received much attention as a research and business tool. On-line searches provide readily available information to formulate a report for decision-making purposes (Morrison & Oladunjoye, 1996).

Through the use of presentation software, information may be presented more effectively. Computer slide shows, overhead transparencies, and multimedia presentations complement a speaker's delivery.

The ability to send and receive a fax directly from the computer work-station, to communicate electronically with people in and out of the organization, and to provide background music while the operator is working are but a few of the reasons computer technology has revolutionized the business operation.

Telephone technology has advanced as rapidly as computer technology. Answering machines, voice-mail systems, pagers, caller identification, and cellular phone technology enable people to use oral communication channels much more extensively.

Answering machines and voice-mail systems provide callers with a medium for leaving messages. Voice answering systems can reduce telephone tag, eliminate lost or incorrect messages, and diminish time-zone barriers (Mueller, 1996). Through remote access, one can check messages away from the office or home using a touch-tone phone.

Pagers and cellular phones provide communication options while people travel or work away from an office. Caller identification enables message receivers to see the name/number of all persons attempting to locate them. Returning calls from individuals who choose not to leave a voice message is simplified. Additionally, such systems provide users with greater security by discouraging crank callers who know they can be identified.

Other frequently cited communication technologies include videoconferencing, electronic meetings, virtual reality, scanners, voice recognition systems and pen-based input devices (O'Connor & Bronner, 1996). Video-conferencing and electronic meetings reduce participant travel time and expense in conducting business. Educational institutions are using forms of videoconferencing for distance learning to reduce student travel time.

Voice-recognition systems, although not yet replacing the keyboard for data input, are becoming more common. Scanners and pen-based input devices convert copy (a signature, for example) into a digitized form that can be stored or transmitted electronically.

Although these communication technologies have been available for several years, their application to productive communication activities is a fairly recent development. Kruk (1992) predicted the first half of the 1990s would be a period of introduction to communication technologies while the second half would be a period of assimilation. That prediction appears to be accurate today.

Diversity issues impact communication. Today's workforce is diverse. This diversity incorporates gender, culture, and ethnicity. Stereotypes and misunderstandings of cultural and social differences frequently lead to miscommunication.

The traditional masculine influence of business has been replaced with a neutral one. In addition to gender issues, race, culture, and personal choice are receiving greater attention in the workplace. Stereotypes of certain positions should be avoided because they usually do not exist today! Business educators should teach students to never assume that the president, the doctor, or the sales representative is male. Pronoun references should not be masculine unless referring to a specific man and descriptors of workers should be neutral—avoid businessman, waitress, stewardess, etc. In the once male-dominated business world, one could address any correspondence to **Mr.** even if the person were unknown or had used only initials. Even as women entered the business world in larger numbers, many communicators chose to cling to the traditional forms of address. Today, such a choice would be risky.

Additional communication issues, however, are perhaps more significant. The nonverbal communication expectations of different cultures create communication barriers. Local customs, norms, and traditions may be violated by a person who is unfamiliar with the local culture (Anderson, 1995). A knowledge of customs such as the importance of the family, eating patterns, and degree of formality expected in certain situations will lessen the chances for miscommunication.

Globalization changes communication. With the rapidly expanding technologies, international business is no longer the exception. Most businesses are either directly or indirectly affected by international trade. Workers entering the job market today will be involved in international business regardless of the firm with which they are associated.

The most frequently mentioned communication issue in globalization is, of course, language barriers. Although English is the language of business in many countries, not all countries transact business in English. Bilingualism is no longer a luxury in business; the ability to speak at least two, if not three, languages has become a necessity. If one wants to communicate effectively, one must speak the host language. Imagine trying to negotiate a contract in a country whose language you do not know. The host company will have a major advantage in that their staff can discuss their position on a proposal in their language and you cannot understand them!

A less significant communication issue that should nevertheless be mentioned is time differences. Although the United States has differing time zones, many people find it difficult to extend the concept of time zones to other parts of the world. Knowing when and how to communicate at an appropriate time is essential for international business.

Changes in Business Communication Practices

Technology, diversity, and globalization issues have changed business activities in general and business communication activities in many areas. The most significant changes involve speed, accuracy, styles, and delivery channels.

Speed. Technology has dramatically increased the speed of communication. Letters that once required five to seven working days for delivery through the U.S. Postal Service may now be faxed to the receiver in less than two minutes. Electronic mail may be used to send messages to people who are not available for oral communication.

Accuracy. Because messages may be sent faster, the communicator must be careful to proofread for accuracy before sending. Traditionally, a communicator had a second opportunity to look at a document later in the day or on the following day; today's technology discourages that time lag. Therefore, accuracy of messages becomes more critical. Usually, the message originator does not have a second chance to review and to edit carelessly chosen words or phrases. Communicators should use nondiscriminatory language and be sensitive to word choices that may have different meanings in different cultures.

Style. Technology has also altered styles of communications significantly. Most current software packages include templates for formatting letters, reports, memos, brochures, and newsletters. These predesigned formats are easy to use but may not necessarily follow the traditional conventions of layout and design.

Letter and report formats have been altered to increase productivity. To support desktop publishing activities, spacing after sentence punctuation has changed from the traditional two spaces to one space. The popular block-letter style is receiving competition from various forms of simplified styles that provide flexibility in letter addresses and salutations.

Triple spacing before report headings has been replaced with double spacing (two lines) or quadruple spacing (four lines) to reduce the keystrokes required in formatting a report.

Charts and tables have been altered because of software limitations. Many popular software packages arrange the pie slices in the order in which the data were input—not necessarily in descending order as was traditionally expected.

Electronic mail messages follow a simple memo format with less attention given to structure and formality.

Ethical and legal issues. Ethical and legal issues also have an impact on communication. Ethical and legal decisions serve as a basis for **all** communication. The first question in all communication endeavors is to determine whether the message is a legal one. Statements that intentionally or unintentionally mislead or deceive the reader may have legal consequences. For example, if a communicator is involved in hiring a new employee, statements regarding salary, position, and job responsibilities are crucial. The procedures for hiring should be consistent for all candidates. Therefore, the same information should be communicated to each candidate to avoid discrimination accusations. Other legal issues result from advertising, product guarantees, credit, and privacy issues.

Closely associated with legal implications are ethical considerations. Therefore, the second point is to determine whether the message is ethical. While it may not be illegal to fire someone by sending a fax message, the process does not seem very ethical. Privacy is an important ethical and legal consideration. While positive messages are preferable, biased or distorted facts in written and visual presentations also discredit the communicator.

Criteria for Selecting Delivery Channels

Changes in communication practices necessitate changes not only in message composition but also in message delivery. A variety of communication channels should be considered for successful communication (Johnson & Bayless, 1997).

Technology has increased the number of channels available for business communication delivery. The communicator may choose to send oral or written messages and may choose to deliver these messages through a conventional or an electronic channel.

Oral communication. Oral messages include face-to-face conferences, telephone conversations, group communications, or mass media. Traditional channels include face-to-face and group communication, whereas electronic means may be used through telephone conversations, voice mail, and mass media.

When immediate feedback is necessary, oral communication is the best delivery method. In addition to the spoken word, nonverbal messages may be assessed in face-to-face and group meetings. Even the telephone enables the listener to hear certain nonverbal messages (the tone used). Conversely, spoken communications may be less precise and grammatical errors may be less obvious. Conventional oral channels are more time-consuming for both the sender and the receiver because common times must be committed to the communication exchange; whereas with electronic channels, messages may be left for people who are not available at the time the sender calls. Voice mail and answering machines reduce telephone tag and provide a suitable channel to deliver short, simple messages.

Written messages. Written communication (letters, reports, memos) provide a record of the communication and should be used when documentation is needed. Traditional written communication is delivered by mail, by messenger, or other physical carrier, whereas electronic delivery may be sent by facsimile or by computer network.

Facsimile communication is one of the fastest growing areas of communication technology. Communicating by fax can be fast and less expensive than conventional mail services. Costs for fax transmission increase when long-distance phone charges are included. Those charges, however, are frequently less expensive than conventional mail services. Confidentiality is a concern with fax messages as many machines are located in a common area rather than in an individual's private office.

E-mail is fast, does not require the receiver to be available at the time of transmission, and can provide a record of communication because the message may be printed. E-mail is considered to be less informal, internal (in many cases), and less confidential. Employers may choose to monitor e-mail messages of their employees. Availability may limit the choice of an e-mail channel because not all people have access to e-mail.

While an occasional grammatical error may be ignored in an oral conversation, correctness is essential in the written word as all errors are recorded for multiple readings. Written communication is considered more formal than oral communication. Written communication does not require the sender and the receiver to be available at the same time; the receiver may read the message when it is convenient.

Criteria. Other criteria may influence message delivery. These factors should be considered in determining appropriate channels.

If speed is essential in the communication, an appropriate channel might be face-to-face, telephone, or voice mail. A fax or an e-mail message could also be appropriate.

If a message is simple, oral channels may be selected. If, however, the message is detailed or complex, a written channel is preferable. The receiver will then have a hard copy to use as a reference. The written message may be transmitted via memo, letter, or fax.

If all recipients of the communication should receive the message at the same time, a group meeting, memo, letter, or posted notice would be effective. Sending the same message by e-mail may be preferred. Those checking their messages from location away from their homes or offices would benefit from that delivery mode.

If the message is one that should be conveyed in privacy, a face-to-face meeting in a private location or a letter delivered in a sealed envelope would be appropriate channels.

When nonverbal responses are desired, face-to-face or group meetings are best. Telephone conversations provide only limited nonverbal cues whereas written messages provide none.

Telephone, group meetings, and face-to-face meetings are the best channels for immediate interaction. Voice mail and e-mail may provide prompt interaction, whereas written messages may elicit delayed reactions.

Consider the resources of the receiver when determining channels. Electronic channels may be less accessible and therefore a poor choice in some situations.

Cost can be a factor in choosing the appropriate channel. If all other elements are equal, a business letter will be more expensive than voice mail or electronic mail. Face-to-face meetings can be extremely expensive if the participant time factor is considered.

The Communication Challenge

Successfully communicating in a changing business environment is a challenge. While some communication elements do not change—correctness, consideration, and content—other elements do. Skillful communicators will recognize the factors influencing communication trends and will effectively use the technology available to prepare and transmit well organized, accurate, and clear messages.

References

Anderson, C.W. (1995). Multicultural teaching in business education. *TBEA Journal, 1*, 91-98.

Johnson, B.S., & Bayless, M. L. (1997). *Business communication*. Houston: Dame Publishing.

Kruk, L. B. (1992, September/October). Office 2000: A glimpse into tomorrow's workplace. *The Balance Sheet, 74(1)*, 10-14.

Morrison, J. L., & Olandunjoye, G.T. (1996). A comparative analysis of change expectations: A profession at risk! *NABTE Review, 23*, 53-57.

Mueller, N.S. (1996, February) What do you say to voice mail? *Managing Office Technology, 41(2),* 49-50.

Nelson, B.H., & Luse, D.W. (1994). Electronic networking available for business communication professionals. In M. L. Bayless (Ed.), *1994 Refereed Proceedings of the Association for Business Communication.* (pp. 29-32). San Diego.

O'Connor, B. N., & Bronner, M. (1995). Facilitating curriculum development: The role of electronic meeting systems. *NABTE Review, 22,* 5-9.

Stipp, D. M. (1996). *Using advanced communication technologies.* Mountain-Plains Business Education Association, Service Bulletin 38.

Sutton, J. C. (1995, June) Teaching with technology: An internet overview. *Business Communication Quarterly, 58 (2),* 8-9.

PART IV

INITIATIVES THAT EMPOWER BUSINESS EDUCATORS

CHAPTER 11

Business Teacher Preparation

Clarence D. White
Radford University, Radford, Virginia

Terry D. Roach
Arkansas State University, Jonesboro, Arkansas

When the publication *The Unfinished Agenda: The Role of Vocational Education in High School* was released, much discussion was given to business education's role in the nation's educational systems. A particular concern was the place of business education courses in a secondary curriculum (Bartholome, 1989).

This report suggested a balance in the curriculum to better serve students' needs so that both academic and vocational courses would become more related and more integrated. The report also stated that "States should not mandate curricular requirements that restrict students' opportunities to participate in vocational education experiences" (Bartholome, 1989). Since business education offers many of these educational experiences, the competencies needed by current and future business teachers became an issue.

Competencies published in 1987 by the National Business Education Association (Bartholome, 1989) indicate that all business teachers should be competent in the following areas:

- Curriculum development
- Evaluation
- Guidance and leadership
- Subject competencies

- Instruction
- Management
- Communication
- Professional development

Furthermore, business teachers must be aware of and able to incorporate into classroom instruction the following five competencies given by the Secretary's Commission on Achieving Necessary Skills (SCANS) (Everett, 1995).

- Resources—effectively utilizing time, money, materials, space, and staff.
- Information—employing a variety of tools to receive and transmit data.
- Interpersonal—working effectively with others.
- Systems—complying with organizational structure to reach goals.
- Technology—using computers, machines, and other tools.

Along with these five competencies, the SCANS report includes three foundation skills (basic academic skills, thinking skills, and personal skills) that make up the "know-how" employees will need for workplace success. The challenge for business teachers is to meet the intent of the SCANS "know-how" and to teach these skills in context, choosing as many activities as possible from the "real" world (Everett, 1995). The educational preparation of business teachers does not stop with the NBEA and SCANS competencies. Business education teachers must know how to teach and how to deliver quality instruction at appropriate levels for students to gain technical and academic competence.

As technology and business education continue to change, the competencies needed by current and future business teachers will also continue to change and will need to be addressed regularly. Two general questions must be answered: (1) What should be the educational preparation for business teachers? (2) What should business teachers know and be able to do before they accept teaching assignments? This chapter addresses these questions.

Professionalism

Dedicated, motivated, and flexible members enable a profession to survive. Scaglione (1994) suggests that business educators

- Identify talents and share them.
- Accentuate the positive.
- Invite interaction.
- Make learning relevant.
- Give fewer grades but more feedback.
- Celebrate success.
- Dare to be different.

Business teachers need to exhibit professionalism in their classrooms and to develop their expertise in the areas discussed below.

Leadership. Business teachers can acquire leadership skills by developing their technical skills, conceptual skills, and interpersonal skills. Technical skills involve both knowledge of the discipline and the ability to impart that knowledge to learners. Conceptual skills can be defined as the ability to view a situation as a whole and to see how the various components interrelate. Interpersonal skills include the ability to get along with and work with people. With these leadership skills, business teachers will be leaders in their business education classrooms and in their professional careers.

Interpersonal/"teacher" skills. The ability to work with people is a critical skill. Business teachers must be able to relate to students and to colleagues. They must be able to give needed support and instruction to students and to receive these same considerations from their peers. Some interpersonal skills, such as empathy, are not readily visible. Teachers must have the ability to comment on the progress and achievement of students, to implement new and exciting ways of instruction, and to challenge students to reach new heights of learning.

Teachers must realize that what they say or do has lasting effects on the lives of students. Teachers must demonstrate dependability and expect students to be dependable. Hence, teachers who give sincere attention to the words and actions of students indicate sincere regard for self-worth and may increase student self-esteem. Teachers who practice self-actualizing skills and higher-order skills from the affective domain of Bloom's Taxonomy can expect students to learn the same skills. These skills may include dependability as well as tolerance, loyalty, perseverance, promptness, and attention to detail.

Many teachers who are considered good teachers are the ones who stay current on teaching methodology. Additionally, professional educators attend workshops and business education conventions, acquire additional training in business technology, complete hours toward an advanced degree, express concern for their profession, genuinely like people (including students), and continue to improve their teaching styles.

Professional organizations. Professional business education organizations provide the means to discover new developments in the field, to learn new teaching methods, to keep technologically current, and to share ideas with colleagues from all levels and areas. NBEA and state business education associations are only two professional organizations dedicated to the improvement of business education and to the preparation of business teachers. Business teachers involved in professional organizations show a willingness to improve their teaching credentials.

Business educators often affiliate with civic and community organizations such as the Jaycees, Chamber of Commerce, Rotarians International, Kiwanis Club, Women of Today, and Business and Professional Women. These associations provide experiences, networks, and resources relevant for classroom instruction. Business educators should encourage student membership and active involvement in professional organizations such as the Future Business Leaders of America or the Business Professionals of America. Through advising student organizations, business teachers have positive opportunities to promote personal growth and develop leadership abilities in students and themselves. Student organizations provide members and advisors with learning experiences that are not readily available in the classroom.

Student Teaching

Student teaching includes observations and participation and is intended to be a learning experience. During student teaching, the beginning teacher applies the theories and techniques learned in college/university courses to real teaching situations. In the classroom the beginning teacher has opportunities to test various teaching strategies and techniques, to build a wide range of teaching skills, and to develop an effective teaching style.

Student teaching experiences may be enhanced when participants incorporate the following resolutions:

- Be bold. Realize that what a teacher says or does has lasting effects.
- Take the initiative. Do what needs to be done before being asked.
- Be dependable. Complete tasks even if unexpected sacrifices become necessary.
- Demonstrate concern. Respond to needs without expecting a reward.
- Be attentive. Show empathy and express concern for others.
- Be tolerant. Accept individual uniqueness.
- Be loyal. Be a team player (Chiodo, 1988).

Student teaching is a time for learning and removing mistakes from the student teacher's delivery style. Many student teachers who do poorly during the first few weeks develop into excellent teachers by the end of their student teaching experience.

Subject Competencies

The Policies Commission for Business and Economic Education (Calhoun, 1995) describes the role of business education at the secondary level and states that business education achieves its goals through:

- Specialized instruction to prepare students for careers in business.
- Fundamental instruction to help students to assume their economic roles as consumers, workers, and citizens.
- Background instruction to assist students in preparing for professional careers requiring advanced study.

A critical decision for business teachers is selecting appropriate methodology for teaching each assigned business course. New business teachers will soon realize that one teaching style may not be appropriate for all courses.

SCANS Chairman William E. Brock (1994) identifies eight areas that all students need in preparation of foundation skills, personal qualities, and competencies. The areas are basic skills, thinking skills, personal qualities, resources, interpersonal skills, information, technology, and systems. Business teachers should develop a teaching style and a curriculum that coincides with these eight areas to help students make the school-to-work transition.

To enhance the school-to-work transition, business teachers must be competent in skills including, but not limited to, communication (speaking, listening, writing, and questioning), technology, problem solving, cooperative learning, team building, and leadership. In addition, business teachers must meet the needs of students and employers by providing a curriculum that emphasizes work ethics, attitudes, and employer expectations, such as motivation, reliability, initiative, and working with others. Business teachers should include career awareness and career exploration in a curriculum that integrates academic and business education. To learn more about how schools successfully implemented the transition of school to work, business teachers may review articles in the *Vocational Education Journal*, *Business Education Forum*, and state and other business and vocational education publications.

Keyboarding. Business educators report that keyboarding is the most popular elective course offered in secondary schools. By using the correct teaching methods, business educators can instruct students to keyboard properly either on typewriters or on computers.

When planning keyboarding instruction, teachers should consider the quantity and kinds of practice materials. The length and spacing of practice time can significantly affect student progress. Students learn and master psychomotor development at different rates and levels. Each element of skill development is best learned in isolation before being put into a composite situation.

Technology/computer applications. Business teachers must be properly trained in the use of computers and all business technology. Computer training for business education teachers includes appropriate computer course work and/or experiences early in educational programs and continuing education in computer training offered at both the state and institutional levels.

Business teachers must understand computer operations, capabilities, and limitations. Teachers should know and correctly use computer terminology and computer application software. In addition, business teachers should teach problem-solving skills using computers.

Equipment needs for instruction as well as software needs will change as technology changes. Currently, teachers are discussing how virtual reality and the Internet are to be taught. Additional concerns are how much and which factions of this technology (including software) need to be taught in the business education courses, what new courses need to be developed, and how content can be integrated across the curriculum.

Accounting. Business teachers should follow three steps when planning for accounting instruction. First, determine learning outcomes that specify what students must do to complete the accounting program. Second, plan learning activities that are consistent with learning outcomes and that follow established learning principles. Third, plan evaluation techniques that will measure the students' performance according to the learning outcomes originally specified.

Teaching methods should emphasize that each new segment of accounting principles and practices builds on previous learning. Accounting instruction should be organized to allow the completion of the accounting cycle several times for different business ownership types, such as sole proprietorship, partnership, and corporations.

Teaching methods should provide for drill and practice, simulations, projects, and homework. Students best learn accounting theory and practice through continual and consistent application—working the problems. When possible, accounting problems should be completed using computer applications software. Many teachers agree that students should first complete accounting problems by using the traditional pencil and paper application and then transfer their accounting skills to computers.

Basic business and international business. Basic business is (or should be) a part of the general education of every person. Although titles may vary by state, courses that may be classified as basic business include consumer education, economics, business law, management, marketing, international business, and general business. The course content aids in developing an understanding of business as a basic institution in the American social process and clarifies each person's economic role in relation to both personal needs and to the economy as a whole. Moreover, basic business content contributes to a functional knowledge of the role of American business in relation to world affairs.

International business concepts should be taught to all American business students. Emphasis should be placed on foreign cultures, mores, monetary systems, religions, customs, family values, economies, and lifestyles. By knowing the competition, Americans are more successful with international business negotiations.

Teachers must be highly selective in deciding which objectives and topics will be included in basic business courses. Many topics require a great deal of time and varying amounts of emphasis. Often special teaching tools, such as laser disks, videos, and guest speakers, are necessary for delivering the most current business activities and practices.

Business English/communication. To develop students' communication skills, business teachers must demonstrate proficiency in oral and written communication processes. With business people spending up to 80 percent of their time in some form of communication, business teachers must remember that communication situations have at least two viewpoints: the intent of the sender and the interpretation of the receiver. Students need instruction in delivering messages, interpreting printouts, reading and interpreting letters and reports, and listening effectively.

Students need to learn which communication channels are the best for delivering messages. Therefore, instruction may include the Internet and other forms of electronic communication and alternative delivery systems. Additionally, students need to be taught how to set priorities for processing and distributing documents and how to use documents to make business decisions.

Topics in a comprehensive business communication course may include communication process and theory; human relations and psychology; speaking, listening, and nonverbal communication; written communication; basic English skills and vocabulary. Students' prior achievements and their needs and interests will help guide business teachers in determining the degree of emphasis in each area. When English teachers and business teachers collaboratively teach in an integrated or applied curriculum, the instruction will not follow a comprehensive, formal communication course. However, business teachers have more opportunities than ever before to demonstrate proficiency and to influence the students' development of communication skills.

Business math. Increasing numbers of students pursue careers that require assembling, manipulating, and interpreting numerical data. Since Tech-Prep offers a new venue for delivering education, secondary students may enroll in courses that have resulted from the integration of mathematical concepts into applied curricula. These courses may include Applied Math I and II and Principles of Technology.

Shorthand/notehand. When shorthand/notehand is offered, business teachers should be familiar with the various symbol, alphabetic, and machine systems.

Business teachers should possess the same skills as those taught to their students. The major emphasis during the first semester is on theory, vocabulary building, and dictation. During the second semester, the emphasis is placed on further speed development and transcription.

Critical Thinking Skills

Cultivating critical thinking skills is a concern of business educators. Critical thinking includes attitudes, knowledge, and skills that enable one to solve problems. This problem-solving process includes determining a problem, gathering information, judging the validity of references, recognizing assumptions, and drawing conclusions.

Teachers have a direct influence on the development of critical thinking skills by:

- Encouraging positive student-teacher interactions.
- Using open-ended questioning techniques.
- Providing immediate verbal and nonverbal feedback.
- Infusing opportunities for critical thinking on all topics.
- Guiding students through the problem-solving process.
- Selecting and using content that enforces critical thinking.
- Modeling critical-thinking behavior.

Because the nature of the way people work has changed, *what* and *how* people learn should also change to expedite preparation for the workforce. Business teachers have the opportunity to guide students in their abilities to think more critically. Consequently, business teachers must help students develop their ability to reason (think) so that the students can produce their own ideas and form logical conclusions and develop workable plans.

Assessment/Evaluation

Evaluation is a vital part of the educational process. Evaluation in the business education instructional program provides feedback to both the students and the instructor and aids in improving students' performances.

Evaluation devices are grouped into two main categories: formal techniques and informal techniques. The best known formal evaluation techniques are teacher-made tests such as oral or written, in-class or take-home, closed book or open book, group or individual, or psychomotor such as in keyboarding. Published tests that may be standardized are other examples.

The most common form of informal testing is observation. Checklists and rating scales are examples of observational tools that may be used to assess students' progress. Other informal techniques for student evaluation include portfolios, case studies, anecdotal records, interviews, self-rating scales, personal data forms, discussions, computer-generated skills assessments, and role-playing incidents.

Classroom Management

Concerns about discipline and the lack of discipline are consistently cited in the annual Phi Delta Kappa/Gallup polls of the public's attitudes toward public schools in America. No one method can be used to effectively discipline all students. Whatever method is chosen, certain characteristics should be present.

Long-term changes. When teachers discipline students who engage in inappropriate behavior, a method should be used that will foster long-term, positive behavioral change. Teachers want students to develop self-discipline measures that will lead them to consistently display good behavior. Preventing problems is preferable to dealing with problems after they occur.

Sensible rules. Frequently, administrators tell teachers to post their lists of rules for proper student conduct in the classroom. Each rule must make sense to students. Any rule viewed as "stupid" is unlikely to be followed. Students will be more willing to adhere to rules that are perceived as beneficial to them. Furthermore, students who are involved in establishing the rules may develop self-discipline.

Student dignity. When the predispositions and needs of teachers clash with those of students, tension will arise. Teachers should never humiliate students in front of their peers. Address the discipline problem, but never attack a student's dignity with sarcasm or threats. Dignity in discipline can often be accomplished by maintaining eye contact with the students, moving closer to students when a corrective message needs to be delivered, or arranging an individual meeting with the students.

Self-modeling. Teachers should model proper behavior and show kindness and concern when speaking with students. When conflict occurs, students should observe the teacher implementing solutions that are respectful, non-violent, and verbally non-aggressive.

Discipline is by no means easy. The discipline method used must stop disruptive behavior, build acceptable social behavior, and provide the students with positive emotional benefits.

Motivation

As facilitators of learning, business teachers have the difficult responsibility of motivating students to learn. Many forces compete for students' attention, thus necessitating strengthening the teacher's arsenal of motivational tools.

A number of teaching methods produce motivational benefits. Design lesson plans that clearly identify lesson objectives. Allow students to discover axioms and truths through planned classroom activities. All classroom assignments and activities should show relevance to actual business practices. Use a variety of teaching styles. A reward system can be used effectively for motivation and may include an honor spot on a bulletin board or oral recognition on the public address system. Congratulatory letters to parents of students who do outstanding work are another good source of motivation (Jackson and Johnson, 1995).

Business educators may also motivate students by using current teaching materials and state-of-the-art business equipment/machines, maintaining attractive classroom decor, and continuously updating reference materials and examples.

Supplies and Equipment

A good indication of effective instructional planning is demonstrated by having all the needed supplies available and ready to use before each class begins. Textbooks, a primary learning tool, can guide or direct a student's learning. According to Callahan and Clark (1988), business teachers will find that textbooks provide:

- Structure for the course.
- Course content and emphasis.
- Activities and suggestions for teaching strategies.
- Information on sources, materials, and tools.

Business teachers also have access to other instructional materials provided by publishers. These materials include test banks, resource manuals, practice sets and simulations, study guides, software packages, and workbooks. Furthermore, chalk or whiteboards, bulletin boards, overhead transparencies and projection panels, and computer-generated presentation software may be used for demonstration in classes to enhance student learning and retention.

Teachers have had interactive learning devices in their classrooms for some time. The use of CD-ROM, digital whiteboards, laser disks, videos, and enhanced display panels using interactive software are also available. Individualized instruction may once again become essential in teaching both the gifted and the exceptional student through use of virtual reality devices.

Discussions by publishers include the possibility of providing computer on-line textbook/learning resources. Instead of buying the software and textbooks, schools could buy data communication time from telecommunication carriers and pay the publisher a user's fee to access materials directly through computerized data banks. This process could make all materials current on any given day. Textbook and supplies expenses may be reduced; however, communication time and access fees will become added expenses.

Special-Needs Students

Business teachers will most likely have learners with special learning challenges in their classrooms. Fogarty (1995) lists these special challenges as the following: primarily speaks a foreign language, hearing impaired, visually impaired, economically disadvantaged, attention deficit disorders, physically impaired, and precocious (highly gifted). To meet the special needs of these students, teachers must adapt their methods, materials, media, and classroom facilities arrangements.

Perhaps states should require instruction in teaching the exceptional learner as a part of the certification requirements. For example, prospective teachers may be taught how to deal effectively with the problems of physically challenged students. Instruction should be included on how to help students use their special equipment, such as wheelchairs, magnifying reading lamps, hearing devices, or voice synthesizers. Furthermore, business teachers will be instructing these students in using voice-input computers. Learning to include interactive video and computer interactive software will be expected of all business teachers.

Additionally, business teachers will have to learn new classroom management skills that require them to delegate responsibilities to teacher aides who will be assisting with the challenged students. This delegation will include training the aides, guiding the aides in what is considered proper help and instruction, and overseeing the work of the aides in record-keeping, health, and other related activities required of these special students.

Cooperative and Service Learning

Cooperative learning fuses technical literacy and workplace skills. Cooperative learning requires students to set group goals. However, each student's contribution to the group is evaluated. Both individuals and groups receive feedback on their performances.

Service learning programs place students into actual work assignments. Business teachers have attempted to place their students into business-only work sites. Service learning allows students to be placed in areas such as health care, horticulture, veterinarian services, restaurants, and other practical work environments.

Cooperative and service learning situations may enhance students' social skills, including communication, conflict resolution, and leadership development. Additionally, through cooperative and service learning activities, students become more responsible for their own progress.

Partnerships with Business/Industry/Government

Business teachers can better meet the needs of their students by involving business, industry, and government leaders in identifying, planning, and delivering instruction. Leaders from the private and public sectors must be encouraged to offer professional skills and resources that will improve the quality of the school experience and thus create a better workforce.

Zahn and Poole (1992) identified areas for cooperation that business teachers, schools, and communities can adapt for local needs. These areas include:

- Establishing mentorships.
- Requesting corporate volunteers.
- Decorating storefronts.
- Showcasing businesses.
- Seeking senior citizen volunteers.
- Initiating apprenticeships.
- Arranging teacher internships.

Business and education must work together to establish goals that are positive, specific, and measurable.

Summary

Two general questions posed in the introduction were explored in this chapter. The two questions were: (1) What should be the educational preparation for business teachers? and (2) What should a business teacher know and be able to do before accepting a teaching position? Areas for teacher preparation included professionalism and student teaching. Topics related to what a teacher should know included subject competencies, critical-thinking skills, assessment/evaluation, classroom management, motivation, supplies and equipment, special-needs students, cooperative and service learning, and partnerships with business/industry/government. The information presented in this chapter will be useful when business educators and business teacher educators read, study, and apply the concepts.

References

Bartholome, L. W. (1989). Preparing and updating professional business education teachers. In B. Kaliski (Ed.), *Asserting and reasserting the role of business education,* (pp. 57-69). Reston, VA: National Business Education Association.

Brock, W. E. (1994). A vision of education. *Vocational Education Journal, 67(7),* 21-22.

Calhoun, C. C., & Robinson, B. W. (1995). *Managing the learning process in business education.* Birmingham: Colonial Press.

Callahan, J. F., & Clark, L. H. (1988). *Teaching in the middle and secondary schools.* New York: Macmillan.

Chiodo, B. A. (1988). Seven solutions for student teachers. *The Balance Sheet, 69(2),* 10-13.

Everett, D. R. (1995). Teaching the SCANS competencies in business education. *Instructional strategies: An applied research series, 11(3),* 1-7.

Fogarty, R. (1995) *Integrating curricula with multiple intelligence.* Palatine, IL: I.R.I./Skyline Publishing.

Jackson, J. H., & Johnson, I. W. (1995). Five basic motivational tools for the high school classroom. *Business Education Forum, 50 (1),* 31-33.

Scaglione, J. (1994). Professional pizzazz: use it or lose it! In A. McEntee. (Ed.), *Expanding horizons in business education* (pp. 168-177). Reston, VA: National Business Education Association.

Zahn, D. K., & V. A. Poole. (1992). Education and work partnerships. In A. Burford, & V. Arnold. (Eds.), *The hidden curriculum* (pp. 191-193). Reston, VA: National Business Education Association.

CHAPTER 12

Retain, Retrain and Reward Business Educators

Dorothy A. Neal

Sacopee Valley High School, Hiram, Maine

The saying that "The more things change, the more they stay the same" should be considered as sage advice for business educators. Business education in the United States can be traced to the very beginnings of colonization, through its formative stages in the 19th century, to its present status as an integral component of American education. The early beginnings of business teacher education occurred primarily through direct work experience, in private business schools, or through self-instruction (Meggison 1989).

The growth of business education in this century has been described by Crank and Crank in this manner: "The expansion of the business education curriculum began in the 1920s, continued into the 1930s and 1940s, was halted briefly in the 1950s, and had its greatest growth in the 1960s and 1970s" (Crank and Crank 1977).

Business education today involves turning our kaleidoscopes of constantly changing patterns and carefully investigating ways that we may retain, retrain, and reward business educators who are an essential and necessary part of our global society.

Connect Business Education to Goals 2000

The Goals 2000 Educate America Act charges the United States with eight major educational goals to be achieved by the year 2000. Goal 3 and Goal 5 apply directly to business education.

Goal 3. American students will leave grades four, eight, and 12 having demonstrated competency in challenging subject matter . . . and every school will ensure that students learn to use their minds well, so they may be prepared for responsible citizenship, further learning, and productive employment in our challenging economy.

Goal 5. Every adult American will be literate and will possess the knowledge and skills necessary to compete in a global economy and exercise the rights and responsibilities of citizenship (Keying In, January, 1995).

While the Goals 2000 Educate America Act helps define what students should know and be able to do in "essential" subjects, the legislation leaves its major standard setting to individual states. The legislation also creates a National Skills Standards Board to define broad occupational clusters and create a system of standards, assessment, and certification for the skills needed in each area. Getting all stakeholders involved, including parents and the business community, in the process of determining these standards can assist in better teacher preparation and continued professional development. Technology integration must play a major role in the entire process.

A portion of the Goals 2000 School-to-Work Opportunities Act has special significance for business education. This act, passed in 1994, focused on integrating vocational and academic education so students would learn realistic problem-solving skills in the classroom for use on their jobs. The School-to-Work Opportunities Act's major focus is not only on students planning to go directly into the workforce but also opening additional opportunities for the college-bound student. Through clearly defined career paths, students can move from school to the work site in a more realistic fashion. The act encourages expanding programs presently in place such as apprenticeships, career schools, cooperative education, simulations, and tech prep (Keying In, January 1995).

Business Education's Relationship to the Job Market

Every two years the U.S. Department of Labor publishes an important document called the *Occupational Outlook Handbook* that contains detailed information on jobs and their growth. Trends are indicated and specific information on all aspects of jobs are provided.

According to the 1996-97 *Occupational Outlook Handbook,* a major factor in job satisfaction will be opportunities for pursuing an associate's or baccalaureate degree. Those who do not possess the necessary skills, especially technological skills, will have difficulty finding employment. Technological skill relates to almost every job in today's market. Business educators teach nearly all the technological skills needed for employment! This fact should give a clear message as to the importance of business educators.

Retain Business Educators

Most people respond positively to a perceived need. Because of the obvious increased need for workers with strong technological and human skills and because business educators teach these skills, the need for retaining business educators will continue to increase. The need is not diminishing; the need is increasing.

One of the best ways to foster the retaining of business educators is through the mentoring process. Mentors are positive, inspiring, and hardworking individuals who touch lives by their personal actions and motivate others to reach out for their dreams. Mentors encourage others to be creative and lead others to new and greater accomplishments—whatever the challenge. Mentors instill pride in others for what they do, and in turn, facilitate the process within others that makes them want to do even better.

Mentors can offer assistance in a variety of ways, including the following:

- Share information freely.
- Listen to the needs of others.
- Turn obstacles into opportunities.

Mentors usually have a wealth of knowledge to share. In business education today, everyone needs to have someone with whom to share knowledge.

Mentors should develop the art of listening to others, which requires constant and vigilant work. A beginning business educator needs an experienced colleague who will listen actively and who will share ideas. The need for effective listening never ends and is crucial for a beginning teacher regardless of age or teaching level.

Obstacles can often be viewed as opportunities. For example, many school administrators at all levels base courses strictly on numbers and forget the far-reaching ramifications of their hastily made decisions. Administrators need to be educated about the benefits of offering courses on skills needed in today's job market. Business educators could offer workshops for updating administrators about the continuing changes in the field. If done with careful preparation, much can be done to perpetuate the important role business educators play in the total curriculum of a school at all levels.

Business educators must communicate with other departments to explain the relationship of business education classes to other courses. The best way for business educators to take the lead in this endeavor is to explore existing opportunities for interdisciplinary instruction. Consider the following possibilities:

- Utilize technology and offer career counseling to students in other courses.
- Collaborate with other instructors and allow students to complete assignments in the business class.
- Team with the foreign language and social studies departments to plan and deliver a unit on international business.

These types of activities with colleagues can provide motivation and satisfaction for students and teachers. Collaborative efforts often result in increased class enrollments, and thus business educators are retained.

One of the most obvious, yet often overlooked, ways to retain business educators is for teachers to work directly with business and industry. The National Business Education Association has a business partnership with Manpower Temporaries.This partnership has been ongoing for several years and has allowed business educators to get hands-on experience in business. Partnership programs abound and can be identified through electronic and printed sources. Partnerships also provide a resource database for establishing advisory committees. Advisory committees can assist in developing positive dialogue concerning both school and individual business needs.

Active professional involvement builds a network of colleagues with similar interests and concerns. This network provides encouragement and helps retain business educators. The National Business Education Association and regional and state business education organizations provide meaningful opportunities for professional enrichment. Other professional and honorary organizations for business educators include, but are not limited to, the American Vocational Association, Association for Business Communication, International Society for Business Education, Delta Pi Epsilon, Phi Delta Kappa, and Phi Kappa Phi.

Retrain Business Educators

An essential focus in a business educator's life is professional development. The constantly changing subject matter in today's technological world mandates continual updating and retraining.

Various groups offer workshops and seminars that business educators may attend. These meetings provide opportunities for business educators to become involved and to network. Examples include local service and civic organizations, publishing companies, parent groups, and religious assemblies. An important concept is that learning is lifelong, changes constantly, and never ends.

What types of professional development activities would best fit current teaching assignments and prepare for future teaching assignments? Consider the following retraining options for business educators:

- Select professional activities that directly relate to current technology.
- Participate in a job internship program, either part-time during the year or full-time during the summer.
- Travel to a foreign country. The International Society for Business Education provides annual programs in countries throughout the world.
- Attend conferences at all levels where speakers address cutting-edge topics. Knowledge is updated, and professional lifelong friendships are formed.
- Earn additional college hours by enrolling in on-campus classes, distance learning, or conference credit.
- Offer in-service training programs to update others.
- Serve on committees at the school and community levels. This involvement is especially important to ensure business-education interests are included in any restructuring.
- Participate on a grant-writing team to demonstrate business educators' interest in the ever-changing world of education.
- Encourage joint efforts of business people and educators to foster increased awareness of relevant subject matter.
- Write an article or proposal for a business-related publication.

Participation in the activities above enhances individual professional development and serves as a motivational model for others.

Reward Business Educators

The power of rewarding and recognizing individuals has a "win-win" effect. Business educators are no exception. Common words associated with the "reward" include award, recognition, and prize. Business educators should focus on the role that recognition plays in empowering educators.

Educators seem to be notorious for ignoring recognition as an essential part of their personal growth, yet they continue to emphasize recognition in their teaching. Everyone needs to be rewarded and recognized for professional efforts, no matter how trivial or monumental.

Recognition can take many forms: written or spoken words and/or monetary award. A simple act of recognition can change a teacher's day.

Try these techniques for rewarding business educators:

- Organize a local teacher recognition process. Form a committee to recognize educators at all levels based on established criteria, including years of service in a particular subject area. Plan a recognition event and advertise the event through the media and other public resources.

- Nominate a teacher for a local, state, or national award in business education or education in general. Encourage the nominee to provide needed information; volunteer to assist in preparing the necessary paperwork. This coordinated effort brings recognition not only to the individual but also to the school and community. This author can attest to the positive effect of winning, having recently won the Maine Teacher of the Year Award in 1994 and a Milken Family Foundation Award in 1995—one of 150 given in the United States.

- Encourage students to become involved in recognition contests for school and community. Students can utilize their business skills to help establish criteria and to help organize the ceremony. When students are recognized, teachers also gain recognition through association with those students.

- Establish an ongoing public relations campaign to recognize professional involvement of educators.

- Maintain both electronic and paper bulletin boards that highlight positive faculty news.

- Encourage department heads and administrators to write congratulatory letters to faculty for positive recognition and reinforcement.

- Utilize the video and/or audio announcement system to publicize teacher accomplishments.

- Select a "teacher of the month" and display information about the recipient in a visible location.

- Encourage service, civic, and professional organizations to establish written and monetary awards for teaching excellence.

- Maintain sabbatical plans that will enable teachers to update skills and broaden educational backgrounds.

- Establish local policies that will allow teachers to participate in professional meetings.

- Initiate an "adopt-a-teacher" program where businesses provide both monetary and in-kind services.

While not all-inclusive, the ideas above provide a springboard for a reward system that will serve to recognize, motivate, and reward educators. The power of recognition is phenomenal!

Summary

Retaining, retraining, and rewarding business educators continue to be vital components in connecting education to today's global society. The implications of retaining business educators as essential professionals in this monumental age of restructuring points out the need for continuous retraining and ongoing professional development. Recognition and rewards afforded business educators should be continuous and serve as examples to others. The secret to bringing all three of these important initiatives together in the learning process is ably stated by Taylor (1955):

Learn to live, and live to learn,

Ignorance like a fire doth burn,

Little tasks make large return.

References

Crank, F., & Crank, D. (1977). Historical perspectives of education for business. In J. Crews, & Z. Dickerson. (Eds.), *Curriculum development in education for business* (pp. 1-18). Reston, VA: National Business Education Association.

Meggison, P. (1989). Business education in years gone by. In B. Kaliski. (Ed.), *Asserting and reasserting the role of business education* (pp. 9-19). Reston, VA: National Business Education Association.

National Business Education Association. (1995, January). School-to-work opportunities act. *Keying In, 5.*

Occupational outlook handbook. (1996-97). Washington, DC: U.S. Department of Labor.

Taylor, B. (1955). To my daughter. In J. Bartlett. (Ed.), *Bartlett's Familiar Quotations* (Thirteenth Edition). New York: Little Brown Publishers.

U.S. Department of Education. (1991). *America 2000: An educational strategy* (Rev. Ed.). Washington, DC: U.S. Department of Education.

PART V

BUSINESS EDUCATION FOCUSES ON CHANGE

CHAPTER 13

Global Economy

Betty J. Brown

Ball State University, Muncie, Indiana

The world has changed within the last decade to a global economy. The United States, like other countries, has seen its share of world exports increase dramatically. Over the past three decades, exports of manufactured goods have increased in percentages and in dollar values for machinery, chemicals, finished products, and various other commodities. Agricultural exports have increased significantly since the mid-1980s. Imports of agricultural products from other countries have remained stable as a percentage of all imports for the past decade. Imports of other goods have steadily increased, rising from a total value of $345 billion in 1985 to more than $600 billion in recent years (*World Almanac and Book of Facts,* 1994, p. 115).

Currently, about one-third of U.S. companies export, and about 50 firms account for more than 40 percent of U.S. exports (*World Almanac,* 1994, p. 188). The last round of the General Agreement on Tariffs and Trade (The Uruguay Round) lowered tariffs to less than 3 percent (from 4.7 percent previously). These tariff cuts affect approximately 85 percent of world trade (*Statistical Abstract of the United States,* 1994). As a result of the agreement, some countries have opened a part of their domestic markets to trading partners. In general, the United States is well positioned to benefit from the new trade agreement. Our world will become more global in concept.

This rapidly changing world has opened career opportunities for Americans and for residents of other countries. Inevitably, even landlocked states have moved toward a global market for their products. Companies in "small-town America" have a world market for their products. American consumers, whether they realize it or not, use products from all over the world. As a result of this move to a world economy or a world market for products, employment prospects have changed. Not only do workers find that more traditional jobs have changed in nature, but also workers find new career possibilities. As American companies compete in the global market, they open facilities in other countries; they send workers to other countries for marketing, production, consulting, and various other purposes.

The United States trades with most of the other countries of the world. Its chief trading partners are Canada, Japan, Taiwan, China, and Germany. As a result of increased trade and new configurations for trade, new terms have become part of our vocabulary: the Pacific Rim countries and the European Community, for example. As trade with such countries as Japan, Taiwan, China, Korea, the Philippines, and Australia has increased, Americans have become increasingly aware of the Pacific Rim countries. In the 1950s some countries in mainland Europe first formed an organization for trading, the European Common Market; that organization (now the European Community) has become much more of a factor in the global economy in the 1990s. The result has been increased awareness of these groups of countries and more dependence on them as consumers of American products and as sources of goods and services not produced in the United States.

Preparing Students for a Global Economy

How can schools prepare students for this global economy? A curriculum for the global economy may not be drastically different in course names and content from courses previously offered. However, the focus of courses that have been offered for years has shifted. Fundamental to an understanding of a global economy is an understanding of our own economy. Business firms that work in a global setting all need employees who have a sound base of business understanding; "international" as a concept permeates all of their business operations. However, "international business" is not different from "business." The concepts complement each other, and the idea of dealing in an international setting builds on a basic understanding of business. Students should learn the geographic location of countries that are part of world trade, especially those that are trading partners of the United States.

In an attempt to bring globalism into focus in preparation for the future, business educators offer courses in international business, international communications, or other "international" topics. As the world economy becomes more apparent, the curriculum will shift away from a few courses specializing in international emphases. The global economy will be such a part of the business system that it is not singled out for special courses. The curriculum will have evolved into one in which globalism permeates the content, in which students take for granted that they will live and work in a global economy.

Our economic system is built on specialization. Workers specialize in providing services, products, and labor. In turn, regions and countries specialize, too. In recent years this concept of specialization has led to increased awareness of and dependence on a global economy. Emerging economies, like developed economic systems, have become part of world trade by furnishing the products that enable them to compete. Students need to understand, initially, why individuals and their countries have a global perspective. When students understand that fundamental concept, they can understand better why nations no longer are isolated from each other and why nations engage in international ventures of all kinds. Individual nations, and business enterprises within those nations, engage in international trade because they find the benefits outweigh the costs. Products that would be unavailable to them are on the global market.

As countries engage in world trade, currencies are exchanged. Because of its stability, currency of the United States is important to world trade. In the spring of 1996, the U.S. government announced a new design for the $100 bill. At the same time, the U.S. government launched an extensive campaign in Russia to reassure the Russian people that the old $100 bill would still be of equal value. Americans were not concerned about a new bill because they assumed that any bill backed by the U.S. government would be good. However, in the past, currencies in other countries have lost their value with a change of government. U.S. currency is often used in other countries for savings because it is stable. Russian citizens whose savings are in U.S. currency needed reassurance that the old $100 bill was still valuable.

This chapter will describe some ideas for preparing students for the global economy by integrating basic concepts into existing courses. In addition, some of the activities will be appropriate for a course called international business or international communication. As a beginning, students need to be aware of geography. What activities can be incorporated into business education courses that will make students aware of where countries are located? The Internet, software programs, maps, and other resources can provide this background. If students know what countries are located around the Pacific Ocean, for example, they can understand the Pacific Rim countries as an important component of international trade. When students can locate the countries that are part of the European Community, they understand better why the elimination of tariffs and trade barriers was fundamental in making the European Community an economic force.

Activities for Integration into Skill-Development Courses

The content of keyboarding courses and courses that build on the foundation of keyboarding need not change as students prepare for a global economy. However, students should be aware of career possibilities that involve other countries and languages. One point of interest of which they should be aware is that keyboards are adaptable to different languages. Information processing packages have options for different languages. When a software package is installed on a computer, user options may include telling the system how to format for a given language.

Within a word-processing package, formatting options for different languages can be chosen. Even this basic knowledge of software features will make students more aware of how the world as a whole impacts on business. For example, the WordPerfect software package provides a language tool. The user can select a spell checker, thesaurus, and grammar checker to match one of almost 30 languages. Students may be interested in knowing that they can select among versions of a single language for those writing tools. English is divided into English for Australia, for Canada, for the United Kingdom, and for the United States. The writing tools are different for English in those four countries. Spanish, French, and Portuguese also have two versions. These features are indicative of how the global economy permeates all aspects of business.

Skill-building assignments can include content on the global economy. Students can be exposed to ways in which different countries address business communications. Letter styles and formatting variations from other countries can be introduced. Ask students to address a letter to Canada or the United Kingdom and note how the ZIP code used in the United States is replaced by codes for routing within those countries.

Incorporate data about global transactions into problems that students are assigned. When working with spreadsheets, students can add information from their research on international trade. Assign a report, complete with spreadsheets and graphs, on the amount of U.S. trade with various other countries, including figures for imports and exports. The *World Almanac and Book of Facts* (1994) and the *Statistical Abstract of the United States* (1994) are two sources of those figures. Ask students to develop a database of companies within their state that are involved in exporting.

Activities for Accounting

Accounting students should be aware that foreign currencies will be a factor for companies as they engage in international transactions. Often companies are paid in U.S. currency, but the exchange rate for that currency is an important matter. As an orientation to the role of exchange rates in transactions, construct an exchange table with spreadsheet software. A table that displays the equivalent U.S. value for various foreign currencies can be updated as often as necessary to show those values. *The Wall Street Journal,* as well as most daily newspapers, publishes a chart of foreign currency values each day; and those values can be inserted into the table. This activity makes students aware of the changing values of money on the international markets.

Students may not be aware that large accounting firms with international clients provide services beyond traditional accounting. These firms assist their clients in registering their products to the ISO 9000 standards. The International Standardization Organization, founded in 1987, includes 91 member countries. The American National Standards Institute represents the United States. Recently, the number of American companies that have registered has increased significantly. An increasing number of buyers throughout the world, particularly in Canada, Mexico, and Asia, require their suppliers to register. Eventually, ISO certification will be a requirement for suppliers in the international market, especially in Europe. An accounting firm's quality system registrars can review a company's quality-control system and assure that it meets the standards. With the required documentation and records available, a company then is qualified to supply goods to foreign customers. Arrange for students to interview accountants who work with companies involved in international trade, and ask about activities related to international trade. These interviews may take place by e-mail, by phone, by letter, or in person.

Activities for Developing Communication Skills

The business community travels worldwide. Even in small communities, companies and their personnel have economic connections with other companies and business employees in dozens of countries. Students who plan an office career probably will use their office skills to make overseas travel plans. They may communicate with people speaking other languages, and they will have other intercultural exchanges. In office procedures courses or units, students should have some preparation for their experiences with other cultures. For example, how will they greet international visitors to their offices? How do body language, gestures, and greetings differ in meaning among different cultures? What differences in spelling of commonly used words occur? Students should be sensitive to such differences. In some countries, gestures such as taking a potential buyer to dinner or giving that person a gift are frowned upon. Role-playing activities can help students recognize differences among cultures.

Activities for Basic Business Courses

In introductory courses such as introduction to business, activities can emphasize the globalism of business in the United States. After students see the differences among economic systems, they can brainstorm about how our business system would be different if it were not a market economy. What are the economies of other countries like? Ask students to choose a country to study and find answers to questions such as these: What is the role of the government in that country? What type of economic system does it have? What are its major industries? What are its size and population? What types of resources does it have? What are the main sources of income for its people? What does it export and import? What can you find out about the lifestyle of its people? What are its major foodstuffs? *The World Almanac and Book of Facts,* available at most bookstores, is a resource that will give students basic information about other countries.

One very visible result of our global economy is the presence of American fast-food restaurants in other countries. Ask students to choose a fast-food restaurant and research its international activities. McDonald's, Coca-Cola, and PepsiCo, for example, have expanded to many other countries. Ask students to study their own business community to determine whether any business firms are owned by foreign corporations. As a project, students can study those firms and their countries to become acquainted with the economic systems.

Contact your state's department of commerce and its international trade division or similar organization for ways in which these organizations assist U.S. companies. For example, U.S. companies may be able to introduce their products to foreign markets through participating in trade shows overseas or in trade shows in the United States for potential foreign customers. Such trade shows are often part of the services of the department of commerce. In Indiana, trade specialists in the State Department of Commerce have linguistic, cultural, and business expertise and work with trade offices in various other countries. The trade specialists help Indiana firms to make business contacts, generate trade opportunities, and participate in trade shows or missions.

Ask students to plan an imaginary trip through foreign countries. As a part of their planning, students should become acquainted with the culture, currency, geography, primary businesses, imports and exports, and sources of income of the countries. During the research process, help students to search the Internet for information about the countries being studied.

Assign students to inventory products that they have bought or have in their homes and list the countries that provided the items. Students will be surprised to find clothing, shoes, food, appliances, etc., often are products of other countries.

Many large banks have international specialists who work with their full-service offices in other countries. These specialists are more than just correspondents with other countries. Ask students to research some of the services offered by those banks, such as multi-currency lines of credit and commercial lending for companies with overseas operations.

Direct students to collect information on their state's exports and imports, the methods by which goods were received from other countries and were shipped to the international market, and companies involved in those transactions. As students find out about their own state, they gain a realization of how global our economy is.

Teachers or students may request a copy of any guides to international trade that are made available to companies in the area through their state department of commerce or economic development office. Use those guides to become acquainted with the extent of international trade among companies in your region.

On the Internet, find Universal Resource Locators (URLs) for information related to services, tourism, travel, and cultures of other countries. The World Wide Web has a site on foreign currency, for example. A list of conversion rates for currencies is updated daily, and a fact sheet is included on dealing with foreign currencies when you travel (http://www.ora.com). Search the Internet on international currency, international finance, currency exchange, and world trade.

Throughout the world, 303 world trade centers operate in 91 countries. These trade centers provide information about international business opportunities. The trade centers' chief objective is to assist member companies in marketing, legal, and transportation aspects of international business and to guide them to foreign trade opportunities. Members can participate in seminars on topics pertinent to international business, receive assistance in participating in trade missions, and meet with consultants from the world trade centers to explore international trade opportunities. Access information about the world trade centers on the Internet at http://www.yahoo.com/International_Trade/World_Trade_Centers.

Guides to individual countries and cities are available on the Web. For example, a guide to Australia includes information about geography, environment, communications, travel, culture, government, and history (http://www.csu.edu.au/education/Australia.html). A Russian travelogue is available that includes photographs, illustrations, and daily writings that give a flavor of Russian culture and environment (Access the site with this URL: http://yahoo.com/Regional/Countries/Russia. Then search only under "Russia" for "travelogue"). Because the Internet grows daily, keeping pace with all the available sites is difficult. Invest in an Internet Yellow Pages book or other directory to get ideas of sites that you can use through the Internet. Searching the Internet on "International Business," students can find a wealth of information on international trade news, international investment, business news, jobs around the world, and currency exchange.

Yahoo offers a guide to dozens of countries under the URL "http://www.yahoo.com/Regional/Countries." The sites have information on business and trade, culture, travel, cities, government, and many other topics about those countries. One benefit from exploring on the Internet or browsing through a reference book such as the *World Almanac and Book of Facts* is that students become aware of the vast amount of information available on dozens of other countries.

Acquaint students with types of businesses closely associated with international business. For example, companies that want to enter the global market can make contacts through trade shows. With increased globalization of business, trade-show marketing is even more important. European businesses, particularly, rely on trade shows as a marketing medium. Specialists in trade-show exhibits have products ranging from portable display systems to complete custom displays, some even as large as a home. Ask students to identify exhibit companies in their state or city.

Awareness of the globalism of our world should be a major emphasis in all business courses. Even though students may not engage in specific activities related to the global market, they should be aware that globalism is a fact of life. They may not be aware of companies in their own community engaged in global trade. Any activities that help students become aware of those business firms and of the impact of the global economy on their everyday lives should be part of course content, even if incidental to the main objectives of the course.

Subscribe to a regional or state business magazine that will provide information to students about local businesses. For example, the *Indiana Business Magazine,* published monthly in Indianapolis, is available for subscription. Periodically, the magazine publishes a corporate directory that lists all corporations in the state with sales of $5 million or more. Students may be amazed to learn that companies with sales of millions of dollars employ only a few people; yet, these companies are very active in global markets. *Indiana Business Magazine* is an excellent source of information about Indiana companies that deal domestically and internationally in various kinds of business services and products. Features include articles on the winners of the magazine's International Business Person of the Year Award and Exporter of the Year Award. Such articles are excellent ways for students to learn about business firms and people in their own communities who are involved in the global economy. Subscribe to similar magazines for your state or region and make them available to students for browsing and for researching projects about the global economy; or check to see if a local company will donate back issues for your classroom.

Workers must have team skills as they enter the business world. Plan some cooperative learning activities focused on the global economy. For example, introduce a "skill of the week" that would be needed in working with people from other cultures. For one week, focus on that skill in class activities. Skills that can be emphasized include conversing on the telephone on an international call, listening carefully and affirming what a speaker has said, and demonstrating gestures and their meanings in different cultures.

Currency differences are an important factor to any company engaged in foreign trade. As a brainstorming activity, ask students to design a common currency, one that might be used around the world. What characteristics must the currency have? What barriers to its acceptance can they identify? Why do we not have a common currency? One of the objectives of the European Community is to have a common currency. What problems can students see that the EC will have in trying to agree on that objective? This activity will require students to research some of the currencies in use around the world and understand differences among them.

Ask students to brainstorm about their perceptions about the global economy and world trade. Ask them to think of all the reasons why a person should "buy American." Then think of all the reasons why a person should "buy foreign-made." Students will find that many products are assembled in the United States from parts manufactured in other countries. On the other hand, a large number of products are assembled in other countries using parts that have been manufactured in the United States. These global products are indicative of the global economy. Many goods cannot be clearly classified as either "domestic" or "foreign."

In an introduction to business class, as a capstone experience to the study of international business, organize a picnic with food prepared from food products of several countries. In their research of different countries, students should identify food products that are exported or that are used extensively in that country, as well as typical dishes for that country. Part of the assignment could be the preparation of a food using those products, which they share with their classmates.

In a class such as international business or business communications, students can develop a project around the global economy; do research through library resources; correspond with companies and industrial development, trade, and tourism agencies in other countries; and search the Internet to compile information about one aspect of the global economy. The assignment could be the study of one country or one company that trades outside the United States. Using all the skills they have acquired through their business classes, the students' final reports should include text, charts and graphs, and documentation.

If students have thoroughly studied a country, their reports should describe the geography, culture, history, wages, labor force, transportation system, and economic system of the country, as well as facts about their imports and exports, multinational companies, and extent of trade with the U.S. If they have studied a company, their reports could include such content as information on the products exported and imported, places in which the company has branches or plants, data collected from the company about its operations, some analysis of its financial data, and types of advertising used in foreign markets. Another possible capstone project would require students to select a product for distribution overseas, do research on where it could be successful, plan for advertising the product, and gather information on what type of image would make the product sell in various cultures.

Structuring the Business Education Curriculum for the Global Economy

The National Standards for International Business (1995), available through the NBEA, are part of a framework for the business curriculum, elementary through postsecondary. The section of the publication on international business identifies nine sets of standards for curriculum about the global economy. Those areas can serve as a structure for developing concepts and activities to emphasize the global economy throughout the business education curriculum. The first set of standards for international business, the awareness level, addresses the role and impact of international business, geography, career opportunities, and travel considerations.

In a class such as introduction to business, provide opportunities for students to learn about the role of local companies in foreign markets and to analyze the impact of their international activities on the local community. In an office-procedures class, assign projects that require students to locate various countries and identify currencies used, time zones, languages spoken, and communications systems. For one country, assign students to research communication systems that would enable them to contact business firms in that country. Require students to identify other factors that would affect them if they worked for a company with business interests in that country. Identify career paths available in local business firms that provide employment in another country. If students can identify employees in the local business community who travel to other countries for their firms, ask students to interview them and report to the class on their findings about travel procedures and career opportunities.

The second area in the National Standards, international business communication, is one in which business educators have developed materials and curricula. Americans have been made aware that they must consider communication differences among various countries and understand that blunders in verbal and nonverbal behavior can be barriers in business. In business communication classes students can be assigned projects that require them to become well-acquainted with the customs, communication patterns, and business protocol of various countries. Sharing the results of their studies with other students will develop an awareness of differences in communication among various cultures.

The international business environment, the third area in the National Standards, outlines many of the areas that should be part of a course in international business. Social, cultural, political, legal, and economic factors may be integrated into other courses. Students in introduction to business will become aware of types of governments and trade policies such as tariffs and quotas.

The fourth area of the National Standards, ethics, is one that introduces a topic different from traditional business. What differences do employees of U.S. companies find in ethical standards when they work in other countries? What is the effect of their actions on trade relationships? Students can study ethics from the viewpoint of a host country and a visiting company. Case problems on ethical situations are a way to emphasize differences among cultures. What is the effect in certain countries of presenting a gift to a prospective customer? In some cases that gift would present a dilemma to the recipient whose culture rejects such gifts as affronts.

The fifth area, finance, includes standards readily identified with international business transactions. In introduction to business, accounting, and computer applications courses, students can calculate values in different currencies used in transactions and can investigate exchange rates. Business magazines and TV news programs furnish currency values; assign students to follow the exchange rates for a period to see changes. The nightly business news on public broadcasting stations is an excellent source of information about local and foreign stock markets, exchange rates, the latest news on international trade, and U.S. companies in the news. Assign students to watch the broadcast, or videotape portions for class use.

The sixth area of the National Standards addresses management of companies engaged in international trade. Management personnel of companies involved in foreign trade have added responsibilities. Managers who have entered foreign markets often have found that learning the cultures of various countries was critical to their success. They understand the importance of staying "in tune with the country's culture," and of working within the parameters of the host country. Assign case studies of companies in foreign markets; ask students to investigate the special problems of managing a company trading outside the U.S.

For international marketing, the seventh area of the National Standards, provide an array of business magazines and ask students to look for advertisements for consumers in foreign markets. Through the Internet, search for information on other countries that will help students to determine what means of marketing would be effective. Ask students to plan a marketing or advertising campaign that would be appropriate in another country.

Some U.S. companies enter the global market only as exporters; they have no overseas facilities. Others may be multinational companies, with facilities in the United States and other countries. The global economy includes several kinds of companies, of which these are two. When importing and/or exporing goods or services, a company will become involved with the U.S. Customs Service and the customs agencies of other countries. International trade agreements may affect their transactions. For example, the General Agreement on Tariffs and Trade (GATT) regulates tariffs. The North American Free Trade Agreement (NAFTA) affects trade with Mexico and Canada. The international trade division of a state department of commerce is a valuable resource for a company that exports goods and services. Contact that division in your state by e-mail, phone, or letter, and introduce students to the services provided to companies. The eighth area of the National Standards, import/export and balance of trade, lists goals that should be accomplished in the integration of these topics into students' preparation for the global economy.

The last section of the Standards on International Business includes guides for the organizational structure of international business. Students in an introduction to business course generally have a good foundation of knowledge about business organizations. Expand that base by introducing them to organizations for international business operations. As large corporations move into the global market, they become involved in joint ventures, subsidiaries that operate in foreign countries, and franchises for international trade.

Postsecondary and college students have opportunities to become even more conversant with global opportunities and experiences. Travel and study opportunities in other countries enable them to have first-hand experience with business firms in foreign countries. Materials on business and investment opportunities in other countries can be incorporated into such courses as introduction to business, international communication, and international business. The Internet is one good source of leads to organizations and companies that have such materials. The World Wide Web includes URLs for other countries that provide information on commercial and investment opportunities. The U.S. International Trade Commission has links to many international trade resources on the Internet. The address for the Trade Commission is "http://www.utitc.gov." That URL will lead to many resources, including information on trade within the U.S. and trade with other countries.

A wealth of information on the global economy and a variety of classroom materials for teachers and students are available. *Creative Teaching Ideas for International Business* (1996), a joint project of the National Business Education Association and the International Society for Business Education, contains 75 teaching ideas for secondary, postsecondary, and college/university courses. Many state departments of education have curriculum guides for teaching international business for teachers in their states. The National Council on Economic Education has developed curriculum guides with lesson plans for international business as a course and as a part of other courses; an example is *Teaching Strategies: International Business* (Wentworth and Leonard, 1989). This book includes 23 lesson plans for teaching about world trade as part of an international business, economics, or social studies course. The activities can also be integrated into other courses. A textbook by Dlabay and Scott, *Business in a Global Economy* (1996), with an instructor's guide, is available for a one-semester or one-year course in international business. These materials can assist teachers to prepare students for a global economy.

The concept of living in a global economy should permeate the entire curriculum. Preparation for a global economy should not be a part of only an international business or international communications course. All aspects of living, working, and managing in the U.S. economy are influenced by the fact that U.S. business firms deal with companies around the world. Jobs will require the ability to interact with people from other countries and cultures. As students become aware of and prepare for the global nature of our economic system, they will find opportunities that a few years ago may have been only dreams.

References

Creative teaching ideas for international business. (1996). Reston, VA: National Business Education Association and International Society for Business Education.

Dlabay, L. R., & Scott, J. C. (1996). *Business in a global economy.* Cincinnati: South-Western Publishing Company.

National standards for business education. (1995). Reston, VA: National Business Education Association, (pp. 101-126).

Statistical abstract of the United States (114th Ed.) (1994). Washington, DC: U.S. Department of Commerce.

The world almanac and book of facts. (1994). Mahwah, NJ: Funk and Wagnalls.

Wentworth, D. R., & Leonard, K. E. (1989). *Teaching strategies: International Trade (Secondary).* New York: National Council on Economic Education.

CHAPTER 14

Entrepreneurship Education

John E. Clow

State University of New York, College of Oneonta
Oneonta, New York

An entrepreneurial explosion occurred in the United States starting in the early 1970s and continuing into the 1990s. As pointed out by Drucker (1985), the United States has been experiencing an entrepreneurial boom not evident in the last 100 years. Dennis (1993) also indicated that 38 million new jobs were created between 1970 and 1990, representing a 50 percent increase in the number of available jobs. What an enormous expansion considering that the growth of the population over the age of 16 was only 35 percent! These jobs were created primarily by the small-business sector due to expansions and new business formations.

Interestingly, this explosion in entrepreneurial ventures was unexpected. After World War II and up to the late 1960s, the focus was on big business and government. These entities added most of the new jobs to the economy and kept the economy healthy. In recessionary times the small businesses displaced workers; the large businesses had few layoffs. Government was expected to provide sufficient intervention to solve the problems of society. Small businesses were considered to be an anachronism.

Why did entrepreneurship ventures and small businesses become the primary job generator from the 1970s to the present? Will this business trend continue into the next century? If so, what curriculum changes need to be made, and how should they be made to assure appropriate student preparation for their world? These topics are the focal points of this chapter.

Reasons for Entrepreneurship Explosion

Several reasons for the new entrepreneurial era indicated by Dennis (1993) are discussed in the paragraphs below.

Changed role of women in the labor market. Since World War II, the percentage of women in the labor force has been increasing. In 1950 about three in 10 women were employed in the labor market; in 1990 the number was six in 10. Dennis believes that the increase of women in the workforce has had two effects on the entrepreneurial explosion. First, as more and more women enter the job market and gain business experience, an increased number of women will eventually develop the confidence level and skills to start businesses. The second effect focuses on the husband's interest in pursuing entrepreneurial ventures when the wife has a permanent job. When the wife is earning a steady income to support the family, the husband generally is more willing to assume the risk associated with starting a business on his own.

Influence of technology and information. Technology has changed considerably in the last few decades; futurists indicate that technology will continue to grow geometrically. Information generation and availability are much greater today than in the past. New businesses are created to address the need of marketing new types of technological inventions. The major opportunities for entrepreneurial ventures emanate from disruptions in the established markets and production processes caused by technology and information. Smaller businesses generally can deal more quickly with these disruptions than can the larger businesses. The disruptions provide a plethora of opportunities for entrepreneurial ventures.

As indicated by Dennis (1993), the development of mailing lists of individuals with similar tastes and interests spawned several new types of entrepreneurial ventures, including special-interest magazines. New technologies also provided cost advantages to the smaller firm compared to the larger firm in some areas. As an example, the development of the personal computer has generated an increase in home-based businesses, generating services at a lower cost than if the same work were completed in a centralized business office. The advent of the Internet will continue to generate a number of new businesses—another illustration of how new technology and information are creating opportunities for entrepreneurial ventures.

Cost of entry. A third long-term effect is the cost of entry, meaning the cost of setting up a business. For several decades the economy of the United States has been shifting from producing goods to producing services. Most new businesses in the United States produce services. The cost of entry for a service-producing industry is on the average lower than for a goods-producing firm because of lower capital equipment costs. According to Dennis (1993) human capital costs seem to be the same. The lower entry cost for service-producing industries enables more people to start their own businesses.

Public receptiveness to entrepreneurial activity. The American culture generally values entrepreneurs and their work. Entrepreneurship has more respect in this country than in many other highly developed countries, such as those in Europe. A 1992 survey of the general public by Princeton Survey Research Associates showed that the American people generally have a favorable impression of the small businessperson. With such a favorable societal attitude, individuals are encouraged to pursue an entrepreneurial venture.

Baby boom and the labor market. The baby boom started in 1946 and ended in 1960. From the mid '60s to the '80s, the baby boomers entering the labor market caused a big bulge in the labor force. As competition for jobs in the corporate world increased, many baby boomers did not find jobs in the corporate sector. Therefore, they selected other ways to earn a living, including self-employment.

Turbulence in the American economy. Starting in the 1970s and continuing into the 1990s, the American economy made a number of changes because of major economic forces, such as inflated oil prices, hyperinflation in the early '80s, increased competition from foreign companies, deregulation of financial services and transportation, and corporate restructuring. As indicated previously, disruptions provide opportunities for the entrepreneur. Indeed, many people with an entrepreneurial interest have started new businesses to meet new challenges. One response of corporate America to increased competition has been the outsourcing of work to small businesses.

Impact of 1960s attitudes. In the 1960s young adults questioned authority and corporate America, expressed individualism, and chose new lifestyles. These perspectives correlated much better with the entrepreneurial way of life than with the corporate mentality. A generation with those outlooks had a greater proclivity for starting one's own business rather than becoming the organization or corporate person.

Entrepreneurial Activity Outlook in the Future

Morrison from the Institute for the Future (1996) indicated that individuals and networks are the organizational pattern for the future. Large businesses will not become extinct; however, the more common pattern may be smaller organizations—many times an entrepreneur working alone.

Some of the factors that brought about the entrepreneurial explosion of the '70s, '80s, and '90s will not be such strong forces in the future. For example, baby boomers will not be flooding the labor market and the percentage of women entering the labor market will tend to stabilize. Yet, the economic turmoil in the American economy will probably continue, especially in regard to increased international competition and technological and information processing changes. The cost of establishing many new businesses will continue to be relatively low. Currently and in the foreseeable future, the public sector will likely implement more policies favorable to the entrepreneur and small business owner.

The business world of today and tomorrow seems to be increasingly geared to the entrepreneur and small business operation. Therefore, integrating entrepreneurship education in schools is justifiable.

Justification for Entrepreneurship Education

Entrepreneurship education develops the skills and knowledge for business initiation and operation. In addition, students develop an understanding of the entrepreneur's role in the American economy.

Why should entrepreneurship education have prominence in the schools? First, the entrepreneurship process is very important for the health of any economy. Kent (1990) identified entrepreneurs as those individuals who bring about an improvement in the human condition and without whom material progress would be nonexistent. Entrepreneurs offer new ideas to others. As creative forces within the economy, entrepreneurs develop products or services that satisfy needs and enable individuals to have jobs. Spending some time in the formal educational program on entrepreneurship education seems only logical considering the importance of the entrepreneur to the economy and the society.

Second, entrepreneurship education can also provide students with an understanding of business—its purposes, its structure, its interrelationship with other segments of the economy and society. An understanding of business is not only helpful for those who will be running a business but also for those working in a business. Employers want individuals who have more than the technical skills—employees who have a comprehension of what a business is all about (Mann, 1992). This understanding generally cannot be gained from studying economics or career education; rather, getting involved in business, preferably experientially, seems to maximize these learnings. Using entrepreneurship education as the means to teach students about business has proven to be an effective path to foster such understandings.

Third, formal educational programs can make a difference in the entrepreneurial skills of students. Some people believe that entrepreneurs are born, not made. Undoubtedly, some people are more blessed with the natural abilities of the entrepreneur. Literature shows that many individuals possess potential entrepreneurial abilities that are not used (Kent, 1990). When schools encourage developing entrepreneurial abilities, more creative change agents will be available in the society.

Fourth, entrepreneurship education focuses on life. Alfred Whitehead, noted educational philosopher, repeatedly said that education should be about life. Education should make life more understandable to people; individuals should be better prepared to live a quality life. As Kourilsky (1995) has indicated, the "make-a-job" mentality instead of the "get-a-job" thinking is much more important in the current and future world. Without the "make-a-job" mentality, schools will not be making an optimal effort toward meeting the needs of our youth and our economy.

Most current theorists in the field believe that entrepreneurship education should be multigrade and multidimensional. The next two sections will focus on the specific content and selected materials to be used in entrepreneurship education programs.

The Grade-Level Content for Entrepreneurship Education

Besides such features as the role of the entrepreneur in the economy and the study of the characteristics and qualities of an entrepreneur, curriculum theorists believe that entrepreneurship education should show the steps of the entrepreneurial process. These steps are:

1. Identifying an opportunity that is an unfulfilled want and developing a good or service to satisfy that want. This step involves identifying a good or service to produce and determining whether a sufficient current or developed demand exists for the item at a price that will enable the entrepreneur to recover costs and make a profit.

2. Securing the resources to start the business. This endeavor involves obtaining funding, capital resources, and labor resources to start the business.

3. Initiating the business. Begin to produce and/or sell the good or service on which the business is based.

4. Maintaining a profitable business. This step involves keeping the records, marketing the products, managing the resources, planning for expansion/contraction, producing the good, etc.

5. Liquidating the firm. This process not only involves timing the liquidation but liquidating the firm to maximize the entrepreneur's profits.

Kourilsky (1995) believes that many times the first three dimensions are missing from traditional entrepreneurship education programs. Instead, the programs or units called "entrepreneurship" are to a great extent the maintenance phase (the fourth step). For example, many teachers think of a school store as being synonymous with entrepreneurship. If the students perform the common tasks of operating a school store—ordering supplies, selling items, keeping inventory records, and preparing advertising—they complete only the maintenance part of entrepreneurship. Students miss those very important steps of entrepreneurship that involve getting an idea for a business and taking the steps necessary to initiate the business.

Many secondary programs in entrepreneurship education do not emphasize the last step of liquidation. Time constraints and a belief that the other steps are more important may be used to justify omitting the liquidation step. In this time of ever-changing markets, this step is critical. Many entrepreneurs do not make a large profit from their operation each year; their primary realization of profit is derived from selling the firm at the right time of the firm's life cycle. This "right-time selling" is important to the entrepreneur and to the potential buyer of the business.

Target audience for entrepreneurship education. Entrepreneurship education is being recommended for everyone in the schools—not just for those interested in starting their own business. Kourilsky (1995) indicates that entrepreneurship education efforts should be perceived as targeted to three majors layers of students—namely, the initiator, the development team, and the constituency.

The initiators are those who actually take the risk to start a business based on an opportunity that they see which others do not. Divergent thinking skills, a willingness to solve problems, a passion for an idea or opportunity, and a willingness to work with ambiguity in creating the idea and setting up the business are some of the other qualities of an initiator. Fewer initiators exist compared to the number in the other two groups.

Development team members are those who work with the initiators. As Kourilsky (1995) points out, this group generally is concerned about the growth of the firm rather than the establishment or initiation of the firm. The traits of development team members generally are very similar to the traits of initiators. In many instances, they may not have the individual confidence level to "fly" on their own to initiate a business. Fluidity exists between the initiator and development team levels. Many individuals serve on a development team before they initiate their own business.

The constituency (the largest group) appreciates what the entrepreneur does for the community and supports the entrepreneurship function. They see themselves as being affected by the entrepreneur even though they might not be working with one. Their actions are reflected in both the marketplace and in the polling booth; their votes in both places are reflective of their attitudes toward the entrepreneur. The initiator and the members of the development team are also members of the constituency.

Specific content for entrepreneurship education. With a grant from the Center for Entrepreneurial Leadership of the Ewing Marion Kauffman Foundation, the National Business Education Association developed standards for entrepreneurship education. The standards are designed to develop the skills, knowledges, and attitudes important for all groups. The standards can and should be used to plan entrepreneurship curriculum for grades K-14. Nine achievement standard areas with broad descriptions of the subcategories under each are listed below:

I. Characteristics
    A. Characteristics of an Entrepreneur and You
    B. Role of the Entrepreneur in Business
    C. Opportunity Recognition and Pursuit
    D. Problem Identification and Solutions

II. Marketing
    A. Identifying the Market
    B. Reaching the Market
    C. Keeping/Increasing Your Market

III. Economics
    A. The Economic Way of Thinking
    B. Characteristics of a Market Economy
    C. The Function of Price
    D. The Role of Profit/Risk
    E. The Role of Government

IV. Finance
    A. Determining Cash Wants
    B. Sources and Types of Funding
    C. Interpreting Financial Statements

V. Accounting
    A. Importance of Keeping Records
    B. Types of Business Records
    C. Establishing and Using Business Records
    D. Interpreting Business Records

VI. Management
    A. Establishing a Vision
    B. Hiring People Who Share the Vision
    C. Building Teams to Fulfill the Vision
    D. Monitoring the Achievement of the Vision

VII. Global Markets
    A. Cultural Differences and Their Effect on Business
    B. Export/Import Opportunities
    C. Trends in Global Marketplace

VIII. Legal
    A. Forms of Business Organization
    B. Government Regulations that Impact the Owning and Operating of a Business
    C. Business Ethics

IX. Business Plan

The National Business Education Standards identifies one achievement standard for each of the nine areas. Performance expectations are then listed for each achievement standard that are developmentally oriented for grades K-14. The finance achievement standard, for example, is "identify and use the necessary financial competencies needed by an entrepreneur."

One of the four subcategories for that achievement standard is interpreting financial statements. The performance expectations for the various levels are:

Level I   Examine a profit-and-loss statement to determine whether a business is profitable.

Level II   Describe why the analysis of financial statements is important for business.

Level III Analyze for decision-making purposes the financial health of a business.

           Analyze for decision-making purposes the cash flow of a business.

           Analyze for decision-making purposes the worth of a business.

           Determine when financial experts should be consulted for the interpretation of financial data.

           Determine the number of products to be sold to make a profit (break-even analysis).

Level IV   Identify factors that cause changes in the financial picture of a business.

The levels correspond to the following key:

Level I   Elementary (K-6)

Level II   Middle School/Junior High (6-9)

Level III Secondary (9-12)

Level IV   Postsecondary/Community College or Technical College (13-14)

The Business Education Standards are used primarily for curriculum planning and student evaluating. If an elementary teacher wants to know the entrepreneurial content that experts in this field believe should be integrated into the elementary level, the performance expectations marked Level I are listed in the nine achievement standard areas. The experts believe that these expectations can and should be mastered by students at that level. A local school curriculum planning team will need to decide the appropriate materials and elementary grade in which to develop the performance expectations and how to measure whether the students have reached the desired level of performance.

The middle, secondary, and postsecondary schools also have performance expectations listed for their respective levels for each of the nine areas. Curriculum planners for each of these levels will need to determine whether their students have developed the performance expectations for the lower levels before planning educational activities for their own level.

The Business Education Standards can also be used for other curriculum-related purposes. Some textbook authors have used the performance expectations for evaluating texts. Teachers have used the performance expectations as springboards for developing lesson strategies/activities for the various grade levels.

A full copy of the entrepreneurship standards can be obtained by requesting the *National Standards for Business Education* from the National Business Education Association, 1914 Association Drive, Reston, VA 20191.

Teaching Materials for Entrepreneurship Education

Extensive teaching materials are available in the area of entrepreneurship education. Several entrepreneurship textbooks with ancillary materials are on the market. Numerous films on various aspects of entrepreneurship education are also available.

An important ingredient in establishing any entrepreneurship program is to provide students with an opportunity to experience entrepreneurship. This experiential philosophy is pervasive in the materials available from the Center for Entrepreneurship Education of the Marion Ewing Kauffman Foundation. The YESS! (Youth Empowerment and Self-Sufficiency) Mini-Society program is geared for grades K-6 and enables direct student involvement in activities. In this program students are asked to set up their own society and identify opportunities for establishing a business. These experiences are then integrated in various subjects offered at the elementary level. The materials correspond with the standards mentioned earlier. Additional information about this program can be obtained from the Center for Entrepreneurial Leadership of the Ewing Marion Kauffman Foundation, 4900 Oak St., Kansas City, MO 64112-2776.

A middle school and lower-high school program (grades 7-10), titled The New Youth Entrepreneur, includes 12 modules relating to various facets of entrepreneurship. This program asks students to identify opportunities in their own environment on which to start a business and then to establish that business. The modules provide assistance for the young people in setting up their business and are consistent with the National Standards for Business Education. Titles of the modules include:

Module One:	Entrepreneur? Who, Me? Yess! You
Module Two:	Opportunities - They Are All Around You
Module Three:	Business Ideas For All Communities
Module Four:	How To Sell Your Idea - The "What's In It For Me?" (WIIFM) Factor
Module Five:	Money To Get Started
Module Six:	Where To Do Business
Module Seven:	Types of Business Ownership
Module Eight:	Where To Get Help
Module Nine:	Records and Books - Did You Make Any Money?
Module Ten:	The Rules of the Game
Module Eleven:	How to Mind Your Own Business
Module Twelve:	You Can Make It Happen - YESS! You (The Business Plan)

The modules were field-tested in business education classes during the 1994-95 school year; teachers were very pleased with their readability, graphics, textbook/workbook format, and student interest in the materials. Students were actively involved as they proceeded through the modules. Recognizing an opportunity and then starting a business based on that opportunity was energizing for the students, especially for underachievers who seemed to appreciate the open-ended, creative aspects of the activities. These materials can be obtained through EDTEC, 313 Market St., Camden, NJ 08102.

For the secondary level, the Center for Entrepreneurial Leadership has contracted with NBEA to develop model lessons for entrepreneurial education for the level-three performance expectations of the entrepreneurship standards. These lessons will be developed and tested in classrooms during the 1996-97 school year, with publication scheduled for 1998.

Another set of entrepreneurship education materials for the secondary level, called PACE (Program for Acquiring Competence in Entrepreneurship) published by the Center on Education and Training for Employment is organized around 21 core competencies:

1. Your Potential as an Entrepreneur
2. Nature of Small Business
3. Business Opportunities
4. Global Markets
5. The Business Plan
6. Help for the Entrepreneur
7. Types of Ownership
8. Marketing Analysis
9. Location
10. Pricing Strategy
11. Financing the Business
12. Legal Issues
13. Business Management
14. Human Resources
15. Promotion
16. Selling
17. Record Keeping
18. Financial Analysis
19. Customer Credit
20. Risk Management
21. Operations

The three levels relate to complexity, not to grade levels. For example, under the business plan, the three levels of complexity are:

1. Describe a business plan.
2. Recognize the steps for preparing a business plan.
3. Analyze the process for developing your business plan.

For each level of complexity, multiple objectives are recommended. Teachers can order 63 booklets that cover the concepts and the levels of complexity for their individual classrooms. Additional information about this set of materials can be obtained from the Center on Education and Training for Employment, 1900 Kenny Road, Columbus, OH 43210-1090.

Another set of materials for the middle-lower high school level is published by the National Council on Economic Education. Entrepreneurship in the U.S. Economy includes a set of conversational, easy-to-understand readings with many student activities and a teacher resource manual. The package contains 35 lessons; many lessons take more than one class period to complete. Materials are more than adequate for a one-semester course but would have to be supplemented for a two-semester course. In these materials economic concepts are fused with various principles in business administration. Unit titles for the materials include:

Unit 1 — The Entrepreneur and Choicemaking

Unit 2 — Entrepreneurs in Different Settings

Unit 3 — Market Forces and the Entrepreneur

Unit 4 —Choosing Among Options for Setting up a Business

Unit 5 — Finances and Operation of the Entrepreneurial Enterprise

Unit 6 — Managing the Factors of Production

Unit 7 — Marketing Considerations

Unit 8 — External Factors Affecting the Entrepreneur

Unit 9 — Developing Entrepreneurial Skills

A story line continues throughout the materials involving an individual who initiates and maintains a business in marketing canvas bags. She encounters many problems and situations involving the use of economics and business principles in the decision-making process. More information about this program can be obtained from Economics America, 1140 Avenue of the Americas, New York, NY 10036.

Opportunities for Business Education

The entrepreneurial explosion provides considerable opportunity for business education. Both the public and educational leadership recognize that entrepreneurship education is increasingly important for young people. Very strong justification for entrepreneurship education in the schools can be found. A recent Gallup poll indicates that young people would like to know more about entrepreneurship (Kourilsky, 1995). Business educators can be a major force for bringing more and better entrepreneurship education into the schools.

Business education should be the major player in entrepreneurship education since the major focus of entrepreneurship is based on business— accounting, economics, finance, business law, management, marketing, and information systems. Entrepreneurship education applies business foundations to the small business rather than the larger one.

What, then, are some specific strategies that business educators can use to integrate more and better entrepreneurship education in schools?

At the elementary level business educators should work with elementary teachers in the integration of sound entrepreneurship education activities in areas such as language arts, mathematics, or social studies. Activities from the National Council on Economic Education, the Center for Entrepreneurial Leadership of the Ewing Marion Kauffman Foundation, and the Standards for Business Education can be used to integrate more entrepreneurship education activities into the elementary curriculum.

Some business educators are currently working at the elementary level teaching keyboarding/computer skills. Perhaps a school district could provide additional time to a business teacher for coverage of entrepreneurship. In today's crowded curriculum, this idea will be difficult to sell. Indeed, business educators will need entrepreneurial abilities to promote this concept to school administrators!

At the middle/junior high school level, two recommendations are made. Since considerable emphasis is placed on career education at this level, middle/junior high school students should study entrepreneurship seriously as an option for career decision-making. For a number of years, career education has focused primarily on *job preparation* with little consideration for *job creation*. Although most students will not start a business immediately after graduation, they should acquire entrepreneurship skills and knowledge since many of their career paths will lead to business ownership.

The second recommendation is to offer a course at the middle/junior high school level on entrepreneurship. In this course students could develop their own small business, dependent on their interests and abilities and the opportunities available in their community. The content of this general education course could include common business understandings, different kinds of thinking (creative/problem solving/decision making), and the entire entrepreneurial process. Students may become interested in the field of business and entrepreneurship when exposed to business foundations taught in an *experiential* format and applied to the entrepreneurship form of business.

At the secondary level care should be taken to determine whether the entrepreneur and the entrepreneurial process are well represented in the curriculum. For example, the accounting principles course might focus on how to set up accounting records for a new business that offers a specific type of good or service. In general business or introduction to business, the entrepreneurial process could be a pervasive part of the coverage within the course.

A second recommendation for the secondary level is to implement a course (semester or year) focusing on more sophisticated applications of entrepreneurial concepts and building upon the course at the middle school level. In many schools a course called business management is deemed to be the entrepreneurship course. Business educators should ensure that the course actually covers **all** of the steps in the entrepreneurship process.

Entrepreneurship, like computer literacy, relates to many other disciplinary areas. Technology, agri-business, and human resource courses focus on various aspects of entrepreneurship. Business educators might offer their services to faculty members in the other areas for coverage of such business areas as accounting/record-keeping procedures, legal aspects of small businesses, and marketing techniques.

If entrepreneurship education is to flourish below the collegiate level, teacher education programs must make sure that certain aspects are in place. Teacher education candidates should have a strong background in the disciplines of business—accounting, economics, finance, information systems, management, and marketing. In addition, they should have a course in entrepreneurship. They should be encouraged to start their own businesses. Perhaps a form of internship credit could be given for this experience.

The teacher education program should provide experiences for the teacher education candidate to become competent in dealing with both convergent and divergent thinking skills. Traditional business-teacher education programs have focused on convergent thinking skills where only one or a few correct answers to different questions exist. If entrepreneurship education is to be successful, teachers must be confident in using these different thought patterns.

Summary

The time has come for the schools to integrate more entrepreneurship education in the curriculum. Multiple justifications exist for including entrepreneurship education in the nation's classrooms. Business educators should be leaders in the implementation of more and better entrepreneurship education in grades K-14. A number of teacher aids for business educators to use in teaching entrepreneurship were discussed in this paper and are valuable for improving schools and the business education profession. The background of business teachers focuses on the underpinnings of business that is the base for entrepreneurship. In the crowded curriculum business educators should use their entrepreneurial ability to secure more attention to entrepreneurship in the schools.

References

Dennis, W. J., Jr. (1993). Is the new entrepreneurial era over? *Journal of creative behavior, 27*(2), 112-29.

Drucker, P. F. (1985). *Innovation and entrepreneurship.* New York: Harper and Row.

Kent, C. A. (1990). Introduction: Educating the heffalump. *Entrepreneurship education: Current developments, future directions.* New York: Quorum Books.

Kourilsky, M. (1995, October). Entrepreneurship education: Opportunity in search of curriculum. *Business Education Forum, 50*(1), 11-15.

Kourilsky, M., Allen, C., Bocage, A., Waters, G., Clow, J., & Rabbior, G. (1995). *The new youth entrepreneur.* Camden, NJ: EDTEC.

Mann, P. H. Entrepreneurship and the world of small business. *Gifted child today, 15*(1) 26-27.

Morrison, I. (1996). *The second curve: Managing the velocity of change.* New York: Ballantine Books.

National Business Education Association. 1995. *National standards for business education.* Reston, VA: National Business Education Association, pp. 1-13, 77-90.

Stafford, A. D., Allen, S. D., & Clow, J. (1994). *Entrepreneurship in the U.S. economy.* New York: National Council on Economic Education.

Whitehead, A. N. (1959). *The aims of education and other essays.* New York: Macmillan.

CHAPTER 15
Future Work

Linda J. Austin
Kingwood College, Kingwood, Texas

Cheryl L. Willis
University of Houston, Houston, Texas

The decade of the '90s has been a hectic one for business educators. The globalization of the marketplace, advances in technology, the end of the Cold War, the downsizing of the workforce, and the accountability movement in education—the implications of all these trends have found their way into our lives. Professional business educators continue to keep track of changes personally and professionally, attempting valiantly to keep ahead of the changes. Even though change produces stress, educators feel a deep need to produce students who are flexible and who have competitive job skills.

Educators should not be surprised by the rapidity of change occurring everywhere—colleagues in past NBEA Yearbooks have described changes, have urged teachers to be the leaders of change rather than simply responding to it, and have warned of the consequences if their words were not heeded. Quoting from a 1968 speech given by William B. Patterson, Norman Kallaus wrote:

> Those who rightly interpret the direction of the changes (in America) and who respond to them, and lead response to them—such persons in history have mostly flourished. Those who remained the same when the same was no longer fitting—they perished, thinking they were holding to the old virtues, which an irresponsible generation had abandoned. For the most part they perished because their minds had become like the body of the dinosaur, unfit for the new climate of the world. Our world is also changing, and few disagree that we are changing to a degree and with a speed that has scarcely ever been recorded (Kallaus, 1970).

Since educators were forewarned of the changes in the world and their concomitant effects on the profession, why is so much more pressure felt now than in decades gone by? Change does not begin to describe what is happening. A better word to describe this scenario is transformation—a major change in appearance or character, i.e., the caterpillar undergoes a transformation into a butterfly. All aspects of society have undergone change but none so dramatically as the world of work, in which business educators have a direct stake. In order to help cope with the current conditions and more importantly to prepare for future work, educators must understand this transformation they are going through and its effects on work, the workplace, the worker, and business education. Once educators shed the cocoon that binds them to old patterns, they will be able to embrace the opportunities that await their students and themselves.

Transformation of Work

The message that work will be changed by information technology, defined generally as computing combined with telecommunications and networking, has been heard for years. Information technology enables workers to do more of their job through an intermediary, such as a computer or an expert system. More profoundly, however, information technology has transformed the very nature of jobs themselves because organizations have reengineered jobs to take advantage of technological capabilities (Hines, 1994). The key information technologies—computer networks, imaging technology, massive data storage, and artificial intelligence—will reshape today's occupations. The views of experts differ, however, on whether the impact of information technology on work, the economy, and the society overall will be positive or negative.

Secretary of Labor Robert Reich asserts that technological advances will have a trickle-down effect. Through the use of technology, the costs of products will be reduced because of the reduction in the amount of labor needed. The prices of the goods or services will fall, thus increasing consumer demand, creating new markets, increasing profits, and putting more people to work in high-wage, high-skill jobs and industries (Reich, 1994).

Jeremy Rifkin, author of *The End of Work*, contends however, that this rosy scenario is wrong (Review of *The End of Work*, 1995). He sees technology as the culprit rather than the savior, driving the productivity improvement schemes that enabled more and more goods to be produced and distributed by fewer and fewer people. Rifkin states that "in the automated economy of the twenty-first century, there simply will not be enough jobs to go around" (Review of *The End of Work*, 1995). He further dismisses the notion that only low-skilled jobs are vanishing from the manufacturing and the services sectors; middle managers and other skilled workers are also being displaced. Other authors see downsizing as a result of advances in technology causing displacement among professional fields. Included in this downsizing are accountants in public firms, in industry, and in government (Mingle, 1994).

Still other analysts believe that organizations are well along the path toward being "de-jobbed," citing that the conditions that caused the emergence of the "job" in the early 19th century—repetitive tasks, large organizations, and mass production—are no longer relevant for this fast-moving economy. "Today's organization is rapidly being transformed from a structure built out of jobs into a field of work needing to be done" (Bridges, 1994, 64). Bridges believes that there will still be plenty of work to do, but jobs will not be packaged "in the familiar envelopes we call jobs." (Bridges, 1994, 64). The present's "good job" is now a very risky business and the past's freelance activity is now in tune with the future (Bridges, 1994, 72.)

In the next decade, corporations will continue to downsize, more permanent employees will be replaced by independent contractors, and technology will evolve at fast-forward speed. The only "security" is in the portability of one's own skills. The way people work will continue to be remade by technology (Jones, et.al., 1995, 32).

Transformation of the Workplace

In the past the workplace for business has been "the office"—a physical place that people drove to from home, remained there for eight or 10 or 12 hours (or more) a day working on tasks and projects, and then drove home at the end of the work day. In the 1980 NBEA Yearbook, Bruno states, "The office is the place where administration, i.e., the management and handling of information, takes place" (1980, 22). The office became the hub of activity, for it was the receptacle for all the important and not-so-important information concerning the business. The workers in the office were, by mere association, important because they knew how to get to the information that resided in the office, how to process that information, and how to distribute it.

The transformed office of the future will not have this tie to location; the information-oriented jobs of the future will involve "W3 work"—work that can be done "whatever, whenever, wherever" (Fryxell, 1994, 18). The human being has become the locus of work, and the notion of the workplace is fading away. The knowledge—and the means of production—is wherever the person is" (Bond, 1995, E1).

Several alternative office strategies have appeared to accommodate W3 work. One such strategy, the virtual office, made possible by rapidly improving technology, is the freedom to work anywhere. The virtual office, along with other types of alternative office strategies, can boost employee productivity, can increase employee's time with clients due to reduced commute time, and also can reduce costs to the organization.

Telecommuting, combining working at the prime business site with working at home or at some other remote site such as the offices of customers at least two days a week, will be done by at least 15 to 20 percent of the office-based workforce by 2000. Approximately 7.6 million workers today telecommute, with that number expected to rise to 25 million by 2000 (Greengard, 1994, 71). Tele-Commuter Resources in the Minneapolis/St. Paul area calculated that a three-day-per-week telecommuter saves $2,071 a year in car costs and gains 156 hours a year otherwise spent on the freeway; additionally, the environment would be cleaner by 6,240 pounds of carbon dioxide. On a national scale, telecommuting is projected to save 1.5 billion gallons of fuel and prevent 3.5 million tons of carbon from polluting the air by 2000 (Greengard, 1994, 71).

Another new workplace arrangement being adopted by companies is "hoteling" arrangements, in which workers retain offices but on a shared basis. Employees who normally spend much of their time away from the main office call ahead to the hoteling support staff to reserve a time slot in a specially designed work area. When the employee arrives, the hoteling staff has made sure that the correct name plate is posted outside the door and that telephone calls are routed correctly. Employees benefit from a work space and schedule that fits their needs; companies benefit from reduced real estate costs, which is second only to salaries as an operating cost item. Ernst & Young, a large accounting firm, has begun a hoteling arrangement in Chicago for its auditors and over the next several years hopes to cut the amount of office space it leases by 2 million square feet. At an average cost of $20 per square foot, savings could total $40 million (Stamps, 1994, 16-18).

Several other alternatives to the traditional office setting include shared space, where two or more employees share a single, assigned workspace; or group addresses, where a designated group or project team share space for a specified period of time; satellite offices used by those employees in closest proximity to them; and remote telecenters that are full-fledged office centers located close to clients but away from the main office. These various office strategies offer many of the same advantages such as improved productivity and customer response; but also many of the same disadvantages such as personality conflicts, perceived worker disconnection from the organization, and management problems resulting from poor communication (Greengard, 1994, 76).

Savings realized on the cost of keeping up the traditional office environment is a major advantage to telecommuting from the employer's prospective. Jack Nilles, president of JALA International, estimates that a person working at home two days a week saves a company $12,000 a year as a result of increased productivity, reduced office space, and lower turnover (Langoff, 1995, 230). Bell Atlantic Corp. cites statistics that 25 hours spent working at home are the equivalent to 40 office hours (Stites, 1995, B11). Many corporations try telecommuting for its flexibility, both for employers and employees.

In the future,

> ". . . firms will avoid occupying expensive offices and instead organize themselves in new forms that use telework, subcontracting, outsourcing, and part-time or consulting work to a greater extent. As teleconferencing spreads and computer networks become more user-friendly and cheaper, executives will have access to company information, hold meetings, and run firms with employees who are not present physically" (Makridakis, 1995, 19).

With the realization that the mobile workforce may possibly be the dominant way of getting the job done in years to come, what new skills must managers have to manage "remotely" and what new skills will be required of workers in the future?

Transformation of the Worker

About 60 percent of today's workforce is categorized as information workers. An information worker will be hard to distinguish from a non-information worker in the future because information technology will have spread across the spectrum of workplaces. "Most workers in 2010 will be primarily information workers who incidentally make widgets, sell clothes, and grow corn. The worker's primary activities will be gathering, creating, manipulating, storing, and distributing information related to products, services, and customer needs" (Hines, 1994, 12-13).

Occupations. No one knows where and what kinds of new jobs will emerge over the next 10 to 15 years, but some indications have been given where the expansion might occur. The list below identifies a number of job titles of "careers of tomorrow" according to Andy Hines of Coates & Jarratt, a firm that specializes in identifying and reporting future trends (Hines, 1993, 55-56).

Artificial intelligence technician	Image consultant
Benefits analyst	Information broker
Business alliance coordinator	issues manager
Business educator	Man/machine interface specialist
CAD/CAM technician	Market development specialist
Career change counselor	Materials utilization technician
CD & video disc librarian	Personal buyer
Certified financial planner	Personal fitness trainer
Communications engineer	Remote sensing
Computer	interpreter
analyst	mapper
designer	technician
graphics specialist	Retirement counselor
microprocessor technologist	Robot
network manager	engineer
security specialist	trainer
E-mail technician	Satellite technician
Fiber optics technician	Smarthouse analyst
Financial consultant	Software talent agent
Home health aide	Strategic planner
Hotline counselor	Systems analyst
Telecommunications	Transplant coordinator
systems designer	Wellness consultant
network manager	

Jobs for computer systems analysts and programmers will more than double in the next 10 to 15 years, while about 20 percent fewer typists and word processors will be needed. The growing number of elderly people will create jobs in the health care, home help, financial services, and travel industries. Rapid technological change means that workers will need to be retrained; therefore, the demand for teacher/trainers will grow. A big expansion in the entertainment and information services industries is predicted (*Technology & Unemployment*, 1995).

Industry sectors that are projected to experience growth and some job titles in each are as follows:

- Medical—positions in equipment sales, pharmaceuticals, physical therapy, home health care, speech pathology, and radiologic technicians;
- Computers—positions in computer engineering, systems analysis; and
- Service industries—positions in hospitality, retail, and finance (Jacobson, 1995, E1).

Working Woman's Tenth Annual 25 Hottest Careers issue covers "the best job options in a work force being reshaped by the twin forces of advancing technology and globalization." Career titles marked with an asterisk (*) are the "10 Best of the Best" since these jobs meet all three selection criteria—they offer "great money, and growth, and are hospitable to both sexes" (Jones, et.al., 1995, 31-44).

1. Bioethicist	13. Lobbyist
2. Biologist	14. Management consultant
3. Computer-software engineer	15. Obstetrician-gynecologist*
4. Environmental manager/ industrial hygienist	16. Rehabilitation counselor
	17. Temporary staffing specialist
5. Fertility specialist*	18. Clergy
6. Information systems manager	19. Corporate librarian
7. Multimedia manager	20. Family practice doctor*
8. Pharmacoeconomist*	21. Film and video editor*
9. Utilities-marketing manager	22. Fund raiser
10. Corporate counsel	23. Intellectual property (copyright) lawyer*
11. Credit card marketer*	24. Labor-relations executive*
12. Elder lawyer*	25. Physical therapist*

According to Samuel R. Sacco, executive vice president of the National Association for Temporary and Staffing Services (NATSS), his industry provides 2 million skilled workers every work day. He sees a continued need for temporary workers while the economy is in transition from industry to service. The positions will be filled by retired workers needing to supplement their income, by laid-off workers who need meaningful work while seeking full-time employment, and by young people looking for a way to try out potential jobs and employers. The member companies and chapters of NATSS have established business-education partnerships throughout the United States. One outgrowth of the partnerships is a program called Preparing Youth For Industry (PYI), which is designed to keep inner-city students in school by giving them practical knowledge about the workplace and business world (Ferberg, 1995, 16-18).

Some think that the core employee of the future is the technician. "With one out of every four new jobs going to a technical worker, the Bureau of Labor Statistics (BLS) forecasts that this army of technocompetents—already the largest broad occupational category in the U.S.—will represent a fifth of total employment within a decade" (Richman, 1994, 7). Furthermore, the number of college graduates who take jobs in technical fields is projected to grow by 75 percent to 2.2 million by 2005.

According to Michael Arthur, a management professor at Suffolk University in Boston, "Technical occupations are becoming the new anchor for people's careers" (Richman, 1994). Arthur goes on to explain the distinction between a jobholder and a careerist. Jobholders performs a limited range of tasks within the context of a specific organization whereas careerists define themselves by the cluster of skills they bring to their work, which, by the way, are transferable from employer to employer (Richman, 1994, 8).

The rationale for the rise of the importance of the technical worker is an outgrowth of the flattening of the organization. No longer are technicians relegated to positions subordinate to managers (a lean and mean organization has fewer of them); nor are technicians seen as just one notch above the less-skilled "blue- and pink-collar masses." Technicians' competence gives them value to the organization rather than their places in the corporate hierarchy.

Organizations turn to technical workers to ensure productivity gains from investment in new technology. Some organizations even are starting to make the mastery of a technical specialty the prerequisite for career growth, preferring their managers to be masters of technical data rather than supervisors of hourly workers (Richman, 1994, 10).

The secretarial/clerical profession has been affected by office automation and by downsizing. According to Burge, there are 521,000 fewer secretaries today (Burge, 1996, 10) than in 1987. Those secretaries remaining in the field have had to make the transition from traditional duties to functions that were formerly performed by managers, such as tracking business-unit performance, attending and participating in week-long sales meetings, or coordinating training for employees. The titles for these new administrative professions have changed also—from secretary to administrative assistant, lead coordinators, office assistant, or office managers. While the traditional skills of time management, organization, and communications are needed now more than ever, the new administrative professional must have skills in additional areas such as project management, budgeting, meeting facilitation, working in teams, using information technology, and decision making (Burge, 1996, 10).

Educators must also come to grips with what kinds of work people will not be doing in the future, largely because of computers and communications technology. Experts estimate that by 2015 the speed of the computer will approach that of the human brain; the density of memory chips will approach that of the human memory; and the speed of computer transmission will approach that of our visual system. As machines took over the manual, repetitive, routine tasks previously done by humans to mark the beginning of the Industrial Revolution, so too will computers perform most standard mental ones. By 2010 computers may read and speak as well as humans and probably "see." By 2015 there will be no need for people to do any repetitive manual or mental tasks that can be performed by computer programs and expert or knowledge systems (Makridakis, 1995, 18-19).

Skills. The worker of tomorrow will be far more independent and self-directed and will not need managing as the term is known today. The qualifications of the worker of tomorrow can be summarized by the letters D.A.T.A.:

- Desire—you really want to do the work.
- Ability—you are good at what the work requires.
- Temperament—you fit that kind of situation.
- Assets—you have whatever other resources the work requires (Bridges, 1994, 72).

To ensure employability, future workers should possess the following skills: basic competence in reading, writing, and computation; computer literacy; good communications skills; good people skills; willingness to work hard;

flexibility; and creativity (Vessel, 1991, 119). Shostak (1993, 30-34) identifies attributes needed in tomorrow's jobs as team-building skills, commitment to continuing education programs, comprehensive and insightful grasp of a business in general and of one's contribution to it in particular.

Successful telecommuters generally have the following characteristics: minimal need for supervision, self-motivation, history of dependability, organization and time-management skills, preference for home environment, high level of skill and knowledge of the job, tolerance for isolation (Bond, 1995, E1).

Experts believe that self-managed careers will assume greater importance in the future. Therefore, 21st century workers must be adaptable and knowledgeable rather than merely "task-trained." Job functions will be shared and titles will be blurred. Multi-disciplinary skills will be desirable: an accountant/software expert, an environment lawyer/hazardous waste management specialist, a geriatrician/health-services administrator, etc. (Ettorre, 1994, 12-17).

To meet the challenges of the exciting future before them, students need foundation skills they can apply immediately—reading, writing, math, and computer skills. Learners need to embrace lifelong learning and be equipped for self-managed careers. The ability to "learn how to learn" and the research skills taught will help students to adapt to rapid technological change. Then they will interact with and contribute to the global workplace whenever work is done, wherever work is accomplished, and with whatever tools are needed.

As Michael Fullan said in *Change Forces*, "The ability to cope with change, learning as much as possible with each encounter is the generic capacity needed for the 21st century" (Fullan, 1993, 136). Similarly, "We are called upon to teach so much to our students to fit them for what is a continually changing work environment. Perhaps the keynote to teaching is to teach students how to be adaptable and how to cope with change" (Wood, 1980, 208).

Phases of Transformation in Business Education: Transformed, Transforming, and Transformer

Throughout its history, business education has thrived on change. In the 1966 Yearbook, Arensman emphasized this point.

> Out of the social and economic upheaval of the 1920s came the expansion of business, the wider use of the typewriter, the liberation of women, and the migration to the cities. . . . During the social and economic collapse of the 1930s business education also responded to change. Vocational business education with its shorthand, typewriting, and bookkeeping enabled good students to obtain whatever jobs could be found amidst massive and continual unemployment. . . . During the war years of the 1940s, the continuing heavy demand for vocational workers resulted in both the acceleration and the expansion of business courses (1966, 303-304).

The stressors that educators feel today were termed "confusion" in the '60s after the launching of the Russian Sputnik in 1957 sent the United States reeling. Arensman (1966, 305) stated that "conscientious business teachers who earnestly tried to keep up with the latest office practices, the latest duplicating devices, and the latest data processing equipment were often swamped by complex inventions, strange terminology, and an exploding technology they were increasingly unable to understand." Does this statement sound familiar?

Business educators must look for the opportunities created by the ongoing transformation and become transformed. Educators must leverage their strengths and improve on their weaknesses. What are these strengths—knowledge of how business makes money (indeed, that it is essential for business to make money); how people work together; how to organize projects; how to find information; how to organize information so that it is communicated well; and in general how to work to get a task done.

The difficulty comes in using this knowledge given the business tools in usage today—networks, communication satellites, imaging technology, voice recognition technology, etc. Business educators know business, but they may not know how organizations conduct business in this new age. Business educators must become trained in how business does business through information technology so that in turn they can interpret for students how business solves problems and creates business using information technology. Whether information technologies are a boon or a bane to workers in 2010 may depend upon the strategies students as employees use to implement those technologies for employers. Depending upon the road taken to implementation, these technologies can create more challenging jobs or they can replace jobs (Hines, 1994, 13).

"Transforming" connotes a dynamic state of being. Consider this statement from the 1990 NBEA Yearbook:

> During the 1990s, business educators will either manage the decline of their discipline or oversee a fundamental structural change in the discipline. If changes are not made in response to new economic conditions and workplace requirements, business education will witness an exodus of students from its programs (Daggett & Jaffarian, 1990, 171).

Have business courses responded to the workplace requirements of the future? How many course offerings in business education have seen increases in enrollment; of those that had an increase in numbers of students enrolled, how many were technology-based? How many other disciplines are now offering technology-based courses versus 10 years ago? How many business education teachers are employed compared to 10 years ago? Have individual business educators managed the decline of the discipline or have they overseen a fundamental structural change (a transformation) in the discipline?

For business educators and business teacher education, the challenge is great to transform individual teachers and the discipline. How change is achieved (when, where, and with what tools) will be decided as the future unfolds and with the input, decisions, and day-to-day work of educators individually and collectively. Educators must lead by example—demonstrating flexibility and commitment to lifelong learning, staying informed, equipping themselves with knowledge for and about business, and collaborating with business partners.

Many of the challenges to be faced in the 21st century are the same ones faced in the '60s, the '70s, the '80s, and the '90s. However, the nature of work has undergone a transformation and so, too, must the nature of business education. To prepare students for the workplace, business educators must be willing to transform themselves and the profession. Wherever, whenever, whatever it takes, business educators must succeed in the transformation so that the discipline can continue to be the transformer of students' lives.

References

Arensman, R. W. (1996). Business education retools for change. In E. W. Lanham & R. W. Arensman (Eds.), *Business education meets the challenges of change* (303-309). Reston, VA: National Business Education Association.

Bond, P. (1995, July 17). The growth of telecommuting. *Atlanta Constitution,* p. E1.

Bridges, W. (1994, September 19). The end of the job. *Fortune,* 62-74.

Bruno, J. N. (1980). Constraints affecting the business office. In M. H. Johnson (Ed.), *The changing office environment* (pp. 22-30). Reston, VA: National Business Education Association.

Burge, J. (1996). Are secretaries a dying breed? Performance in practice. *American Society for Training and Development Forums,* 10.

Chambers, N., Hermelin, F. G., Nelson, A. V., Weiss, E., & Woodruff, V. (1994, July). 25 hottest careers. *Working Woman,* 37-44.

Daggett, W. R., & Jaffarian, R. A. (1990). Business education in the 1990's: A window of opportunity. In S. L. O'Neil (Ed.), *Strategic planning for the 1990's* (pp. 166-171). Reston, VA: National Business Education Association.

Epstein, G. (1995, April 10). The demise of job security in the U. S. Is more fiction than fact. *Barron's,* 22.

Ettorre, B. (1994). Where will the new jobs come from? *Management Review,* 12-17.

Fernberg, P. M. (1995, June). The skills shortage: Who can fill these shoes? *Managing Office Technology,* 16-18.

Fryxell, D. A. (1994, May/June). Telecommuting: It has its plusses and minuses, but the "virtual office" may be where many of us work in the future. *Link-Up,* 17-19.

Fullan, M. (1993). *Change forces.* London: The Falmer Press.

Greengard, S. (1994). Workers go virtual. *Personnel Journal,* 71, 76.

Hines, A. (1994, January/February). Jobs and infotech: Work in the information society. *The Futurist,* 9-13.

Hines, A. (1993, April). Transferable skills land future jobs. *HRMagazine,* 55-56.

Jacobson, J. (1995, August 21). Future jobs. *Pensacola News Journal,* pp. E1, E3.

Jones, M., Chambers, N., Kalis, L., Nelson, A. V., Scher, H., & Schorr, M. R. (1995, July). 25 hottest careers for women. *Working Woman,* 31-44.

Kallaus, N. (1970). The changing levels of office occupations. In R. G. Price & C. R. Hopkins (Eds.), *The emerging content and structure of business education* (pp. 49-59). Reston, VA: National Business Education Association.

Langhoff, J. (1995, October 30). Telecommute America: Get ready for business in the fast lane. *Fortune,* 229-235.

Makridakis, S. (1995, April). Impact of information. *Executive Excellent,* 18-19.

Mingle, J. C. (1994). The shape of firms to come. *Journal of Accountancy,* 39-46.

Reich, R. B. (1994, April). Jobs: Skills before credentials. *Training,* 38-40.

Richman, L. S. (1994, August). The new worker elite. *Fortune,* 10-12.

Ritkin, J. (1995). *The end of work: The decline of the global labor force and the dawn of the post-market era.* New York: G. P. Putnam's Sons.

Shostak, A. B. (1993, November/December). The nature of work in the twenty-first century, certain uncertainties. *Business Horizons,* 30-34.

Stamps, D. (1994, February). The virtual office. *Training,* 16-18.

Stites, L. (1995). More corporations try telecommuting for its flexibility. *Philadelphia Business Journal,* B-11.

.Technology and unemployment: A world without jobs? (1995, February 11). *The Economist,* 21- 23.

Temporary help/staffing services support business education partnerships. *Managing Office Technology,* A6-A7.

Topolnicki, D. M. (1995, May). Five trends. *Money,* 102-103.

Vessel, H. (1991, November/December). Excelling in workplace 2000. *The Black Collegian,* 114-119.

Wood, M. W. (1980). Curriculum challenges of secondary business education. In M. H. Johnson (Ed.), *The changing office environment.* Reston, VA: National Business Education Association.

CHAPTER 16

Job-Seeking Process

Zane K. Quible

Oklahoma State University, Stillwater, Oklahoma

For many years, human resources management was largely unaffected by technology, especially technology involving computer usage. Over time, numerous areas of human resources management have become computerized, beginning with the maintenance of various personnel records in computerized databases. Until fairly recently, one area of human resources management that seemed virtually impervious to technology usage was employee hiring.

Job-seekers and companies engaged in the hiring process now are making extensive use of the new technology. The result is task simplification for everyone involved with either job hunting or employee hiring.

This chapter discusses a number of relevant topics, including the following: descriptions of relevant key terms and concepts, a scenario that discusses how new techniques and technology are used in the job-seeking process, and new job-seeking techniques that make use of technology.

Descriptions of Key Terms and Concepts

Among the key terms and concepts described in this section are the following:

An *electronic resume* is a specially designed resume that makes widespread use of nouns rather than action verbs (a characteristic of traditional resumes). Its contents are scanned (using optical character recognition) into a company's computerized resume bank. The nouns facilitate keyword searching, which is the primary reason for preparing electronic resumes.

A *video resume* is a video recording of a person discussing his or her background. The information typically parallels that found in a traditional resume. Although companies are prohibited by law from using a video resume to discriminate against applicants on the basis of their age, gender, race, etc., the video resume has been a useful tool in demonstrating one's oral communication capabilities.

A *resume database service* is provided by an independent company specializing in employee job placement. Clients provide the resume database service with their resumes and perhaps a completed application blank that are then scanned into the database service's resume bank. Employers use the database service to obtain the names of potentially qualified applicants who are selected using the keyword search process. The greater the number of keywords applicants possess, the more likely they are considered to be better qualified for the position. A number of companies that specialize in providing these services are listed in a later section of this chapter.

An *in-house database service* is maintained by a company in which all applicant materials and all employee materials of a job-related nature are scanned into its resume banks. Then, when a position opens, the resume banks are scanned using a keyword search. Individuals who have the greatest number of qualifications are identified as being desirable potential applicants.

Online job hunting on the Internet uses the Internet to facilitate the job-hunting process. Companies that have an opening post information about the position in the job-bank section of the service. Individuals who are looking for employment place relevant information about their backgrounds in the resume bank section of the service. Both those looking for employment and those looking for employees can "surf the Web" regularly to examine the job bank and resume bank. E-mail is a common communication medium when messages must be transmitted between the potential employer and the potential applicant. A later section of this chapter includes a list of service companies that allow the posting of information about openings as well as the resumes of job seekers.

Computerized job interviewing is used in some companies today to conduct a preliminary computerized interview with several applicants before they actually begin the process of on-site interviews. Computerized interviewing gives the company one more opportunity to obtain additional information before committing to an on-site interview. Generally, the information request is sent to the potential employee by means of an e-mail message; the potential employee responds with an e-mail message that contains the requested information. Another type of computerized job interview is held on-site prior to the conducting of an interview with a company employee. A common purpose of this type of computerized interview is to compare the similarity of applicants' responses on their application blanks and their responses provided during the computerized interview.

Job-related electronic bulletin boards are maintained by individuals and associations to assist companies looking for employees. Companies post relevant information about the positions on the bulletin board. Likewise, individuals who are looking for employment post information about their backgrounds and qualifications. Both groups regularly scan the bulletin board messages. A number of these bulletin boards are listed in a later section of this chapter.

Job-related newsgroups provide a valuable service for both the company seeking employees and the individuals seeking employment. Some of these newsgroups focus on a specific field: an example is a newsgroup that provides information about open positions in the computer area as well as information about individuals who are looking for a computer-oriented job.

Job-Seeking Scenario Using New Techniques and Technology

The following describes how an employer makes use of a number of the new techniques and technology in the hiring process as well as how individuals who are looking for employment use a variety of the new techniques and technology.

XYZ Company, a manufacturer of modular work stations, movable panels, and other components used in designing open office-space work areas, is interested in hiring a new employee to fill a sales representative position. Approximately 750 employees are presently on XYZ's payroll. The manager of human resources plans to use a broad-based, widespread search to identify potential employees. Therefore, the manager decides to augment the traditional search process with new technologically oriented recruiting techniques.

The following sources are used to identify potential applicants in the search for a sales representative:

1. Job-vacancy notices outlining the requirements for the open position are posted on conventional company bulletin boards, run in the company newsletter, and placed in local and area newspapers.

2. Job-vacancy notices are posted electronically on the company's e-mail system and electronic internal bulletin board, making them available to any present employee who has access to a desktop computer and the appropriate software.

3. XYZ Company's computerized personnel database is used to identify which present employees might possess the qualifications needed by a sales representative. By using keywords, the database is searched to identify the employees who possess the needed qualifications. These individuals will be invited to apply for the position.

4. Job-vacancy notices are also posted on a number of online job placement services (job banks) used by XYZ Company. Individuals seeking employment regularly scan these resources (using a computer with a modem and software that enables them to access the Internet) to determine whether any openings exist for which they wish to apply.

5. An individual in the human resources department also regularly scans online resume banks (again, using a computer with a modem and software that provides Internet access) to identify viable applicants for the sales representative position.

6. The company also notifies the various resume database services with which it contracts that a vacancy for a sales representative exists. These services scan their resume banks to determine which of their clients possess the qualifications required by XYZ Company. (This process is similar to the one outlined in No. 3 above, except that the earlier-discussed process is an internal search involving present employees; this process involves an external search of potential applicants.) The identified clients are informed about the opening and are invited to apply.

Application materials (completed application blanks, resumes, etc.) of the prospective employees are scanned as they arrive, using optical character recognition (OCR) scanning equipment. The results are stored in the company's applicant computerized database. XYZ Company uses a specially designed application blank that simplifies scanning. A growing number of job applicants are submitting an electronic resume, perhaps along with their traditional resume, that facilitates scanning. Generally, the electronic resume provides a better match between applicant qualifications and job requirements than the traditional resume because the electronic resume is specifically designed for that purpose.

Companies also scan into the applicant database printed application materials from viable applicants. These are downloaded from the online resume database services. Eventually, the technology will likely develop to the point where the information available about applicants does not have to be downloaded, then printed, and finally scanned. Rather, the technology will permit individuals to have their application materials directly downloaded into the company's computerized resume bank.

Among the applicant information stored in the database is the following: applicants' educational attainment, work experience, and other desirable attributes and characteristics. The job-vacancy notice for the sales representative position in XYZ states that three to five years of relevant work experience in sales are required, in addition to a bachelor's degree in marketing or a related area, excellent oral and written communication skills, and knowledge of work space design.

After the closing date for receiving applications passes, XYZ Company begins the process of identifying within its applicant pool the best-qualified candidates from both inside and outside of the company. Therefore, a keyword search involving the most important job qualifications is entered into the computerized applicant database system. Of the applicants, those whose qualifications best match the job requirements (stated as keywords) are identified. At this point, the individual responsible for hiring the new sales representative will likely read through the applicants' materials to determine which ones will be interviewed for the position.

The technology, in addition to facilitating the inputting of considerable amounts of applicant information into the company's applicant database, also expedites correspondence creation. If additional information is needed from an applicant, a form letter can be used to request the desired information. Technology also can be used to prepare the correspondence that invites the finalists for an interview as well as to notify all unsuccessful applicants.

New Job-Seeking Techniques Using Technology

This section discuses a variety of new technology-based job-seeking techniques. Using these techniques generally results in more efficient procedures for both the job-seeker and the company seeking employees.

Electronic resume. The use of electronic resumes is expanding as ever-increasing numbers of job seekers are using resume database service companies. Many companies today are also creating databases to store information about job applicants, and this has had a positive impact on the interest in electronic resumes. The primary reason for creating an electronic resume as a supplement to a traditional resume is the use of the electronic version in undertaking a keyword search.

Among the distinguishing factors or characteristics of electronic resumes are the following:

1. Electronic resumes use nouns and some adjectives; traditional resumes use action verbs.

2. Electronic resumes should not have any design characteristics that might impede the accurate scanning of their contents. For that reason, the following design

characteristics are important: use of a readily scannable font (such as Helvetica or Univers), use of a font size ranging between 10 and 14 points, and avoidance of such font attributes as shadow lettering, italics, underlining, etc.

3. Electronic resumes, because of their primary function as a scannable document, are structured differently from traditional resumes. The job-seeker should isolate important keywords (nouns and adjectives) by placing them at the top of the document immediately after the individual's name and address. The rationale is that some of the software used in undertaking the keyword search is limited to 50 key terms. By putting the important keywords at the beginning of the document, the applicant has a better chance of maximizing the number of important matched terms. If the keywords are spread throughout the document, with some of the more important ones at the end of the document, the 50-word maximum may be filled before the important keywords are found. This procedure will likely result in an applicant's being considered less well-qualified than others, simply because he or she had fewer hits on keywords.

Figure 1 illustrates an electronic resume.

Figure 1

Mary D. Brown
894 Grant Avenue
Madison, WI 65434
(313) 474-5555

Keywords: Accountant. Cashier. Bookkeeper. Accounts receivable ledger. Accounts payable ledger. Financial reports. Business Administration. Lotus 1-2-3. Windows 95. Excel. French. CPA examination. Wisconsin. Beta Gamma Tau. Leadership. Phi Beta Kappa. President's Honor Roll. Excellent oral communication skills. Excellent written communication skills. Highly motivated. Quick learner. Detail oriented. Excellent work ethic. Trustworthy. Top 2 percent of class. IBM-compatible computers. DOS. University of Wisconsin. Madison, WI.

Goal: To work in a Big Six accounting firm, with the eventual goal of becoming a partner.

Education:	University of Wisconsin - Madison. 1994 - 1997 Accounting major. Bachelor of Science degree in Business Administration to be awarded with distinction June 1, 1997.
Experience:	Anthony's Department Store, Madison, 1992 - 1997 Part time during school year, full time during summers. Performed bookkeeping and cashier duties. Maintained accounts receivable and accounts payable ledgers. Prepared variety of financial reports.
College Activities and Honors:	Beta Gamma Tau Honorary, 1996-1997. Alpha Kappa Psi, 1994-1997. President, 1997. Phi Beta Kappa, 1997. President's Honor Roll, each semester, 1994-1997.

In designing an electronic resume, keywords should be considered for inclusion in the following areas:

- Titles of jobs held by the applicant.
- Names of job-related tasks performed by the applicant.
- Special skills or knowledge possessed by the applicant.
- Degree(s) earned.
- High school program or college major (if a college graduate, information about the high school program can be eliminated).
- High schools or colleges attended.
- Special awards or honors received.
- Nature of interpersonal skills the applicant possesses.

Traditional resumes are often folded and mailed along with the letter of application, but an electronic resume probably should not be folded. Folding may cause some of the letters on the folds to "break up" during the scanning process, which might result in misreading. Many applicants are now sending in a large envelope both types of resumes, suggesting to the employer that the electronic version is well suited for scanning.

Perhaps the easiest way to prepare an electronic resume is to identify words on the traditional resume that need to be included in the key-terms section of the electronic version. Another helpful suggestion is to look at a job vacancy notice of the position for which a person is applying, making sure that his or her electronic resume addresses each of the items listed in the vacancy notice.

Video resume. Video resumes, first used several years ago, are receiving increased attention. They can be recorded using two different mediums: video-cassette recorder tapes and compact disks. Tapes will likely decrease as the medium of choice when CD recording technology becomes readily available and affordable. Eventually technology will be available that enables job applicants to transmit their electronic resume electronically to the company(ies) to which they are applying. At the receiving end, all individuals applying for the same position will have their resumes recorded on the same CD. The members of the screening team can easily pass the CD from person to person. However, until the technology is available for transmitting video resumes electronically, the VCR tape or CD on which the resume is recorded has to be delivered personally or by mail.

If the video resume concept becomes popular as a viable job-seeking tool, small CD recording studios will likely be available just as small teleconferencing studios are available in some copy and duplication centers. Individuals wishing to make a video resume will simply rent the studio to make the recording. Job-placement firms will also likely install CD recording studios for use by their clients.

Video resumes are prepared using two different formats. One format involves the job seeker talking about himself or herself, basically providing information commonly found on the resume. With the other format, an interviewer asks the job applicant a variety of questions, resembling an interview. Both seem to be equally effective in enabling the potential employer to assess the applicant's communication skills, poise, etc.

One of the significant advantages of the video resume is that it eliminates to a considerable extent the number of unsuccessful screening interviews a job applicant will have. The hiring company should be able to determine on the basis of the video resume if an applicant appears to possess the desired communication skills, background, etc., to be given further consideration. But herein lies the most significant potential disadvantage of video resumes. If the job applicant was denied further consideration because of gender, race, age, appearance (unless stated as a bonafide occupational qualification, such as might be required for a position as a model), the applicant unknowingly might be discriminated against. For this reason, some applicants and employers view the video resume as too significant a risk for routine usage.

The actual content of the video resume might be as follows:

1. The applicant states his or her name and the title of the position for which he or she is applying.

2. The applicant provides biographical information, mentioning geographical background, high school and college attended, the diplomas or degrees earned, the college major if applicable, and work experience details.

3. The applicant discusses the qualifications possessed for the specific position available, in addition to any general qualifications potential employers will likely find desirable among their applicants.

4. The applicant might display examples of work, if applying for a position for which a portfolio might be useful in evaluating employment suitability. Such positions are advertising representatives, technical writers, graphic artists, photographers, etc.

Resume database services. Resume database services assist individuals looking for employment as well as companies interested in hiring employees. These independent database service companies match the needs of individuals seeking employment with the needs of companies seeking employees.

Among the common types of information stored about their clients in the resume database are the following:

1. Resume (either traditional or electronic, although the electronic version will likely be more useful).

2. Profile (similar to an application blank used by many companies engaged in the process of hiring employees).

Although some information found on both documents will likely be repetitive, other information will be unique to the document in which it is found.

The information stored in the resume database is placed there in three basic ways. One common way is for the database service to scan the client's documents. A second way is for an employee of the resume database service to key the relevant information into the database. A third method involves scanning the documents, and a computer program extracts the desired information, storing it in predetermined categories, including such categories as education, work background, desired location, special skills, etc.

Individuals typically have several choices for transmitting their information to the resume database service. The information can be mailed, faxed, or hand-delivered. Technology is available that enables individuals who have access to a computer with a modem to transmit the information electronically.

In some cases, the information will go directly into the database; in other cases, it will likely be "massaged" before it is put into the database.

A company that uses resume database services in the job-hiring process simply contacts the service company to make arrangements for obtaining information about possible applicants to fill open positions. Most likely the company will need to identify the keywords that should result in the identification of several well qualified candidates. At this point, several alternatives are possible. Perhaps only the names, addresses, and phone numbers of the top candidates are sent to the company that has the open position. In other cases, a copy of the summary profile of each top candidate is sent to the hiring company. In still other cases, copies are sent of all documents submitted by top candidates at the time they register with the resume database service.

Because resume database services are usually for-profit enterprises, a fee will likely be charged to the job-seeker or the employing company, with the fee being assessed more often to the employing company than to the job seeker. If individuals are charged, they will likely be able to use the database service for a certain length of time (perhaps six months) by paying a flat fee (perhaps $75).

Among the names and addresses of resume database services are the following:

Access, 1900 West 47th Place, Suite 215, Shawnee Mission, KS 66205
(913) 432-0700

Career Placement Registry, Inc., 302 Swann Avenue, Alexandria, VA 22301
(800) 368-3093

Electronic Job Matching, 1915 N. Dale Mabry Highway, Suite 307, Tampa, FL 33607
(800) 749-4100

SkillSearch, 104 Woodmont Boulevard, Suite 306, Nashville, TN 37205
(800) 252-5665

In-house database services. Many companies today are inundated with paperwork received from job applicants, a sizeable portion of which consists of unsolicited applications. Some companies have a policy of discarding all unsolicited applications, keeping only the materials they received from applicants who are applying for advertised openings. Regardless of how the mountain of paperwork is handled, considerable human resources are required to manage the information effectively.

With the availability of software that enables companies to track their applications—both solicited and unsolicited—considerable efficiency is gained. No longer do humans have to read through the application materials when they are received to make a determination about whether to give each applicant further consideration.

When materials are received from applicants, the items can be scanned, which facilitates storing the contents electronically. Whether the applicant is applying for a known opening or is submitting an unsolicited application, the materials will be treated equally during the initial screening process that involves the use of keyword searching. The result is that all applicants will be screened for all current openings as well as all future openings, perhaps for a period of six months or so. When traditional non-computerized screening techniques are used, individuals submitting solicited applications are likely considered only for the opening for which they applied; individuals submitting unsolicited applications may not be considered for any openings, either now or in the future. Because some applicants are likely qualified for a number of positions in a company and would consider an offer, the in-house database service is extremely useful. In most traditional systems, applicants are considered only for the position for which they applied.

The software identified at the end of this section has an additional advantage of preparing automatically for each applicant a letter confirming receipt of application materials. With traditional systems, the number of applications received, especially unsolicited, may be extensive; and preparing confirmation letters becomes a difficult if not impossible task. Thus, the applicant never knows if the materials were actually received by the company. If the applicant decides to call the company for confirmation, the manual searching of files to determine whether the materials have been received is often a laborious process.

When an opening becomes available, the contents of the in-house database are scanned using the keywords appropriate for the specific opening. As is the case with other database searches, the greater the number of desired keywords found for an applicant, the better qualified the applicant likely is for the open position.

Because most companies today have a policy of promoting from within, present employees are often given an opportunity to apply for open positions. Some companies do not consider outside applicants for an opening until all present employees have been removed from consideration for the vacancy, either because they lack qualifications or lack interest in the job. Other companies will consider both present employees and outside applicants simultaneously. When the later approach is used, the personnel database that contains records about present employees and the in-house database service that contains the records of applicants are run simultaneously. Some software programs offer companion databases: one for present employees, the other for applicants. Using this software provides greater uniformity in the information available about present employees and the outside applicants who are applying for the opening. In most cases, those responsible for detailed screening of the top candidates identified by the software examine a hard copy of the contents stored electronically.

Among the names and addresses of companies that produce the software useful for maintaining an in-house database service are the following:

- ATS-Pro, Human Resource Microsystems, 160 Sansome Street, Suite 1450, San Francisco, CA 94104
  (800) 972-8470

- Human Resource Information Center, Computer Management Inc., 2346 South Lynhurst Drive, Suite C-101, Indianapolis, IN 46241
  (317) 247-4485

- Resumix, Resumix, Inc. 2953 Bunker Hill Lane, Santa Clara, CA 95054
  (408) 562-4444

Online job hunting using the Internet. The Internet has experienced a very rapid growth in the quantity of resources and in the number of individuals who use it for a variety of functions, including job hunting. Today a large number of individuals use the Internet to locate information about openings for which they are qualified and in which they are interested.

The Internet can be used in several ways for online job hunting. As the Internet continues to develop, additional job-hunting services will likely emerge. Among the ways it is used are the following:

1. A job-seeker can search various Internet resources (most likely resources on the World Wide Web) to determine whether any of the companies in which the applicant would like to work lists job openings in their home page. This search will be most efficient if one or more of the WWW search engines is used with the company name as the keyword. Many companies include a variety of information about job or employment opportunities. ·

2. The job-seeker can search various Internet resources (again, most likely the World Wide Web) to determine available open positions. One or more search engines can be accessed with the position title of interest as the keyword. One disadvantage is that many resources will likely be found, resulting in the job seeker's need to do a time-consuming reading of the provided information.

3. The job-seeker can subscribe to one or more of a number of online services that provide their subscribers with information about job openings.

4. The job-seeker can use a number of specialized services, including those listed below. Specific information about how to use the services can be obtained by calling the telephone number listed for each.

   • Access . . . FCO On-Line (specializes in openings in the federal government)
   703-281-0200

   • Career Link Worldwide (global online database)
   602-973-2002

   • Classifacts (nationwide database of newspaper classified ads)
   303-322-0711

   • E-Span (nationwide database of open positions)
   800-682-2901

5. The job seeker can use a rapidly growing number of job-placement companies that post openings on the World Wide Web. This valuable service enables a company to post relevant information about the opening. The job seeker then "surfs the Web" to determine what openings exist for which he or she is qualified and in which he or she is interested. The job seeker can also post a resume in the databases maintained by many of these job-placement companies, which enables the companies with openings to "surf the Web" looking for suitable applicants.

Among the job-placement companies with a Web presence, along with the URL needed to access these companies using a Web browser, are the following:

America's Job Bank	http://www.ajb.dni/us/index.html
National Career Search	http://www.rpi.edu/dept/cdc/homepage.html
CareerWEB	http://www.cweb.com/
IntelliMatch	http://intellimatch.com/
The Internet's Online Career Center	http://www.occ.com/
The Monster Board	http://www.monster.com/home.html

Computerized job interviewing. Computerized job interviewing will likely become more commonplace as a component of the hiring process. One type of computerized job interviewing involves sending an e-mail message either to a select group of applicants or perhaps to all of them if the applicant pool is fairly small. Each applicant gets the same list of questions, and their responses can be sent by a return e-mail message. This type of interview helps determine which of the applicants will likely be a best fit, thus reducing the number of interviewees who are found during an on-site interview to be unsuitable for employment. In addition to assessing the quality of the applicants' responses, e-mail messages will provide one more way to assess writing skills when these competencies are an important component of job success.

Another type of computerized interview takes place immediately before an on-site interview is conducted by a company employee. Generally, the applicant will not be aware of the opportunity to participate in the computerized interview until being escorted into the room where the computer and appropriate software are located. Two companies, Aspen Tree Software, Inc., located in Laramie, WY, and Dovetail, located in Atlanta, GA, have highly regarded software used in facilitating these kinds of computerized interviews. The software developed by these companies contains the interview questions. The software is also capable of providing analyzed data useful in assessing the job applicants' responses.

Each applicant for the same position is asked the same questions during these interviews. This procedure is used primarily to pinpoint any discrepancies between their completed applications, resumes, and their responses provided during the computerized interview. When a discrepancy arises between the information provided on the application blank and answers provided during the computerized interview, the interviewer will likely want to assess the reason. Because these questions are generally multiple choice in nature, the selection of certain responses by applicants will also "raise a flag," which will likely cause the interviewer to delve more deeply into the applicant's response.

Some companies have found that computerized interviews are useful for asking legally appropriate questions of a sensitive nature because many applicants may feel more comfortable providing certain answers to a computer than to a person. Another benefit of using the computerized interview is the consistency in providing each applicant with the same questions. During interviews conducted by humans, some applicants may get some questions but other applicants get other questions, which conceivably can give certain applicants an unfair advantage over others.

Job-related electronic bulletin-board services. Many individuals have found the use of job-related electronic bulletin boards helpful in their employment-search pursuits. Although the exact number is difficult to determine, a reasonable estimate is that more than 100,000 of these boards pertaining to a vast array of topics now exist; and new ones are being added daily. Anyone with a computer, a modem, and the necessary communications software can access electronic bulletin boards. All of the earlier discussed online services used the World Wide Web; electronic bulletin boards are not part of the WWW, nor are they accessed using the WWW.

Electronic bulletin boards, which are sponsored by individuals, associations, companies, and governmental units, allow individuals seeking employment to post messages regarding their qualifications. Businesses that have openings can post appropriate notices and scan the messages of job seekers for suitable applicants. Some bulletin boards can store large amounts of information that can be downloaded. For example, some bulletin boards provide a wealth of information about finding a job, planning a career, etc.

Most electronic bulletin boards are free. However, depending on the location of the user in relation to the location of the bulletin board, the user may have to pay for a long-distance call. A few bulletin boards have special areas available to users only on a subscription basis. Therefore, the user will have to pay a charge when accessing these special areas. Generally, a user can subscribe to these special areas using the telephone, with the access fee charged to an individual's account.

Listed below are a number of career-oriented bulletin boards, along with their telephone numbers. To access a bulletin board, the user simply uses the communication software program to dial the telephone number of the bulletin board. Once the connection is completed, the user will begin receiving information on the computer screen.

Bust Out BBS: (510) 888-1443 (California)

Career Board: (214) 931-5792 (Texas)

Career Connection BBS: (214) 247-0675 (Texas)

Career Connections: (415) 917-2129 (California)

Computer Careers: (704) 554-1102 (North Carolina)

Federal Jobline: (818) 575-6521 (California)

Job-related newsgroups. In some aspects, the services provided by job-related newsgroups are similar to the services provided by online job-hunting services. The primary difference is that newsgroups are free, whereas the online job-hunting services often charge for placing a resume in a database. In many cases, newsgroups are maintained by individuals who enjoy working with the technology. Job seekers are able to post relevant information about their backgrounds; employers can post relevant information about the positions they wish to fill.

When using a newsgroup, the user simply accesses the desired newsgroup through a server connected to the Internet. Any news reader, including a browser, can be used. An Internet connection provides the link between the user's computer and the host computer. Upon accessing the desired newsgroup, the user sees the subject of each message, the name of the individual who posted the message, and the time and date the message was posted. To read a message, the user simply provides the appropriate command. The user has the opportunity to post a reply to a given message or is able to create a new message about an entirely new topic.

Among the job-related newsgroups are the following:

misc.jobs.offered

misc.jobs.misc

misc.jobs.jobs.contract

biz.jobs.offered

Summary

Augmenting one's job-seeking efforts with technology will become the rule rather than the exception in the future as more individuals become aware of the vast number of new technologically oriented resources available to them. As time passes, new resources most likely will be developed, giving job-seekers even more avenues to use. Generally, individuals who have access to the technology and who are proficient in its use will find job-hunting much more convenient than in the past when job-seeking was restricted to the use of traditional, often-laborious procedures. Tomorrow's job-seeking processes will undoubtedly make today's processes seem quite archaic.

PART VI

CHAPTER 17

Career Vision: A Process for Lifelong Learning

Linda L. Gamble
Washington High School, Pensacola, Florida

In July 1993, the Task Force for Career Education was established in Escambia County, Florida. Comprised of district staff, principals, teachers, guidance counselors, parents, a school board member, postsecondary educators, school advisory board representatives, and members of the community, task force members began developing a comprehensive career education plan. Faced with the realization that nine out of 10 workers in the year 2000 will not have the skills to work the jobs that will be in existence unless they plan well and continue to learn, the task force mission statement became ". . . to use all school, home, and community resources, both human and technological, to prepare students to be lifelong learners who contribute to a global, dynamic, and culturally diverse society" (Career Vision, Draft Copy, p. 3).

Essential Elements and Goals

Members of the task force searched nationwide for materials, locating and studying career models that were already in place in California, Kentucky, Alabama, Oregon, and South Carolina. In small group sessions, the task force members shared ideas and reached a consensus on the elements essential to a restructured approach to education, as shown in Figure 1.

Figure 1

ESSENTIAL ELEMENTS FOR RESTRUCTURING SCHOOLS THROUGH CAREER EDUCATION

- Restructuring needs to involve all stakeholders.
- Outcome-based/career-focused curriculum that prepares students for real world and global economy relevancy must be developed and implemented.
- Students actively participate with teachers as facilitators.
- Community-wide student support services must be integrated.
- The role of teachers should be organized so that they have authority with responsibility.
- Achievement should be continuously monitored.
- Students must be educated for jobs.
- Curriculum must be changed and integrated, with delivery system modifications.
- Instruction in the classroom, student/teacher role changes, program focus on students, sensitivity to different learning styles, collaborative learning, expectations for students will change—so must assessment.

- Instruction must be organized around a concept-based curriculum that utilizes an interdisciplinary approach through teacher teams.
- Students must decide early to follow district subject majors organized around careers/applied technology clusters.
- Radical changes in the daily scheduling of students will involve the use of the block scheduling approach.
- Methodology must shift from lecture to more student-centered learning.
- Technology-based instruction must increase.
- Greater community involvement must be utilized.
- Career centers need to be established in each high school.
- All high school students will be required to complete a workplace readiness course.
- High school curriculum needs to be articulated with postsecondary majors.
- Equity must be provided in middle school career exploration opportunities.
- A comprehensive guidance plan for grades K-12 must be developed.
- The role of guidance personnel in the career education process needs to be enhanced.

The essential elements for restructuring schools, shown in Figure 1, were used to formulate the goals identified in Figure 2.

Figure 2

GOALS OF CAREER VISION

CREATING CURRICULAR PATHS

- Establish learning outcomes in all subject areas.
- Develop program majors: tech prep, academies, schools within schools.
- Integrate curriculum wherever possible.
- Incorporate activities within the curriculum that promote an appreciation of the arts, technical achievement, and the creative process.
- Integrate computers and other technology in all curriculum areas.
- Infuse into the curriculum, where applicable, career education.

DEVELOPING POWERFUL TEACHING AND LEARNING

- Develop interdisciplinary instructional programs.
- Emphasize student-centered instruction with teacher as facilitator/coach.
- Instruct students utilizing state-of-the-art hardware and software.

ESTABLISHING A COMPREHENSIVE ACCOUNTABILITY/ASSESSMENT SYSTEM

- Establish an assessment system that regularly and continually evaluates student progress that allows individual students to accurately assess their own knowledge, skills, and abilities.
- Establish an authentic assessment program that measures the student's proficiency in all curriculum areas: exhibits, projects, performances, written scenarios, etc.
- Develop performance-based assessments of subject matter competencies that require students to use a variety of technological devices.
- Develop an assessment program that evaluates the effectiveness of the total school program.

RESTRUCTURING THE SCHOOLS

- Create school schedules that are tailored to the type of learning experience: flexible and adaptable scheduling that allows for a variation in curricular and instructional delivery, such as clusters and blocks.
- Establish multiple learning sites that are developed and connected by technology and community-based learning.
- Develop a facilities plan to accommodate curriculum, instruction, and structural changes addressed in the school restructuring plan.
- Promote interdisciplinary team teaching with common planning periods.
- Realign curriculum and teaching methodology during summer staff development.

ESTABLISHING RELATIONSHIP BETWEEN SCHOOLS,
BUSINESS, AND COMMUNITY

- Create a variety of opportunities for participation by parents, community, and school personnel in school decisions.
- Create extended day opportunities for students through a collaborative effort between the school and community-based organizations and agencies: community service, 4+2 programs, articulation, etc.
- Establish funding sources to finance various programs and internal restructuring implementation.
- Develop a plan to articulate restructured programs to feeder schools, community colleges, state colleges, parents, community, and businesses.

Career Vision Model

The product of the task force was a student planning guide entitled Career Vision: A Process for Lifelong Learning. Dr. W. L. Maloy, the superintendent of Escambia County Schools, prefaced the guide by writing " . . . there is no doubt that education must never stop; continuous and lifelong learning must become the commitment of our students . . ." (Career Vision, p. 1).

In 1994 and 1995, middle school students were tested, using the ACT Career Planning Program (ACT-CPP). Students' interests, abilities, experiences, plans, backgrounds, and needs were assessed; the students were given the results so that they could study career options based on specific job clusters best suited to them. Guidance counselors also received copies of the students' results so that they could work with students to prepare flow charts for the future (Career Planning, p. 3).

The Escambia County School District Career Vision Model is divided into six career clusters:

Arts/Communication

Business Contact/Marketing/Management

Business Operations/Information Systems

Science/Medicine/Engineering/Technology/Environment

Social/Health/Education/Government/Recreation/Consumer Services

Technical/Agriscience/Natural Resources

Structured paths prepare students for entry-level, mid-level, and skilled/professional careers within the chosen clusters. All clusters include both tech-prep and college-prep courses of study, with an emphasis on blending academics and applied technology to ensure that students will be prepared for entry into both the workplace and the institution of higher learning. Each cluster begins with a short description, followed by questions for students to ponder. The cluster is then divided into major areas of interest, with entry-level, mid-level, and skilled/professional careers listed. Typical majors and related school/community activities are then identified. The two clusters most closely aligned with business occupations are summarized in the following discussions.

Business Contact/Marketing/Management Cluster. Careers in this cluster include professions from entry-level sales clerks to the highest level of administrative and managerial positions. Many careers are available in the areas of real estate, insurance, business administration, and merchandising. Examples of such are hotel manager, office manager, and urban planner. People in these occupations deal with people and data. Students would consider these questions:

- Do you enjoy planning and directing activities?
- Is competition fun for you?
- Are you disciplined and hardworking?
- Are you enthusiastic and self-confident?
- Have you ever been told that you are very persuasive and can convince people of your point of view?
- Are you naturally a "people person," finding it easy to meet and talk with new acquaintances?
- Are you organized, efficient, and comfortable doing detail work with numbers or words?

Major interest areas for students choosing this cluster include Marketing/Sales and Management/Planning. Some of the entry-level, mid-level, and skilled/professional employment opportunities available in those interest areas are shown in the tables below.

Table 1

MARKETING/SALES

ENTRY-LEVEL	MID-LEVEL	SKILLED/PROFESSIONAL
Bill Collector	Claims Adjuster	Buyer
Fashion Model	Insurance Agent/Broker	Securities/Financial Services Rep.
Product Demonstrator	Manufacturer's Rep	Services Sales Rep
	Sales Manager	
	Travel Agent	
	Travel Guide	

Table 2

MANAGEMENT/PLANNING

ENTRY-LEVEL	MID-LEVEL	SKILLED/PROFESSIONAL
Administrative Assistant	Building Manager	Advertising Manager
Auto Service Station Manager	Caterer	Airport Manager
Food Service Supervisor	Construction Contractor	Bank Office/Manager
Postmaster	Credit Manager	Business Manager
	Customer Services Coordinator	City Manager
	Employment Interviewer	Controller
	Funeral Director	Director (Industrial Relations)
	Hotel/Motel Manager	Educational Administrator
	Importer/Exporter	Health Services Administrator
	Store Manager	Labor Relations Specialist
	Office Manager	Personnel Recruiter

Students would typically choose majors from business administration and management, fashion-marketing management, finance, health-services management, hospitality management, human-resources management, real estate, industrial management technology, insurance/risk management, labor relations, and marketing.

Possible related extracurricular activities are Cooperative Education Clubs of Florida, Distributive Education Clubs of America, Future Business Leaders of America, Future Homemakers of America/Home Economics Related Occupations, athletics, band, chorus, foreign language clubs, church organizations, student employment, volunteer jobs, Junior Achievement, and job shadowing.

Business Operations/Information Systems Cluster. A second area, closely aligned with business occupations, is the cluster Business Operations/ Information Systems. Careers in this cluster include positions that attend to the details of a business operation. Jobs in this group are found in government, industry, social-educational systems, and businesses; positions included are billing clerks, air traffic controllers, and financial analysts. People in these careers usually work with data and technology.

Students would consider these questions:

- Do you like talking and working with other people?
- Do you enjoy solving problems?
- Are you disciplined and hard-working?
- Are you organized, efficient, and comfortable doing detail work with numbers and words?
- Do you prefer your work to be structured with clear guidelines?

Major interest areas for students choosing this cluster include Records/Communication, Financial Transaction, Storage/Dispatching, and Business Machine/Computer Operation. Entry-level, mid-level, and skilled/professional employment opportunities are shown in the tables below.

Table 3

RECORDS/COMMUNICATION

ENTRY-LEVEL	MID-LEVEL
Receptionist	Court Reporter
Stenographer	Legal Secretary
Hotel Clerk	Library Assistant
Postal Clerk	Medical Records Tech
	Personal Assistant
	Secretary

Table 4

FINANCIAL TRANSACTION

ENTRY-LEVEL	MID-LEVEL	SKILLED/PROFESSIONAL
Accounting Clerk	Bookkeeper	Accountant
Bank Teller	Loan Officer	Actuary
Cashier		Auditor
Payroll Clerk		Financial Analyst
Ticket Agent		Insurance Underwriter
		Real Estate Appraiser

Table 5

STORAGE/DISPATCHING

ENTRY-LEVEL	MID-LEVEL	SKILLED/PROFESSIONAL
Dispatcher	Warehouse Supervisor	Aair Traffice Controller
Mail Carrier		Flight Dispatcher
Railroad Conductor		Traffic Manager
Shipping/Receiving Clerk		
Store Clerk		
Warehouse Worker		

Table 6

BUSINESS MACHINE/COMPUTER OPERATION

ENTRY-LEVEL	MID-LEVEL
Data Keyer	Computer/Peripheral Equipment Operator
Statistical Clerk	Motion Picture Projectionist
Telephone Operator	Word Processor Operator
Typist	

Students would typically choose majors from accounting technology, court reporting technology, health-information management, health-unit coordination, medical secretarial technology, office-systems technology, real estate, office systems, accounting, finance, insurance and risk management, and management information systems.

Possible extracurricular activities are Future Business Leaders of America, Future Homemakers of America/Home Economics Related Occupations, Future Farmers of America, Cooperative Education Clubs of Florida, athletics, band/chorus, foreign language clubs, church organizations, student employment, volunteer jobs, Junior Achievement, and job shadowing.

School-to-Work Opportunities

An integral component of the Career Vision Plan is the integration of academic preparation with tech prep. Eleventh- and 12th-grade students have access to many school-to-work opportunities designed to strengthen their individual skills and provide them with leadership training. Because students need both strong academic skills and rigorous technical preparation in order to function effectively in the ever-changing world of work, many high schools have integrated English with practical keyboarding skills/practical computer skills and geography, or English with biology and business computer applications. Students can type English and geography papers in their business classes, with both teachers proofreading their work—one teacher for content and the other for mechanics. Teachers have planning time together to coordinate their lesson plans. Apprenticeship programs combine academics with on-the-job training; thus, students work with a team of teachers who can plan coordinated lessons. Employer advisory boards are utilized to ensure relevant and practical instruction.

The following school-to-work opportunities are provided in Escambia County schools:

- Agribusiness Cooperative Education—OJT
- The Banking and Finance Youth Apprenticeship Program
- The Building and Construction Youth Apprenticeship Program
- Business Cooperative Education—OJT
- Cooperative Home Economics Education—OJT

- Diversified Cooperative Training
- Health Occupations Cooperative Education—OJT
- Industrial Cooperative Education—OJT
- Marketing Cooperative Education—OJT

Academic Excellence Incentives

The State of Florida has initiated two programs for students who plan to continue their education at a postsecondary institution. The Florida Gold Seal Endorsement and Scholarship recognizes and rewards student achievement in vocational education. Students who complete a vocational program of study, meet academic requirements, and plan to attend a Florida public university, community college, area vocational center, or accredited private postsecondary vocational, technical, trade or business school can qualify for up to $2,000 per year in renewable scholarship funds. In addition, the students receive a medallion to be worn during commencement exercises, a gold seal to be affixed to the diploma, and a framable certificate.

The Florida Undergraduate Scholars' Fund is a scholarship award for academic achievement for students who plan to pursue their educations at a Florida institution of higher learning. Receipt of the Florida Academic Scholars' Certificate entitles students to automatic admission to a state university or community college if all requirements are met. The program includes an annual award of up to $2,500 per year.

All students are encouraged to explore postsecondary educational opportunities as part of their plan for the future; therefore, information about the Gold Seal Endorsement/Scholarship and the Florida Academic Scholars' Certificate/Florida Undergraduate Scholars' Fund is included in the Career Vision booklet.

Comprehensive Career Guidance Plan

Task force members agreed that the Escambia County Comprehensive Career Guidance Plan needed to be revised in order to incorporate the Career Vision Plan. The guidance plan is now based on the premise that career education should begin in kindergarten and continue throughout the productive life of a student, uniting students, teachers, parents, counselors, and the community (Comprehensive Career Guidance Plan, p. 1). The plan is based on the following assumptions:

- Career Guidance is a program that supports academics and provides direction for students.
- Career Guidance is a program for all students inclusive of the special needs population.
- Career Guidance is designed to help students set and reach life goals.
- Career Guidance is a team effort uniting counselors, teachers, students, parents, and the community in the provision of services for students.

In Grades K-5, the emphasis is career awareness, and objectives include helping students develop positive feelings about themselves and developing the work ethic concept. Recommended activities include inviting career speakers, participating in a career fair, and working with self-esteem activities.

In Grades 6-8, the emphasis is career exploration. Objectives include identifying career clusters; helping students perceive the relationship between education, life roles, and life styles; enabling students to discover and make appropriate decisions about future education and continuing preparation for life; and communicating with students and parents in order to involve them in making sound decisions for the future. Recommended activities are exploring career clusters through academics, taking the ACT-CPP, planning a career day, working with self-esteem activities, attending a planning conference for all eighth graders and their parents, and developing the four-year plan (based on students' interests, personalities, and academic abilities).

In Grades 9-12, the emphasis is on career preparation. Objectives include identifying a career cluster for in-depth study, identifying necessary abilities required in selected careers, and planning an educational/training program to attain the necessary skills for a chosen lifestyle with career options. Recommended activities are participating in a career fair, utilizing a career lab, updating the four-year plan card/course of study, participating in college night programs, retaking and reviewing the ACT-CPP in Grade 10, and participating in a parent/student conference in Grade 10.

Expected Outcomes

The Escambia County Career Vision Plan is now in effect. Expected outcomes are:

- Students will possess the knowledge and skills essential for transition into work and/or further education.
- Students will apply technological skills and concepts to current business and industry.
- Students will apply basic educational concepts to specific tasks or to job-related situations.
- Students will apply those leadership skills that are reflective of a positive self-concept.
- Students will demonstrate in the classroom and/or at the work station those cooperative and human relation skills required to function effectively and responsibly in society and at the workplace.
- Students will apply the knowledge and skills needed to create change, adapt to changes in the workplace, and evoke a positive work ethic.
- Students will use problem-solving and decision-making skills essential for career advancement and self-sufficiency.

As students make the transition to postsecondary institutions, they continue to follow their career plans. Representatives of the Escambia County school district and the local junior college developed a tech-prep course sequencing guide to lead students through the academic and technical courses needed for 47 different careers, divided among the six clusters of Career Vision. The Accounting Technology Program, shown in Table 7A and Table 7B, is one example of the tech prep programs presented in the sequencing guide. Completion of a planned course continuum leads to an associate degree or technical certificate at the junior college or to a technical certificate at a vocational center (Tech Prep Pathways for Success, 1996, p. i).

Table 7A

ESCAMBIA COUNTY TECH PREP

GOLD SEAL PROGRAM: Accounting
CLUSTER: Business Operations/Information Systems

SECONDARY			
9	10	11	12
Algebra I Applied Math I Pre Algebra	Geometry Applied Math II Algebra I	Algebra II Geometry Geometry	Trig/Pre Cal Probability & Statistics Algebra II Liberal Arts Math
English I	English II	English III or Applied Communications I	English IV or Applied Communications II
Earth Science Physical Science Applied Biology	Biology I Applied Biology Prin of Tech I Physical Science	Chemistry Prin of Tech I Applied Chemistry Applied Chemistry	Physics Applied Chemistry Science Elective Program Related
Geography 1/2 L.M.S. 1/2 or Elective 1/2	World History	American History	Am Gov. 1/2 Economics 1/2
Personal Fit 1/2 Team Sports 1/2	P.E. 1/2 Elective or I.M.S.	Elective or Co-op	Elective or Co-op
KEYBOARDING AND DOCUMENT PROCESSING	**BUSINESS COMPUTER APPLICATIONS I**	**ACCOUNTING I**	**ACCOUNTING 2**
Elective	Elective	Business Computer Applications 2	Bus. Mgmt. & Law
Workplace Essentials 1/2 or Blueprint for Prof Success 1/2 or Elective	Elective	Elective	Elective

All specified courses must be successfully completed to receive a certificate of completion. Recommended course sequence is flexible and may be modified to meet individual student needs (upon guidance approval). Honor courses are recommended to meet individual student strengths. Recommended Cluster Electives: Foreign Language, Band, Chorus, Military Programs, Athletics, Art, Practical and Performing Arts should be considered and are recommended for all clusters to meet individual interests and abilities.

Gold Seal Courses are in **BOLD** and **CAPS**
Appropriate Vocational Student Organization: Future Business Leaders of America (FBLA)

Table 7B
ESCAMBIA COUNTY TECH PREP

PROGRAM: Accounting Technology
POSTSECONDARY INSTITUTION: PJC (AS Degree)

POSTSECONDARY			
FRESHMAN	FRESHMAN	SOPHOMORE	SOPHOMORE
Accounting I ACG 2001	Accounting II ACG 2011	ACO 1806 Payroll	ACG 2071 Introduction to Managerial Acct.
CGS 1060 Introduction to Data Processing	CGS 1510 Spreadsheet	ACG 2450 Accounting Applications for the Microcomputer	ACG 2002 Accounting Software Applications
6EB 1011 Introduction to Business	OST 1100 Keyboarding	TAX 2000 Income Tax Procedures	ACO 2948 Accounting Work Experience
ENC 1101 English Comp I	Com 2101 Business Communications	Natural Science (Category IX, X, or XI)	BUL 2241 Business Law I
Mathematics (Any category III)	Cultural Heritage (Category I, II, or III)	College Credit Elective	
	ECO 1000 Intro to American Economy		

All specified courses must be successfully completed to receive a certificate of completion. Recommended course sequence is flexible and may be modified to meet individual student needs (upon guidance approval). Honor courses are recommended to meet individual student strengths. Recommended Cluster Electives: Foreign Language, Band, Chorus, Military Programs, Athletics, Art, Practical and Performing Arts should be considered and are recommended for all clusters to meet individual interests and abilities.

The school district, the junior college, the university, and the business community have joined forces to form the Tech-Prep Consortium. Members of the consortium have produced materials to promote tech-prep programs, have enabled teachers to do on-site studies of local businesses and industries, and have procured grant monies to provide additional services to teachers and students.

As Career Vision becomes fully operational, the process will be analyzed. As job conditions change, the plan will be revised. Data on the effectiveness of the plan will be collected. A career center will be established in each high school so that students will have access to a wealth of material on various careers and educational opportunities. Additional youth apprenticeship programs will be established so that students will graduate from high school with documented and quantified job skills. Postsecondary educators will help students achieve a smooth transition from high school to the workforce by emphasizing the integration of academic and vocational studies, by providing co-op work experiences, and by providing increasing numbers of distance learning classes. Students will be encouraged to understand the fact that the better they plan and prepare, the better their chances will be of finding and keeping good jobs in the future.

References

American College Testing Program. (1994). Career planning: making successful transitions in the world of work. Iowa City, Iowa.

Escambia County School District. (1994). Career vision: A process for lifelong learning (draft copy). Pensacola, Florida.

Escambia County School District. (1994). Escambia County comprehensive guidance plan. Pensacola, Florida.

Escambia County School District. (1996). Tech Prep pathways for success. Pensacola, Florida.

Escambia County School System. 1996. *Escambia County School District's tech prep pathways for success.* 1996. Pensacola, Florida.